A PROPAGANDA SYSTEM

How Canada's government, corporations,
media and academia
sell war and exploitation

BY YVES ENGLER

Copyright © 2016 Yves Engler

All rights reserved. No part of this book may be reproduced or transmitted in any form by any means without permission in writing from the publisher, except by a reviewer, who may quote brief passages in a review.

First printing September 2016

Cover by Working Design

Printed and bound in Canada by Marquis Printing

A co-publication of

RED Publishing

2736 Cambridge Street

Vancouver, British Columbia V5K 1L7 and

Fernwood Publishing

32 Oceanvista Lane, Black Point, Nova Scotia, B0J 1B0

and 748 Broadway Avenue, Winnipeg, Manitoba, R3G 0X3

www.fernwoodpublishing.ca

Fernwood Publishing Company Limited gratefully acknowledges the financial support of the Government of Canada through the Canada Book Fund and the Canada Council for the Arts, the Nova Scotia Department of Communities, Culture and Heritage, the Manitoba Department of Culture, Heritage and Tourism under the Manitoba Publishers Marketing Assistance Program and the Province of Manitoba, through the Book Publishing Tax Credit, for our publishing program.

Library and Archives Canada Cataloguing in Publication
Engler, Yves, 1979-, author
A propaganda system : how the Canadian government, corporations, media and academia sell war and exploitation / by Yves Engler.
Issued in print and electronic formats.
ISBN 978-1-55266-946-4 (paperback).--ISBN 978-1-55266-947-1 (epub).--ISBN 978-1-55266-948-8 (kindle)
1. Communication in politics--Canada. 2. War--Public opinion.
3. Propaganda, Canadian--History. 4. Corporations--Political aspects--Canada. 5. Mass media and war--Canada. I. Title.

JA85.2.C3E64 2016	320.01'4	C2016-905895-6
		C2016-905896-4

Contents

Glossary of Acronyms 4
Note on Names, References 5
Acknowledgements 6
1. Introduction 8
2. Canada's Largest PR Machine — The Military 18
3. Military Institutes and Think Tanks 40
4. The Academic Connection.. 60
5. 'Arms-Length' Institutions... 98
6. Owning the Media 120
7. Case Studies — Propaganda During War 154
8. Conclusion 186
Bibliography 200
Endnotes 210
About the Author 240

Glossary of Acronyms

ANMH	L'Association Nationale des Médias Haïtiens
AUCC	Association of Universities and Colleges of Canada
BSIA	Balsillie School of International Affairs
CCIC	Canadian Council for International Cooperation
CCUPIDS	Canadian Consortium for University Programs in International Development Studies
CDA	Conference of Defence Associations
CGAI	Canadian Global Affairs Institute
CIDA	Canadian International Development Agency
CIGI	Centre for International Governance Innovation
CIIA	Canadian Institute of International Affairs (Canadian International Council)
CIIEID	Canadian International Institute for Extractive Industries and Development
CISS	Canadian Institute for Strategic Studies
CWM	Canadian War Museum
DI	Dominion Institute (now Historica Canada)
DND	Department of National Defence
FIPA	Foreign Investment Promotion and Protection Agreement
IDS	International Development Studies
IDRC	International Development Research Centre
GAC	Global Affairs Canada
NFB	National Film Board of Canada
NGOs	Non-governmental organizations
NPSIA	Norman Paterson School of International Affairs
NSI	North-South Institute
PAOs	Public Affairs Officers
PIRG	Public Interest Research Group
PPC	Pearson Peacekeeping Centre
PR	Public relations
R2P	Responsibility to Protect
RCI	Radio Canada International
R&D	Rights and Democracy
RIIA	Royal Institute of International Affairs, or Chatham House Study Group
RL	Réseau Liberté
RMC	Royal Military College of Canada
RPF	Rwandan Patriotic Front
SDF	Security and Defence Forum of the Department of National Defence
WIB	Wartime Information Board.

Note on Names and References

Names

I sometimes use former names External Affairs (1909-1993), Foreign Affairs (1993-2015) and Canadian International Development Agency (1968-2013). External Affairs morphed into the Department of Foreign Affairs and International Trade and then CIDA was added to the fold, creating Foreign Affairs, Trade and Development Canada. At the end of 2015 the foreign service–aid agency–international trade juggernaut was renamed Global Affairs Canada (GAC). The previous distinction between the aid agency and foreign affairs departments is often more relevant for this book.

References

Since this text is not about particular foreign policy moves I've sought to be as brief as possible with details. While I've included extensive end note sourcing on the subject at hand, details about specific Canadian foreign policy initiatives can be found in my previous books or by punching "Canada's support for US war in Vietnam", "Canadian ties to apartheid South Africa", "Canada's role in overthrowing Haiti's elected government" etc. into Google. Details on most claims in this book are accessible online.

Acknowledgements

I would like to thank Nadia Hausfather who has long encouraged and enabled my research habit. I would also like to acknowledge Dru Oja Jay and Nik Barry Shaw for allowing me to draw from Paved with Good Intentions.

I would also like to acknowledge my uncle Al Engler and mother Bernadette Stringer for looking over the manuscript, my father Gary for his endless help and my wonderful partner Bianca Mugyenyi.

Most of my research and writing has been conducted in university and public libraries. The people who work in them are my too-often-unsung heroes.

Finally, I would like to acknowledge the dozens of individuals (Ken Stone, Susan Clarke Robert Massoud etc.) who've set up public events for my books. In a hostile media climate, their work makes it possible and worthwhile to continue researching and publishing. Their activism gives us hope for developing a genuinely justice-oriented Canadian foreign policy.

A Propaganda System

1. Introduction

"Propaganda is to a democracy what the bludgeon is to a totalitarian state."

Noam Chomsky

In six previous books I've detailed Canadian military, diplomatic and corporate abuses abroad. To summarize this history briefly: Until the end of World War II Ottawa was closely tied to the British Empire, which saw many Canadians dispatched to wars in Sudan (1884), South Africa (1899) and Europe (1914 and 1939). Throughout this period Ottawa backed British colonialism in Africa, the Caribbean and elsewhere. Since World War II the Canadian elite have promoted and profited from the Washington-led world order. Ottawa played an important part in creating Washington-centered institutions such as the World Bank and International Monetary Fund and Canadians fought in Korea, Iraq, Yugoslavia, Afghanistan and Libya, as well as providing less overt support to US war aims in Vietnam and Iraq (2003).

Since the late 1800s Canadian banks and insurance companies have dominated the Caribbean while Canadian firms controlled significant interests in the Mexican and Brazilian economies in the early 1900s. Today our banks are world leaders and Canada is the global mining superpower, responsible for resource exploitation and environmental degradation across the planet.

Canada has seldom been a benevolent international actor. Rather it's been close to the centre of a hierarchical international economic, political and military system that is particularly exploitative of ordinary people in the most vulnerable areas.

When confronted with these facts, many of those who come to my talks express surprise. Often they ask about the discrepancy between what they've been led to believe about Canada's role in the world and the facts I lay out. Their query is usually some variation of "why do nine in 10 Canadians think this country is a force for good in the world even though our governments have long advanced corporate interests and sided with the British and US empires?" This book is an attempt to answer this and other related questions.

***

I seek to make my books accessible by writing in a popular rather than academic style. One way to do this is "to make it personal." While I've scoured the web, newspapers and the academic literature for information concerning 'ideas formation' and suppression in Canadian foreign policy, this text is also informed by a decade and a half of activism. During this time I was heavily involved in student and Haiti solidarity struggles, worked as a researcher for a labour union and wrote six books critical of Canadian foreign policy (as well as two others). I've dealt with a number of the institutes mentioned below and have witnessed biased foreign policy coverage firsthand.

My experience writing on domestic versus foreign policy topics highlights the media bias. When I began writing in the early 2000s, I published a half-dozen opinion pieces in the *Montréal Gazette*, *Hamilton Spectator*, *Ottawa Citizen* and *Globe and Mail* criticizing different domestic issues. During a stint working for the Communications, Energy and Paperworkers Union a decade later, I published a dozen op-eds in corporate dailies. Signed by the union president, these articles accompanied the institutional heft of the union and, while some definitely pushed political bounds, they all criticized domestic policy. My submission to publishing ratio on foreign policy issues is a great deal worse. Since 2004 I've submitted dozens of op-eds critical of Canadian foreign policy and have only had four published in daily papers. So, nowadays I rarely waste time shaping (toning down) my message in the hopes of publishing in a corporate daily. But every so often I delude myself into thinking a newspaper will find an argument or piece of information so compelling that they will publish my 650 words. They invariably decline, but occasionally the process is revealing.

In the lead-up to the Saskatoon launch of *Canada in Africa: 300 Years of Aid and Exploitation* I submitted a piece about PotashCorp's role in buying the non-renewable resources of Africa's last remaining colony in violation of international law. The *Saskatoon Star Phoenix* opinion editor, who I'd communicated with on a few occasions as a union researcher, told me he was considering it and then responded a week later. "Hi Yves, Thanks, but I will pass on your op-ed. This issue has been on our pages in the past, with both sides of the debate making their points." But when I searched the *Star Phoenix* database for articles on the Saskatoon-based company's ties to Morocco's occupation of Western Sahara there was a single 264 word letter to the editor criticizing PotashCorp's policy two and a half years earlier (and a rebuttal from a company representative).[1]

At the start of 2016 I submitted a piece about Manitoba Hydro International's role in privatizing Nigeria's electricity system to the *Winnipeg Free Press*. The article referenced dozens of stories in the Nigerian press about Manitoba Hydro's diplomatic backing, conflicts with local officials and disputes over its four-year contract to manage the Transmission Company of Nigeria. The individual responsible for the *Free Press* perspectives and politics section edited it and asked me to look over her changes. A second editor then asked me to clarify/rewrite a sentence, which was done. The story was then spiked. In response, I published the piece online with a note about the *Free Press*'s actions and told the opinion editors that refusing to cover Manitoba Hydro's controversial policies in Nigeria was racist. After ignoring the issue for four years, the *Free Press* published two wishy-washy articles about Manitoba Hydro in Nigeria a week later.

While they've run some of my articles, Huffington Post has refused to publish, buried or edited numerous submissions for

A Propaganda System

political reasons. A number of articles critical of Canadian support for Israeli expansionism have been rejected and after Nelson Mandela died they refused a piece detailing Canadian complicity with apartheid South Africa. On two occasions Huffington Post blocked any reference to Canadian officials citing the Responsibility to Protect (R2P) doctrine to justify destabilizing and overthrowing Haiti's elected government. In a 2015 article linking newly elected Prime Minister Justin Trudeau to past Liberal governments' foreign policy I wrote: "Canadian officials also cited R2P to justify cutting off assistance to Haiti's elected government and then intervening militarily in the country in February 2004. In discussing the January 2003 Ottawa Initiative on Haiti, where high level US, Canadian and French officials discussed overthrowing elected president Jean-Bertrand Aristide, Liberal Secretary of State for Latin America and Minister for La Francophonie Dennis Paradis explained that 'there was one thematic that went under the whole meeting ... The responsibility to protect.' Similarly, in a highly censored February 11, 2004 cable from the embassy in Port-au-Prince to Foreign Affairs, Canadian ambassador Kenneth Cook explained that 'President Aristide is clearly a serious aggravating factor in the current crisis' and that there is a need to 'consider the options including whether a case can be made for the duty [responsibility] to protect.'" While I supplied a link to the interview between independent journalist Anthony Fenton and Dennis Paradis and another to the documents Fenton uncovered through access to information, the editor said "we need mainstream sources to verify the facts in your blog and unfortunately the facts below are only in the publications cited (or printed elsewhere by the same authors)." I replied, "Huffington Post cannot publish something if it has not been in the corporate media. This seems like a fairly major flaw/admission and I'm very curious to know if it is official policy?" Rather than answer my question, they published the piece but removed the paragraph on Haiti, taking the position that since the corporate media had ignored the destabilization of Haiti's elected government during the previous decade they should too. (In fact, *l'Actualité*, Quebec's equivalent to *Maclean's*, mentioned R2P when it reported on Ottawa, Paris and Washington's plan to oust President Jean-Bertrand Aristide 13 months before the coup.)

Of course, I'd long known Haiti was a sensitive subject. After visiting Haiti eight months after the February 2004 coup I sent a news article to a number of major papers. Even though the article was politically tame, well edited and of proper length, no paper was interested. The foreign affairs editor at the *Toronto Star* wavered and then told me they already had a freelance journalist there while his counterpart at the *Globe and Mail* said he couldn't use the article "as it has a lot of commentary and opinion woven through it."

Three weeks after I submitted my piece to the *Globe* they published a wildly propagandistic article puppeting the coup government's perspective. In a story headlined "Backyard Baghdad", Marina Jimenez wrote that ousted President Aristide "from his South Africa exile" is "funding" and "directing" a "war."[2] She reported about a purported pro-Aristide campaign to murder police officers, "Operation Baghdad", but the story made no mention that independent observers said this was an invention of the coup government to justify their attacks on the pro-Aristide slums. Or that a month before her article appeared more than ten thousand pro-constitution demonstrators marched in Cap Haitien behind a banner claiming "Operation Baghdad" was a plot created by pro-coup forces to demonize Aristide supporters.[3]

These and other experiences convinced me there was some sort of "propaganda system" at work — how else could one explain the divergence between belief and reality regarding Canada's role in the world? Journalists were prepared to criticize governments and corporations to a certain extent on "domestic" issues, but the spirit of "challenging power" largely disappeared regarding foreign policy. Why? Was there an "I won't criticize Canadian foreign policy" test that editors of major media outlets had to pass? And if so, who administered it?

***

Some are fond of explaining how most people come to believe what they believe by elaborating theories that involve hidden messages and secret government departments. Others see no propaganda system at all, only individuals "naturally" learning about the world through daily experience.

While this book draws on various theories of the media, think tanks, public relations etc., it takes a unique approach to these issues. In a late-night phone conversation with my father while working on this book, one of us compared Canadians' faith in their country's international role to hockey fans faith in "their" team, whether that be the Canadiens, Maple Leafs, Senators, Jets, Oilers, Flames or Canucks. This got me thinking about how the passion for a particular team is manufactured and the possibility of a hockey analogy excited me. As a former junior player, I decided that rather than draw on the Chomsky/Herman "propaganda model" to analyze Canada's foreign affairs propaganda system, I'd employ the Les Canadiens de Montréal paradigm.

I do apologize to those who hate hockey and those who love it too much, but comparisons to the country's most popular professional sports league seem like the best way to make my arguments to the largest possible audience. Below I briefly describe the "propaganda" structure of a professional hockey franchise and then use that to explain the propaganda system that convinces Canadians this country is a benevolent force in world affairs.

Why do Montrealers overwhelmingly support the Canadiens, not the Boston Bruins or Anaheim Ducks (or for that matter the Sherbrooke Phoenix junior team)? In recent years these teams have had more success, more Québecois players and play (arguably) a more exciting brand of hockey. Yet Montrealers overwhelmingly stick with the Habs.

The reasons for the popularity are multifaceted and historically rooted. The choice of "Canadiens" when the term was associated with Francophones, the 1955 Rocket Richard riot's contribution to Québec's Quiet Revolution and the Habs' historic success have all contributed to the club's popularity. But the primary reason is that a $1.1 billion US corporation, part of a $15 billion league, promotes itself to fill a stadium, sell broadcasting rights and license retail shops, sports bars, condo towers etc.[4]

To sell its various initiatives the team advertises heavily in local media. Additionally, the Habs' large marketing department feeds reporters and broadcasters with stories and statistics, as well as organizing events, fan forums and team history commemorations.[5] In one of a long list of major marketing initiatives, the Habs partnered with Montréal on "the City is Hockey" campaign through the 2000s. It associated the team with Montréal architectural references and delivered educational kits to schools.[6]

Alongside the city of Montréal, many local businesses drive support for the Canadiens. The TV and radio stations paying to broadcast games have a substantial financial interest in promoting the team. So do a number of other media outlets with Habs partnerships. Hundreds of bars and restaurants across the city have informal team partnerships. Hoping to draw fans in to watch games, they decorate with Habs memorabilia. Many other businesses seeking to profit from the team's popularity — while simultaneously driving it forward — contract players or name products after them.

Ranking just after general news and provincial politics, 12% of Québec news in 2013 was about the Habs.[7] Two years earlier a study found that players, coaches and executives were among the most covered personalities in Québec. Incredibly, 12 of the 25 personalities who received the most media coverage in Québec in 2011 were Canadiens.

A Propaganda System

Considering the attention, the team's popularity is not surprising. But, the hype is hard to justify. With players from around the world, the success or failure of the Habs says little about the quality of Montréal/Québec hockey. Nor does it say much about the quality of life in the city. It really doesn't matter who puts the black rubber behind the goalie more times. Similarly, the popularity of the notion that Canada is a benevolent international force says little about this country's role in the world.

This book details the obstacles Canadians face in understanding their country's place in global affairs. Most significant is the marketing. In the same way the Maple Leafs sell its product, every year the Department of National Defence (DND), Veterans Affairs, Canadian Heritage and Global Affairs Canada (GAC) spend hundreds of millions of dollars in public funds articulating a one-sided version of Canada's foreign policy. The corporate set spends tens of millions of dollars more.

Many "security" and "defence" think tanks and university programs are funded by the military. GAC's predecessors, Foreign Affairs and the Canadian International Development Agency, also spawned and financed "ideas" institutes and university programs. Alongside government-backed efforts, wealthy Canadians have set up a number of internationally oriented think tanks and university departments. The foreign affairs school at Canada's leading university was financed by a mining magnate with an important personal stake in a particular foreign policy while the Canadian International Council, Canada's leading foreign policy 'think tank' for most of a century, was collapsed into another billionaire's university/think tank initiative.

With 10,000 employees, Foreign Affairs has been well-positioned to disseminate its views to the world. Through Radio Canada International, cultural initiatives and Canadian Studies programs Ottawa has promoted its worldview. GAC has also operated a history department and vast media operation.

But it is the military that has Canada's largest PR machine. The Canadian Forces aggressively protects its image and promotes its worldview. DND operates a history department, postsecondary institution and media outlets, as well as spending lavishly on war commemorations. Beginning with South Africa, then World War I, World War II, Korea, Iraq, Somalia, Yugoslavia, Afghanistan, Libya and Iraq/Syria, the military has aggressively controlled information during war. Formal censorship existed during WWI, WWII and the Korean War.

The idea of a benevolent Canadian foreign policy may be intellectually hollow, but it's well-grounded in structures of propaganda. It rests on a web of state and corporate generated ideas institutes and a media sphere largely owned and dependent on mega corporations. Even without formal restrictions, the corporate media (and CBC) permit only a narrow spectrum of opinion regarding Canadian foreign policy. Various factors explain the media's biased international coverage. Most importantly, a small number of mega corporations own most of Canada's media and depend on other large corporations for advertising revenue. Less dependent on advertising, CBC relies on government funds and has long been close to the foreign policy establishment. All major media firms rely on easily accessible information, which is largely generated by GAC, DND, internationally focused corporations and US wire services. Finally, the military, foreign affairs and major corporations have the power to punish media that upset them.

***

What I describe below constitutes a 'propaganda system'. Most of its various constituent parts acknowledge their purpose is to influence public opinion and its various elements are interconnected and reinforcing.

A Propaganda System

2. Canada's largest PR machine — The Military

> "History will be kind to me for I intend to write it."
> **Winston Churchill**

What would be the foreign affairs equivalent to the hype-generating and self-consciously influence-peddling NHL team PR department? Unquestionably the military. Its tentacles reach into every sort of institution shaping public opinion. Like the Habs' PR department it has close relations with the media and sponsors an incredible variety of events designed to generate public sympathy.

The Canadian Forces take public relations very seriously. Operating the largest PR machine in the country, DND runs various media, academic, think tank and cultural initiatives. "It is the responsibility of the Department of National Defense to build and maintain a constituency for defence among Canada's citizens," noted a headline in the military backed Journal of Conference of Defence Associations Institute.[1] In the 1990 article former Chief of the Defence Staff, General Ramsey M. Withers, explained: "In its attempts to place the facts before the public, DND has done a great deal of good, honest work. Prompt, professionally compiled press announcements; the creation of a speakers bureau; an endowment of chairs of strategic studies at universities; the production of special videos; the provision of expert testimony to parliamentary committees; the support given associations and organizations such as the Conference of Defence Associations and the Canadian Institute of Strategic Studies."[2]

While hard to fathom, media relations may be DND leaders' single biggest concern. Briefing files for two new defence ministers in 2014 and 2015 prioritized PR above any other consideration.

A Propaganda System

Describing the 2015 briefing, *Embassy*'s Marie-Danielle Smith noted: "In a book about 'Key Strategic Issues,' about 70 pages long, there are 17 pages worth of public opinion and media analysis, complete with graphs tracking Canadians' perceptions of the department over years of polling data. Conversely, only two pages of the document appear to be entirely devoted to Operation Reassurance in Central and Eastern Europe, two pages to Operation Impact in Iraq and Syria, four to NATO and two to NORAD."[3]

As part of their PR strategy, the CF is secretive about the breadth of their media activities. But internal files provide some sense of their scope. A government document *Embassy* uncovered through an access to information request says DND has "over 13 independent public affairs organizations."[4]

In 2010-11 the CF admitted to spending $354 million on public relations and related military commemorations.[5] Six hundred and sixty-one staff members worked on this effort.[6] According to another 2011 report, DND's Public Affairs had 286 staff.[7] Public Affairs Officers (PAOs) work from Public Affairs Headquarters at National Defence Headquarters in Ottawa and a-half-dozen regional offices across the country. Additionally, every CF base, army division and naval headquarters employs PAOs.[8] DND's website lists contact information for 50 different media relations offices.[9]

PAOs write press releases, organize press conferences, monitor the news, brief journalists, befriend reporters and editors, or perform various other media-related activities. A large proportion of the news stories about the military are based on CF statements and events.

The CF also devotes significant energy to media training. With a 25 person staff, the Defence Public Affairs Learning Centre (DPALC) has two television studios, two radio studios, editing suites, a control room and a small library. The Gatineau, Québec-based DPALC seeks "to develop a cadre of professional Public Affairs Officers in the Canadian Armed Forces, and to give defence personnel, especially Canadian Armed Forces members, the training and expertise they need to connect effectively with Canadians and provide communications advice to senior leaders of the Canadian Armed Forces."[10] DPALC offers 6-10 month courses for PAOs, who often possess experience in the field or a communications related degree. The learning centre also offers day or weeklong media training courses to hundreds of officers every year, which is on top of the media training offered at Canadian Forces College, Royal Military College and Royal Military College Saint-Jean.[11]

"The Canadian Forces studies the news media, writes about them in its refereed journals—the Canadian Army Journal and the Canadian Military Journal — learns from them, develops policies for them and trains for them in a systematic way," explains Bob Bergen, a professor at the University of Calgary's Centre for Military and Strategic Studies.[12] "Canadian journalists simply do not access the Canadian Forces in the scholarly fashion that the military studies them. There are no peer-reviewed journals to which they contribute reflections on their success or failure as an industry to cover the 1991 Persian Gulf War or the 1999 Kosovo Air War."[13]

The CF closely follows the coverage of military affairs. "DND's sprawling media relations machine keeps tabs on tens of thousands of newspaper articles a year," reported *Embassy*.[14] During fiscal year 2012-13 DND monitored a whopping 29,519 newspaper articles.[15] Journalists' questions, who contacts the department most frequently, the information released to each reporter etc. is compiled and made available to relevant officials.[16] Building reporter profiles helps Public Affairs respond to the thousands of media requests DND receives annually. Depending on Public Affairs' assessment of the reporter and question/request they may fulfill it, stall, release partial information etc.

Having the resources to monitor the media helps the CF shape the public conversation of military affairs. DND's heft influences coverage in other ways. With the CF regularly hiring former journalists and journalism students, many PAOs have a personal connection to those covering military affairs. This tends to dampen critical coverage, especially in base communities.[17] In some smaller communities the CF is among the few employers offering communications work and the possibility of future employment tends to lessen a reporter's zeal to question/embarrass the military.

As part of a plan to induce positive coverage and deter critical reporting, in the fall of 2015 David Pugliese revealed the top soldier's call for the "weaponization of public affairs." On the positive side, new Chief of Defence Staff Jon Vance proposed to leak "good news" stories to "friendly" journalists hoping they would portray the military in a positive light. Reporters were expected to participate in the scheme because a leak can lead to a high profile story (with little effort) and "friendly" journalists would gain access to the chief of defence staff and other top officials.

While leaking official documents is run-of-the-mill in government PR, the repressive element of the "weaponization of public affairs" was more controversial. Journalists producing unflattering stories about the military were to be the target of phone calls to their boss, letters to the editor and other 'flack' designed to undercut their credibility in the eyes of readers and their employers.[18]

The CF didn't stop at complaining to journalists' bosses. The top brass repeatedly asked the military's National Investigative Service (NIS) to investigate reporters' sources. In 2011 NIS investigated prominent CTV journalist Robert Fife after he uncovered documents about Chief of Defence Staff Walt Natynczyk spending over $1 million in public funds flying to hockey games and a Caribbean vacation.[19] Pugliese described this as a blatant "intimidation tactic by the NIS against a journalist who was clearly not playing military cheerleader."[20]

In a similar incident, NIS spent more than a month investigating how Pugliese obtained information about a major Pacific Ocean military exercise in spring 2012. While the *Ottawa Citizen* defence reporter said the information came from a US Navy release, which the NSI investigation ultimately supported, DND officials believed Pugliese was tipped off by a friendly PAO. *Esprit du Corp* editor Scott Taylor pointed out that the investigation had nothing to do with operational security. "No classified information was divulged. No operational security jeopardized. No Canadian sailors' lives were put in peril as a result of Pugliese's rather innocuous story, but [defence minister Peter] MacKay's timetable for release [of the information] had not been strictly adhered to."[21]

According to Taylor, NIS was employed on at least four occasions to investigate the source of information for stories.[22] Yet in none of these instances was classified material reported.

The military is sensitive about embarrassing leaks. In 2014 *Embassy* reported on ministerial briefing notes concerning the "problem" of "leaks" and former soldiers speaking with the media.[23] A year earlier the CF required soldiers wounded in Afghanistan to sign a form saying they wouldn't criticize senior officers on Facebook or other social media. Given to injured personnel transferred to the Joint Personnel Support Unit, the form stated "it must be clearly understood that the inappropriate use of social media can have serious ramifications for the CAF; it can erode public trust, cause serious breeches of security and destroy team cohesion."[24]

Former soldiers are a concern since active CF members are restricted in what they can say publicly or post online. Under the Defence Administrative Orders and Directives and Queens Regulations and Orders, soldiers are not allowed to discredit the CF or discourage other troops from their duties.[25] While officers can speak to journalists about subjects under their command, any "enunciation, defence or criticism, expressed or implied, of service, departmental or government policy" is forbidden.[26] With the rise of social media the chief of defence staff ordered CF members to obtain authorization before posting information on Facebook or other online outlets. In 2006 Rick Hillier wrote, "[CF] members are to consult with their chain of command before publishing [CF]-related information and imagery to the internet, regardless of how innocuous the information may seem."[27]

To enable democratic oversight of public institutions the Access to Information Act provides individuals and institutions the right to government records for $5 per request. In the 2012-13 fiscal year DND reviewed 60,055 pages released under access legislation.[28] The Directorate of Information Support of the Strategic Joint Staff can restrict information for numerous reasons, including if deemed "injurious to the conduct of international affairs, the defence of Canada or the detection, prevention or suppression of subversive or hostile activities."[29]

Sensitive information is rarely released and censorship is often employed arbitrarily or to avoid embarrassment.[30] In 2006 David Pugliese detailed the results of 23 access requests in which 87 pieces of information were censored for "security reasons", which had previously been released or were available on government web sites.[31]

DND has repeatedly broken access laws. In 2015 the Federal Court of Appeal reprimanded the ministry for responding to an information request concerning the sale of military assets by saying it would take 1,100 days to retrieve the information.[32] Under access law public institutions must produce records within 30 days or inform the requester of a reasonable extension.

Informed that an officer attended a talk Rideau Institute director Steven Staples delivered about the war in Afghanistan on January 26, 2006, Pugliese requested all CF documents mentioning public speeches in Halifax between January 15 and 30 of that year. Department officials claimed they did "a thorough and complete search" and couldn't find any record of an officer who attended the function and wrote a report.[33] But, the officer assigned to Staples' speech inadvertently left a record. When the *Ottawa Citizen* turned it over to the information commissioner, DND acknowledged the record existed.[34]

The secrecy is long-standing. In 1996 Information Commissioner John Grace pointed to a "culture within ND[national defense]/CF of secrecy and suspicion of those seeking information."[35]

The military also has a more explicit means of bypassing access rules. Since the early 2000s DND has massively expanded special forces personnel partly because they are not required to divulge any information about their operations. Ottawa can deploy these troops abroad and the public is none the wiser. But, noted the late right wing *Toronto Sun* columnist Peter Worthington, "a secret army within the army is anathema to democracy."[36]

CF-created content directly shapes the media sphere and broader public discussion. Combat Camera provides news organizations with video footage and photographic stills of remembrance services and military engagements, but Combat Camera and Public Affairs don't generally release images of Canadian soldiers killing civilians or other controversial actions.

The military produces dozens of publications. Among the more significant, *The Maple Leaf* is distributed weekly to bases across Canada while *Trident* and *Lookout* cover the naval bases in Halifax and Esquimalt respectively.[37]

The military's many websites make articles, speeches, reports and other types of information easily accessible to the public. DND/CF websites generally give one-sided, nationalistic, accounts of military actions. "Canadians in Korea: Valour Remembered", for instance, omits the millions of North Koreans and Chinese killed in a war partially motivated by Washington's desire to pump prime its economy.[38] (Secretary of State Dean Acheson later admitted that the decision to fight in Korea was "a purely political one" that "had made it politically possible for the United States to secure congressional and public support for a quick and great increase in defense expenditures."[39])

As part of its online strategy, in 2008 the CF launched two YouTube channels.[40] In an article titled "The Canadian Armed Forces 'YouTube war': A cross-border military-social media complex" Tanner Mirrlees points out that the military employs Facebook, Twitter, Pinterest, Linkedin, Flickr and other social media platforms to promote its positions and recruit new members.

DND spends $10-$20 million annually on recruitment.[41] The CF advertises on Xbox video games and Twitter, as well as bus shelters and Stanley Cup playoff broadcasts.[42] Describing it as "one of the primary windows through which Canadians view their military", Lieutenant-Colonel Michael Goodspeed calls "recruiting advertising … the most powerful form of PR available to the CF."[43] Its "Fight Distress, Fight Fear, Fight Chaos—Fight with the Canadian Forces" recruiting campaign won a series of marketing awards in the late 2000s.[44]

Recruitment and community outreach are closely intertwined. With millions of Canadians watching Snowbird airshows every year, DND calls them an "important public relations and recruiting tool."[45]

At the height of the war in Afghanistan the CF launched Operation Connection to mobilize the whole armed forces to "make contact and attract recruits."[46] A message sent to soldiers in 2006 explained: "As a member of the Canadian Forces, we count on your presence at the hundreds of activities we will participate in over the next year … festivals, ship visits, visits to schools, car shows, job fairs, air shows, sports events … Telephone your children's schools or your grandmother's seniors' residence and ask if you and/or your unit could be of help planning a Canadian Forces Day event or setting up a Remembrance Day program."[47] Operation Connection showcased the CF at Canada Day festivities, Santa Claus parades, NHL games etc. CBC Our World host Brian Stewart described the "information machine" responsible for Op Connection as "a public affairs unit that dwarfs all other government promotion offices."[48]

Ottawa also promoted specific war celebrations. In 2012 the federal government launched a $28 million initiative to commemorate the 200th anniversary of the War of 1812.[49]

Commemorating "glorious" wars can boost the CF's standing. Bruised by the long and unpopular war in Afghanistan, the CF sought "several positive, proactive communication opportunities" to shore up its image.[50] According to an internal file Canadian Press uncovered, the military had "plans for commemorative activities, including a series of World War I events", which were to receive millions of dollars of CF money through 2020.[51]

Alongside specific war commemorations, the federal government spends tens of millions of dollars on war monuments. Ottawa is home to a National War Memorial, Korean War Monument, National Victoria Cross Memorial, Veterans Memorial Highway, National Aboriginal Veterans Monument, Boer War Memorial etc. There are more than 7,500 memorials registered with Veterans Affairs'.[52] Veterans Affairs allocates tens of millions of dollars annually to war memorials and related "awareness" activities. Between 2006 and 2014 the department's Community Engagement Partnership Fund dished out $13 million for hundreds of small projects recognizing veterans such as $5,000 for a Remembrance Day service at the University of British Columbia.[53] During 2010-11 fiscal year $41 million was spent on Canada Remembers, which included "awareness and participation of Canadians in remembrance activities" and "maintenance and improvements of memorials, cemeteries and grave markers."[54]

Veterans Affairs produces "learning resources" designed for different grades. A Veterans Affairs education officer explained: "At the beginning of the school year, we send a promotional kit to all schools, containing an example of each of the learning resources available for that year. ... There is also a Veterans' Week Speakers Program and DND co-ordinates visits by Canadian Forces members to schools."[55]

Part veteran commemoration and part war memorial, the Canadian War Museum (CWM) re-opened in 2005. The $136 million institution near Parliament includes the Royal Canadian Legion Hall of Honour and is designed for light to shine on the headstone of the Unknown Soldier at 11 am on Remembrance Day. Officially, CWM says it "helps tell the story of Canada's military history to Canadians through its collections, its research, its exhibitions, and its public and education programs."[56] Its re-launch was highly successful and 500,000 visitors a year have passed through the new museum, which dates to 1880 when the militia began displaying military artefacts and archival materials. A 55,000 square foot building, CWM houses a large collection of war art and CF Artists Program works. The museum also has an arrangement with DND to showcase obsolete military equipment.

With a 100-person staff and $65 million a year budget, CWM hosts military history conferences and public lectures.[57] It lends schools free learning kits, which contain artefacts related to World War I and materials to support in-class activities and lessons. It also includes a Military History Research Centre, which has 55,000 volumes.[58] At the academic level, CWM supports Wilfrid Laurier University's *Canadian Military History* journal and the University of British Columbia Press *Studies in Canadian Military History Series*.[59]

CWM works with other museums and historical institutions. Its exhibition titled "Canvas of War: Masterpieces from the Canadian War Museum" was visited by half a million people in nine art galleries and museums across the country between 1998 and 2004.[60] An accompanying book sold 7,000 copies.[61]

CWM regularly partners with the more than 60 CF museums.[62] Accredited CF museums receive space in a DND establishment and financial assistance. According to CF Administrative Order 27-5, "the role of CF Museums is to preserve and interpret Canadian military heritage in order to increase the sense of identity and esprit de corps within the CF and to support the goals of the Department of National Defence."[63]

DND's Directorate of History and Heritage also supports the Organization of Military Museums of Canada.[64] The 50-year old organization seeks "to preserve the military heritage of Canada by encouraging the establishment and operation of military museums."[65]

***

Just as the Montréal Canadiens are in the business of moulding everything written about the Habs, official military historians have shaped foreign policy consciousness. They dominated academic discussion of war into the 1960s and have published at least 40 official volumes and dozens of other works.[66]

At the end of World War I the Department of Militia and Defence established a historical section.[67] Wanting its historians to write the "foundational studies" of Canadian wars, World War I and II records were tightly controlled. Only "accredited regimental historians" and military researchers could access the documents.[68] In *Clio's Warriors: Canadian Historians and the Writing of the World Wars* Tim Cook writes, "it has been the official historians of the Department of National Defence who, for much of the 20th century, have controlled the academic writing on the two world wars."[69]

But, official historians' influence has extended far beyond the "Great Wars". In 1919 the historical section published the first in a three-volume series titled "A history of the organization, development and services of the military and naval forces of Canada from the peace of Paris in 1763, to the present time." Immediately after the Korean War official historians wrote two books on the subject and published another in 1966.[70] (Academics all but failed to revisit Canada's role in Korea until the late 1990s.)[71]

A Propaganda System

During its first four decades the historical section greatly influenced the discussion of military matters. "From 1915 to 1960," Cook writes, "it was the official historians, augmented by only a few others — memoirists, regimental historians, and a handful of journalists — who controlled this burgeoning field [military history]."[72]

The historical sections had both direct and indirect influence. Official historians published a large share of the early books on Canadian militarism. Additionally, they greatly influenced academia. The historical section was the "graduate school in military history", notes DND historian William A. Douglas, until "university departments started producing postgraduates."[73] Roger Sarty echoes this opinion in "The Origins of Academic Military History in Canada, 1940-1967". The article traces the roots of the most important publications in establishing Canadian academic military history. "The main impetus [of the seven publications]", Sarty writes, "came from the Canadian Army's official history programme in the Second World War, and the Army's decision to establish a history department at the Royal Military College of Canada. These initiatives opened opportunities for gifted young and mid-career scholars, whose interest in military subjects originated or was sharpened by their military service during the Second World War. These scholars became some of the most prominent historians in the country."[74]

In the two decades after World War II individuals who worked in the military's historical sections filled many academic posts in military history and associated fields.[75] And they were often influential in their field.[76] Head of the War Artist Program and deputy-director of the Historical Section at Canadian Army Headquarters in London, George Stanley led the history department at the Royal Military College after World War II.[77] During his career Stanley was president of the Canadian Historical Association and Kingston Historical Society, as well as a member of the Massey Commission Committee on Historic Sites and Monuments and the Archaeological and Historic Sites Board of Ontario.[78] He was also chairman of the federal government's Centennial Publications Committee.

At the military-run Royal Military College Stanley taught Jack Granatstein and Desmond Morton. These two individuals, who both worked in DND's historical section, published hundreds of books and articles on Canadian military history and foreign policy.[79]

A military historian for two decades, Colonel Charles Stacey has had "more influence on how Canadians view their nation's military history" than any other individual.[80] He published a dozen books and in 2000 Granatstein wrote that Stacey's "books continue to be read and to have great influence on military and foreign policy historians."[81]

During WWII Stacey took charge of the historical section at Canadian military headquarters in London and directed the army's historical section for 14 years after the war.[82] (Stacey returned to DND between 1965 and 1966 to consolidate the army, air force and navy historical sections into a Directorate of History.) Stacey operated under strict conditions. Superiors often interceded in his work and the minister approved publication of his books.[83] On a number of occasions cabinet discussed and recommended changes to Stacey's work.[84] After reading an early draft of a Royal Canadian Army Medical Corp history, Stacey told a new member of the historical section to tone down his criticism. "You cannot conceive the sensitiveness of official people concerning records for publication. ... Even the most apparently harmless comments can arouse a surprising amount of suspicion and resentment."[85]

During his time at DND Stacey led the Canadian Historical Association and after leaving the military in 1959 he taught — and became "close friends" with — Robert Bothwell and Norman Hillmer at the University of Toronto.[86] Hillmer and Bothwell have significantly influenced Canadian foreign policy historiography.[87] In

A Propaganda System

a 2010 article titled "Where have all of Canada's diplomatic historians gone?" Adam Chapnick says its "rare to find a new historical book on Canada's external relations that is not somehow linked to Bothwell or Hillmer."[88]

Chapnick describes Bothwell and Hillmer, who was at DND's Directorate of History for 18 years, as the "first generation" of Canadian diplomatic historians.[89] "The second is largely found in the Department of Foreign Affairs and International Trade. DFAIT is home to a senior departmental historian and adjunct professor at Carleton University, Hector Mackenzie, and a historical section, previously led by John Hilliker and now ably coordinated by Greg Donaghy. Mackenzie, Donaghy, and others, including Mary Halloran and Janice Cavell, publish regularly in leading academic journals and collections."[90] Foreign Affairs' historians also speak at conferences and help other academics write books. Every year the research division offers a Norman Robertson Human Security and Cadieux-Léger Fellowship to two PhD students working on "a topic of relevance to Canada's foreign policy priorities."[91]

***

Created in 1950, the Directorate of Historical Research and Reports was tasked with overseeing and publishing External Affairs documents. Since 1967 the Foreign Affairs historical section has published 26 volumes of documents on Canadian external relations.[92] Each book in the series covers a handful of years beginning in 1909 when External Affairs was established. Targeted at academics and journalists, the reference books are largely donated to research libraries, senior scholars and Canadian Studies centres abroad through the government's depository library program.[93]

Decades later the directorate still tightly controlled damning information. In an article titled "Documenting the Diplomats: The Origins and Evolution of Documents on Canadian External Relations" Greg Donaghy writes, "[under-secretary of External

Affairs] Norman Robertson, forbade [head of the Historical Division George Parkin] Glazebrook from printing material from the First World War that discussed the possibility that Canada might assume direct control of the British West Indies, an obviously sensitive subject as the Caribbean Islands marched toward their independence in the early 1960s."[94]

DND's Directorate of History and Heritage is big brother to its Foreign Affairs counterpart. A dozen historians are part of the directorate's 50-person staff "mandated to preserve and communicate Canada's military history and foster pride in a Canadian military heritage."[95] They answer "1,000 questions of an historical nature" annually, helping high school students with assignments and academics navigate archival inquiries.[96] The directorate also works with the media. In the early 1990s, for instance, senior military historian Brereton Greenhous was a special advisor during production of the CBC film *Dieppe 1942*.[97] Similarly, director of the historical section Charles Stacey vetted *Canada At War*, the first television miniseries to document Canada's part in the Second World War, before the National Film Board produced program played on CBC.[98]

The directorate also helped veterans exert political pressure. After a backlash to a Canadian War Museum exhibit that mentioned the WWII Allied Bomber Command targeting civilians, senior DND historian Serge Bernier was asked to write a report. Bernier concluded the exhibit was hurtful to the veterans.[99]

Alongside the directorate of history, DND funded the Royal Military College of Canada (RMC). Dozens of its 150+ faculty teach history, political science and other humanities. They publish articles and books on foreign policy themes and have schooled a number of prominent foreign policy commentators. The only federally run university, DND provides about $70 million annually to RMC and the defence minister is chancellor.[100]

RMC, as well as the historical sections at DND and GAC, influence academic debate about Canada's place in the world. Adding to the military's influence within academia, they occasionally hold scholarly conferences such as the navy's "Submarines in Canada: Past, Present and Future." The Canadian Defence Academy Press and the Canadian Special Operations Forces Command Professional Development Centre publish scholarly books while the *Canadian Military Journal* and *Canadian Army Journal* publish peer-reviewed articles.[101]

The reach of the military extends deep into the halls of academia. The Department of National Defence's Security and Defence Forum (SDF) was established in 1967 to "develop a domestic competence and national interest in defence issues of relevance to Canada's security."[102]

Previously named the Military and Strategic Studies Program, SDF includes a Scholarship and Internship program, Special Projects, a Chair of Defence Management Studies and funding for "centres of expertise". SDF's scholarship and internship initiative ploughs $300,000 a year into academic awards that "supports graduate and post-graduate studies in Canadian defence and security issues."[103] SDF also funds a handful of 12-month internships each year "for students with Master's degrees who are interested in working in security and defence-related organizations."[104] Scholarship recipients have worked with General Motors Defence (now General Dynamics), the Canadian War Museum and Conference of Defence Associations.[105]

SDF channels hundreds of thousands of dollars annually into special projects. These include an International Conference Fund and National Conference Fund as well as other efforts to facilitate collaboration among "security" scholars. It also includes funds to give "members of the SDF community an opportunity to visit Canadian Forces operations or bases" and to "bring students from SDF centres and SDF award recipients to National Defence Headquarters."[106]

Adding to its special projects budget, in 2015 SDF gave the University of New Brunswick Milton F. Gregg Centre for the Study of War and Society $488,000 to produce educational material about Canada's Victoria Cross recipients who demonstrated "conspicuous bravery" fighting on behalf of the British Empire between 1856 and 1945.[107]

The SDF's major activity is to fund a dozen "centres of expertise", including Dalhousie's Centre for Foreign Policy Studies, University of New Brunswick's Gregg Centre, Queen's Chair of Defence Management Studies and Centre for International Relations, Carleton's Centre for Security and Defence Studies, York's Centre for International and Security Studies, Wilfrid Laurier's Centre for Military, Strategic & Disarmament Studies, University of Manitoba's Centre for Defence and Security Studies, University of Calgary's Centre for Military and Strategic Studies, University of British-Columbia's Centre of International Relations, Université de Montréal/McGill's Groupe d'étude et de recherche sur la sécurité internationale, Université du Québec à Montréal/Concordia's Centre d'études des politiques étrangères et de sécurité and Université Laval's Institut québécois des hautes études internationales. To receive SDF funding departments generally commit to offering a minimum number of courses with "significant security and defence content."[108]

In some instances military money makes up a significant share of a department's budget. In 2008-09, for instance, Dalhousie's Centre for Foreign Policy Studies received 56% of its budget from SDF and other DND channels.[109] The centre received a little more than half its $323,636 in military funding from SDF and $153,000 indirectly from the navy, which paid the salary of a Dalhousie Defence Fellow affiliated with the Centre for Foreign Policy Studies.[110]

Alongside its support for "centres of expertise", SDF funded a Chair of Defence Management Studies. DND gave Queen's University's Defence Management Studies more than $200,000 annually.[111] As chair of the Queen's program through the 2000s

Douglas Bland received $825,000 to "conduct outreach activities with the Canadian public ... and Parliament about security and defence issues."[112] Bland called the mid-2000s counterinsurgency war in Afghanistan "the right mission for Canada and the right mission for the Afghan people" and criticized "years of Liberal [party] neglect of ... defence policy and the Canadian Forces."[113]

Dozens of academics writing on military, security and foreign policy issues received SDF funds. They generally articulated pro-military positions, which caused a minor controversy during the war in Afghanistan. In a 2008 article University of Ottawa professor Amir Attaran wrote, "when DND needs a kind word in Parliament or the media —presto! — an SDF sponsored scholar often appears, without disclosing his or her financial link."[114] Even SDF proponent and ardent militarist Jack Granatstein admitted in a 2011 op-ed "what the government seems to want from SDF academics is uncritical support for its partisan policies."[115]

DND identifies what it receives from SDF. Various DND reports breakdown the number of courses, publications, outreach events, media interviews and op-eds SDF funding enables. According to a 2009-10 review, the program "sponsored 444 events, reaching more than 18,000 people" and SDF scholars "conducted over 1,550 media interviews and produced nearly 116 op-ed articles on a wide range of topics."[116] SDF subsidized numerous books and supported 230 courses, which educated 10,000 students. A 2010 DND report evaluating the program concluded: "Without the presence of the SDF, university resources would most likely not be allocated towards hiring security- and defence-minded academics and the Centres indicate they would cease to be replenished when current SDF scholars retire."[117] The defence minister made the same point about SDF's predecessor in a 1984 House of Commons debate. Jean-Jacques Blais said "ten years ago it was difficult to attract students to Military and Strategic Studies programs. Today there are 598 undergraduates taking military and strategic studies at three teaching centres. ... The Military and Strategic Studies program has been remarkably successful, considering its relatively low-budget."[118]

SDF funds launched a number of university departments. Université du Québec à Montréal's Centre d'études des politiques étrangères et de sécurité was created with funds from the Military and Strategic Studies Program in 1991 while Queen's Defence Management Studies "was established in 1996 with financial support from the Canadian Department of National Defence."[119] MSSP and the Donner Canadian Foundation (see chapter 3) funded the establishment of Dalhousie's Centre for Foreign Policy Studies (CFPS) in 1971.[120] In a 1992 article on the history of CFPS professor Danford W. Middlemiss wrote, "the principal source of continuing financial support for the CFPS since its founding has been the Department of National Defence's MSSP."[121] Middlemiss also points to CFPS' "liaison activities with National Defence Headquarters" and says the department "continues to cooperate closely with Maritime command."[122]

York's chair in strategic studies was also established with MSSP funds. With former Brigadier General George Bell taking a senior administrative position at the university, York attracted military funds in the early 1970s. Ken Bell and Desmond Morton write, "his influence helped ensure that York's 'chair' gradually developed into a lively centre for strategic studies, even at a time when universities were being forced to retrench."[123]

MSSP was established partly to replace the Canadian Officers Training Corps, University Naval Training Division and Royal Canadian Air Force University Reserve Training Program. In the 1950s and 60s most universities had a unit of the Canadian Officers Training Corps, which was launched at McGill, Queens and the University of Toronto in 1912.[124] According to Lee Windsor, deputy director of the University of New Brunswick's Gregg Centre for the

A Propaganda System

Study of War and Society, the Canadian Officers Training Corps "introduced university undergraduates to a form of military service on campus, providing them with leadership and other military training and preparing them to join the reserve or the regular force if they wished to do so."[125]

Often under pressure from antiwar activists, these programs were "closed down in the Sixties to be replaced by 'chairs in military studies'", write Bell and Morton. "While the innovation helped establish military and strategic studies in some Canadian universities, the results were mixed, and the arm's-length relationship necessary to preserve academic autonomy sometimes galled senior officers at NDHQ [national defense headquarters]."[126]

In 2011 the Senate standing committee on national security and defence recommended re-establishing the Canadian Officers Training Corps. The University of Alberta agreed to host a trial of a program that "allow[s] people to simultaneously obtain a university degree while also gaining leadership experience in the Canadian Armed Forces (CAF) Reserves."[127] The four-year Civil Military Leadership Pilot Initiative was "co-directed by the University of Alberta and the CAF" and the government hoped to export this "test model" to other universities.[128] Launched in September 2013, the Civil Military Leadership Pilot Initiative was to be completed in 2017. "We are delighted with the strengthening of links between Canada's military and our institution," said University of Alberta Provost Martin Ferguson-Pell.[129]

In recent years the SDF budget ranged from $2–2.5 million annually. But, that doesn't include the cost of administering the program or hundreds of thousands of dollars in bursaries SDF distributes each year through the Association of Universities and Colleges of Canada.[130]

The committee that doles out SDF funds is composed of security studies professors and "members of the community" who often have "direct links with the military-industrial complex."[131] In 2008 this included a former vice–president of military firm CAE, Arthur C. Perron, and retired general and senior military advisor to EnCana, Cameron Ross.[132]

SDF and military funds have significantly increased the academic space devoted to "security studies". But this highly politicized funding also makes universities cautious about developing programs that could anger the CF. In a 2001 Peace.ca article University of Western Ontario professor Peter Langille wrote, "one major impediment to peace studies in Canada has been the near monopoly on related issues controlled carefully by DND's Security and Defence Forum through 15 well-funded university SDF centres. Most of our larger university programmes in international relations, conflict and security are very dependent on the DND $ and nervous of any new development that might challenge their access and influence."[133] Six years later Langille told an IPS reporter "[DND] has a near monopoly over discussion and programmes not only of defence issues, but also IR [international relations] within Canadian academe."[134]

Adding to its influence with academia, the CF also directs tens of millions of dollars in less politicized university research funding. DND has a Research Partnership Program with Natural Sciences and Engineering Research Council of Canada (NSERC) and Defence Research and Development Canada (DRDC) collaborates with many universities.[135] With 1,400 employees and a $350 million budget, DRDC scientists have postings at many universities and participate in various co-op programs.[136]

The military also has other ties to post-secondary institutions. In 2006 the Canadian Defence Academy helped a number of colleges add military diplomas and programs formerly provided at military institutions. The Canadian Armed Forces College Opportunities Program offers diplomas in Military Arts and Sciences. As part of this shift, in 2012 the Association of Canadian Community Colleges provided input to the House of Commons Standing Committee on National Defence on "Maintaining the Readiness of the Canadian Forces."[137]

Some defence procurement contracts require companies to sponsor university research. Boeing helped Memorial University set up a Mechatronic Development and Prototyping Facility while Lockheed Martin gave Dalhousie $2-million for research into "quantum computing, physics and material sciences."[138] (Dalhousie is a member of the Aerospace and Defence Industries Association of Nova Scotia while the University of New Brunswick is a member of that province's branch.)[139]

Many Canadian universities also receive US military funding. According to the Canadian Military Industry Database Report, most large Canadian universities have received funding from American military agencies such as the US Navy, US Air Force, US Strategic Defense Initiative or US Defence Threat Reduction Agency.[140]

While not directly related to foreign policy idea formation, funding science research seeps into the politics of these institutions. More directly, the Security and Defence Forum gives the military influence in the social sciences. So does the RMC, official historians and, as we'll see, a network of DND-backed think tanks.

3. Military Institutes and Think Tanks

While the military is the single most powerful driver of public opinion on foreign policy, the Canadian Forces are not satisfied with the influence of their massive bureaucracy and have helped set up various associated institutions as part of their propaganda system. The advantage of military "arms-length" organizations is they create the illusion of a diversity of voices and offer synergies by involving non-military personnel. One could compare such an arrangement with the fan clubs NHL teams promote.

The following are the most important arms-length military organizations set up since Confederation:

Royal Canadian Military Institute

For more than a century the Royal Canadian Military Institute (RCMI) has operated as a social club for military officers and (later) "civilians with like interests". In 1890 the RCMI was set up "to provide in an Institute for the defence forces of Canada a Library, museum and club for the purposes of the promotion of military art, science and literature, to gather and preserve the records of the defence forces, and develop its specialized field in Canadian history."[1] Today, it claims to be "the pre-eminent Canadian forum for discussion, research and education on defence, security and foreign affairs."[2]

The Toronto-based institution publishes a journal, policy papers and books. It also operates a library and museum and holds Military History Nights, a lecture series and annual concert at Roy Thomson Hall (the 25th anniversary show was titled "Sacrifice & Glory: Commemorating a Legacy"). In recent years the vice chair of its Security Studies Committee has contributed regularly to the

40

Ottawa Citizen, Globe and Mail and other media outlets. To get a sense of Eric Morse's politics, one op-ed by the former External Affairs official carried the headline "The deadly chaos behind Putin's mysterious acts".[3]

Toronto Garrison officers who suppressed the Riel Rebellion and First Nations independence on the prairies established RCMI. The driving force behind the institute was Lieutenant-Colonel William D. Otter who led a force that attacked Cree and Assiniboine warriors on May 2, 1885 near Battleford, Saskatchewan, in the Battle of Cut Knife. Without orders to do so, Otter asked permission to "punish [Cree leader] Poundmaker."[4] Close to the RCMI until his death in 1928, the Canadian-born son of English settlers would later command the Royal Canadian Regiment of Infantry in the 1899-1902 Boer War and came out of retirement during World War I to oversee the internment of 8,500, mostly Ukrainian, individuals living in Canada from countries that were part of the Austro-Hungarian and Ottoman empires.[5]

RCMI promoted Canada's participation in the Boer War, which strengthened Britain's position in southern Africa and control over rich mineral resources. In *Royal Canadian Military Institute: 100 years,* Ken Bell and Desmond Morton write, "The Canadian Military Institute would be part of the pressure that sent Canadians to South Africa."[6]

The institute was dominated by ardent imperialists. In *The Sense of Power: Studies in the Ideas of Canadian Imperialism*, Carl Berger described RCMI as the "centre of martial imperialists" in the early 1900s while the institute boasted that most of its 500 members in 1910 were descendants of United Empire loyalists.[7] As Canada moved away from its British imperial roots, the organization added the "Royal" prefix to Canadian Military Institute in 1948.[8] RCMI executive member Major George Drew proclaimed, "let us who know what the love of Empire really means keep before us the vision

A Propaganda System

of a great United Empire of from two or three hundred million white Britons to cooperate in peace as well as in war."[9]

RCMI's early leaders were well connected. Its initial patron was Governor General Lord Stanley (namesake of a cup the Maple Leafs may never hoist again). The institute received early financial support from Eaton's, Bank of Commerce, Toronto Street Railway, Simpson's, Imperial Bank and the Osler and Hammond brokerage firm.[10] In 1892 the Ontario and federal governments began giving the institute a $100 ($1,500 today) annual subsidy.[11] During a mid-1970s controversy over its exclusion of women, chief of the defence staff, General Jacques Dextraze, "warned he could no longer be vice patron of an organization that barred women. Nor was it likely that the Institute could continue to receive its [federal government] grant if it continued to discriminate."[12]

Partly sponsored by RCMI, the Canadian Defence League agitated for universal military training and service in the lead up to World War I.[13] Its founding mandate called for "a non-political, educational campaign looking to the adoption of the principle of patriotic, unpaid, or universal naval or military training, in the belief that such training conduces to the industrial, physical and moral elevation of the whole people."[14] According to Defence League president William Merritt, universal military training would bring "safety to the Dominion and Empire."[15] The league published a monthly magazine from mid-1909 to mid-1914 and periodically during World War I."[16] It also organized conferences and speaking tours across the country.[17]

The Defence League had powerful backers. Longstanding MP and future Minister for Militia and Defence, Sir Frederick Borden, and federal MP and future Premier of Ontario, Sir George Ross, spoke at the league's launch.[18] It was financially supported by retail store owner John C. Eaton and Bank of Commerce head Sir Edmund Walker.[19]

Conference of Defence Associations

Established in 1932, the Conference of Defence Associations (CDA) describes itself as a "non-partisan, independent, non-profit organization [that] expresses its ideas and opinions with a view to influencing government security and defence policy."[20] The Ottawa-based lobby/think tank is not a registered charity, but the CDA Institute is.

Since its inception CDA has been indirectly or directly financed by DND.[21] Initially, member associations paid a small part of the funds they received from the Defence Department to CDA. But, three decades later the role was reversed. CDA received a block grant from DND and parcelled out the money to its various member associations.[22] A 1950s Board of Officers report called for increasing funds to CDA members, noting that the defence "associations are performing a vital role in furthering the defence efforts and that they should receive the fullest support both financial and otherwise."[23]

CDA also receives funding from corporate sources, primarily arms manufacturers and military service providers. CDA's 2015 conference in Ottawa received "generous support of … General Dynamics, NATO and the Department of National Defence … ADGA Group, Boeing Canada, Ernst and Young, Porter, Rheinmetall, United Technologies, AUG Signals."[24] Previous annual conventions received the backing of Lockheed Martin Canada, ATCO Structures & Logistics and Irving Shipbuilding.[25]

CDA represents over 50 military associations ranging from the Naval Association of Canada to the Canadian Infantry Association, Royal Canadian Legion to the Military Intelligence Association. The CDA is run by high-ranking former officers, including individuals with close ties to arms manufacturers. CDA Institute president between 2004 and 2008, Paul Manson, was former chairman of Lockheed Martin Canada and Chief of the Defence Staff.[26] In *Joining Empire: The Political Economy of the New Canadian Foreign Policy*,

Jerome Klassen summarizes CDA's makeup and work: "With a Board of Directors that condenses the state-corporate–military nexus in Canada, it organizes conferences around security and defence issues, lobbies for military spending increases, publishes papers on defense strategy, and funds sympathetic research on University campuses."[27]

CDA publishes Security and Defence Briefings, Vimy Papers and Presentations and Position Papers. The organization's quarterly journal *ON TRACK* "promotes informed public debate on security and defence issues and the vital role played by the Canadian Armed forces in society."[28] CDA has also published influential books such as Queens professor Douglas Bland's *A Nation at Risk: the decline of the Canadian Forces*.

To encourage militarist research, CDA awards a number of prizes. It puts on an annual graduate student symposium where $3,000 goes to the winning paper, $2,000 to second place and $1,000 to third place. CDA co-sponsors the Ross Munro Media Award to a "journalist who has made a significant contribution to understanding defence and security issues" and gives the Vimy Award to a "Canadian who has made a significant and outstanding contribution to the defence and security of Canada and the preservation of (its) democratic values."[29]

While CDA was officially established during the Great Depression, its genesis reaches back to a 1911 conference Minister of Militia and Defence Sam Hughes organized to unite the various government-funded military associations.[30] Hughes was an ardent imperialist and militarist. According to *Sam Hughes: the public career of a controversial Canadian, 1885 – 1916*, "Hughes told the Board of Trade of the Eastern Townships in 1913 that war always produced periods of national brilliance in any country."[31]

While World War I and jealousies among the various military associations stalled Hughes' effort, the CDA would come to fruition with the backing of Minister of Defense Donald Matheson

Sutherland.[32] Since its creation, defence ministers and governor generals (as commander in chief) have regularly appeared at CDA's annual conference.[33] The governor general, prime minister, defence minister and chief of the defence staff are honorary patrons or vice patrons of the organization.[34]

CDA advocates militarism. Its first official resolution noted "the urgent need for an increased appropriation for national defence."[35] At almost every CDA convention between 1946 and 1959 a resolution passed in favour of compulsory military training.[36] A 1968 resolution called for universal military training, expressing concern that a generation of Canadians had become "unused to the idea of military service."[37]

In the 1980s CDA developed the idea of the "Total Defence of Canada". In 1985 Colonel H. A. J. Hutchinson told a CDA meeting: "I would say that the Total Defence of Canada requires much more than just the support of the Canadian Armed Forces, it involves the organization of our total economy, our industrial base, towards a single objective — the defence of this country."[38] Hinting at the need to talk up US President Ronald Reagan's revival of Cold War rhetoric, Hutchison said this "can only be made [possible] if the Canadian people perceive that it is necessary and that, in fact, it is the only course of action open to them."[39]

A 2000 CDA report funded by the Business Council on National Issues, the Molson Foundation and DND advocated increased military spending to defend free trade. It claimed "the defence establishment, including the Canadian Forces, plays a key role in an international policy which provides the insurance and the means which allow the national interest to flourish. It contributes to stability at home and abroad, thus supporting the development of an environment congenial to trade."[40]

During Canada's war in Afghanistan the president of the CDA Institute lambasted the media, claiming it undercut the mission. John

Scott Cowan told a crowd that included future military leaders and Defence Minister Peter MacKay: "[The] media give new depth to the word 'shallow' ... Unlike 40 years ago when journalists were amongst the best-educated and best-informed citizens, today many of them are neither literate nor numerate, and do us the huge discourtesy of assuming we aren't either."[41] Cowan further complained about "the narcissism of portions of the media who report incessantly on themselves" and bemoaned journalists who ask average Canadians their opinion on political subjects. "[Reporters] stick microphones under the noses of whatever slack-jawed gum-chewing vagrants they can find on the street to ask them what they think about oil prices or border security or equalization payments."[42]

At the height of Canada's war in Afghanistan CDA received a highly politicized five-year $500,000 contract from DND. University of Ottawa professor Amir Attaran wrote, "that money comes not with strings, but with an entire leash."[43] To receive the money CDA committed to producing 15 opinion pieces or letters to the editor in major Canadian newspapers, generating 29 media references to the organization and eliciting 100 requests for radio/television interviews. The media work was part of a requirement to "support activities that give evidence of contributing to Canada's national policies."[44] CDA didn't initially disclose its 2007–12 DND sponsorship agreement, which was reviewed by cabinet.[45]

Canadian Institute for Strategic Studies and Pearson Peacekeeping Centre

An associate member of CDA, the Canadian Institute for Strategic Studies was founded in 1976.[46] CISS' mandate was to "provide a forum for, and be the vehicle to stimulate the research, study, analysis, and discussion of the strategic implications of the major national and international security issues, events, and trends as they affect Canada."[47] In 2007 CISS was folded into the Canadian

International Council (see chapter 4), creating the CIC Strategic Studies Working Group.

CISS published a journal, *Strategic Profiles, Strategic Datalinks*, a bulletin and an annual *Canadian Strategic Forecast*. The institute also published dozens of books and financed research fellows, a student internship program and university liaison officer on campuses across the country.[48] CISS also operated a speakers bureau and in the late 1980s had "agreements with NATO's Information Service to conduct a national/regional speakers tour."[49]

CISS promoted militaristic positions. In the late 1980s, according to professor Peter Langille, CISS developed a "high school curriculum program to counterbalance the peace movement."[50] A few years later it aggressively opposed Ottawa's move to close the Baden–Soellingen base in Germany.[51] The CF base gained importance in 1963 when Paris declared that all nuclear weapons located on its soil would fall under French control, prompting the hasty departure of the nuclear-capable Royal Canadian Air Force No. 421 Squadron to Baden.[52] But, the collapse of the Soviet Union made it hard to justify maintaining the German base.

CISS officials often expressed an aggressive strain of militarist thought. In 2007 CISS head Alex Morrison criticized Ottawa for emphasizing the military's role in peacekeeping, telling the *Toronto Star*, Canadian soldiers were viewed as "simply a bunch of do-gooders ... The government (convinced) a heck of a lot of Canadians that our military weren't real military when, of course, they are and they're proving it in Afghanistan."[53] The organization also boasted about Canadian special forces' killing capacities. CISS director David Rudd said special forces are trained "to infiltrate into dangerous areas behind enemy lines, look for key targets and take them out. They don't go out to arrest people. They don't go out there to hand out food parcels. They go out to kill targets."[54] And Canadians should be proud of their work.

A Propaganda System

Retired officers dominated CISS. A 37-year veteran of the air force, Brigadier-General Don W. Macnamara played a central role in creating the institute. After 35 years with the RCAF, Major General Fraser Holman became director and chairman of CISS' Board in the late 1990s.[55] He would be joined by former chief of the defence staff General Ramsey Withers.[56]

Individuals also moved in the other direction. CISS' last president, David Rudd, was hired as an analyst by the Canadian Forces' Operational Support Command.[57]

CISS claimed to be "a member-based, non-profit, organization with no government affiliation."[58] But, former military officers largely ran the organization and its initial sponsors were CDA, the Royal Canadian Legion and DND.[59]

The idea for creating CISS emanated from a CDA meeting and a number of Canadian Institute for International Affairs (see chapter 4) members participated in CISS' creation.[60] CISS was heavily reliant on government funds. It operated a number of joint initiatives with DND "to promote the White Paper [on bolstering the military] and explain the Soviet threat."[61] As part of this effort, CISS trained more than 300 officers for a DND Speakers Bureau in the first quarter of 1988.[62]

CISS also worked with DND and Foreign Affairs to set up the Pearson Peacekeeping Centre (PPC) in 1994. A 2007 DND evaluation explained: "DND and the Department of Foreign Affairs and International Trade (DFAIT), through the aegis of the Canadian Institute of Strategic Studies, established the PPC to conduct national and international multidisciplinary research, education, and training in all aspects of peacekeeping. Both DFAIT and DND agreed to provide annual financial contributions totalling $10M ($5M each) to support the establishment and initial operations of the Centre."[63] An international peacekeeping training centre was established on the site of a disbanded CF Base in Nova Scotia.

PPC closed in 2013 when it lost the last of its federal funding. For most of its two decades a little more than half of PPC's core funding came from DND and the rest was from CIDA. PPC received more than $50 million in government money.[64] Its board of directors was mainly appointed by DND, DFAIT and CIDA.[65] PPC's founding president was Lieutenant Colonel Alex Morrison, who served for 30 years in the Canadian military, including posts at UN Peacekeeping Force Headquarters and a position as an advisor to Canada's permanent representative to the UN.[66] After leaving the military Morrison served as executive director and president of CISS between 1989 and 1997.[67]

In addition to training and educating soldiers, PPC produced the Pearson Papers series, which focused on UN missions in different countries. The centre also published a number of books and its faculty conducted research.

DND's financial support for PPC — and subsequent withdrawal — reflects a debate within the military over peacekeeping. Until the early 2000s many in the military saw peacekeeping as the best way to convince the public to support military expenditures. Canadians strongly support "peacekeeping" and some within the military promoted the idea that a strong force was necessary to participate in UN missions.

Popularly viewed as a benevolent form of intervention, peacekeeping missions have generally been motivated by broader geopolitical interests. Maintaining the seven-year-old NATO alliance was external minister Lester Pearson's priority when he pushed to intervene in Egypt. After Britain, France and Israel invaded in 1956, Ottawa was primarily concerned with disagreement between the US and the UK over the intervention, not Egyptian sovereignty or the plight of that country's people.

Most often peacekeeping was Canada's contribution to the Cold War. Sean Maloney explains "During the Cold War, the United States, the United Kingdom and France, all permanent members of the Security Council, remained aloof in several difficult circumstances as a sort of plausible deniability. Canada was the West's champion in the Cold War U.N. arena."[68]

Coinciding with Ottawa's move away from peacekeeping was the growing clout of the Third World at the UN. *The Canadian Way of War* explains: "By 1967 the sun was setting on the utility of the U.N. as a tool to contain communist influence ... decolonization was nearly over. This increased the number of Third World non-aligned states in the U.N., altering the character of the organization and its willingness to be used by the West."[69]

Since the end of the Cold War and the decline of the Soviet bloc's role in checking US power there has been a resurgence of peacekeeping in the interests of Western imperialism. While peacekeeping was generally motivated by larger geopolitical objectives, the missions in Egypt and Cyprus proved generally positive. But this hasn't always been the case, as the deployments to Korea (1950), Congo (1960) and Haiti (2004) illustrate.

Dominion Institute (Historica Canada) and Donner Canadian Foundation

Founded in 1997, the Dominion Institute (DI) portrayed itself as an advocate of cultural memory and historical education. But, the corporate and military funded institute focused on promoting the notion "that citizenship is constructed primarily through experiencing and appreciating Canada's military past."[70] In 2009 DI merged with Historica Foundation to create Historica Canada.

DI promoted a variety of education initiatives. It partnered with the Canadian Defence and Foreign Affairs Institute to produce an hour-long documentary titled *Foreign Fields: Canada's Role in the World*. The documentary aired on Global TV in 2002.[71] During Stephen Harper's government, DI convinced federal officials to declare a national day of commemoration when the last World War I veteran died and they helped rewrite the citizenship study guide for new immigrants.[72] The updated citizenship handbook *Discover Canada: the Rights and Responsibilities of Citizenship* praises this country's military history and includes more than a dozen photos of armed forces personnel.[73]

DI mostly targeted its educational efforts at schools. Begun in 2000, the Canadian Forces Memory Project has reached over 1.5 million Canadians, mostly students.[74] The initiative brings veterans and CF members to schools and its digital archive offers educators more than 3,000 firsthand stories and 1,500 original artefacts chronicling Canadian military history.[75] In *Memory, Militarism and Citizenship: tracking the Dominion Institute in Canada's military-cultural memory network,* Howard Fremeth writes, "the Memory Project is a perfect example of the banal militarism behind Operation Connection that brings the military into public spaces not only on solemn events like Remembrance Day or during disasters, but throughout the year."[76]

Established partly as a response to the popularity of social history, DI focuses on military life instead of the class politics that may drive war or how militarism can spur racism and patriarchy. In *Warrior Nation*, Ian McKay and Jamie Swift describe the Memory Project message to students: "In essence, the story goes, warriors, made us what we are today. Warriors led us in the past and should govern in the future; and, if you are lucky, you too might grow up to be a warrior."[77]

The Memory Project received significant funds from Veterans Affairs, Canadian Heritage and DND.[78] Since the early 2000s these three arms of the federal government have ploughed millions of dollars into the Memory Project.[79]

While the federal government has been an important source of financial support, the Donner Canadian Foundation gave DI its start-up funds. In its first year DI received $200,000 from Donner, beginning a long-term relationship with the large funding agency and its chairman, Allan Gotlieb, a businessman and former Canadian ambassador to the US.[80] Donner has given hundreds of thousands of dollars to DI. While softening the harder edge of its politics, the 2009 merger with Historica Foundation greatly increased DI resources.

"Paymaster to the right", Donner financed the creation of a number of pro-corporate think tanks in the mid-1990s.[81] In 2005 Donald Gutstein noted, "the reactionary right would have made little headway in Canada in the past decade without Donner's backing. Stephen Harper would be a nobody, for instance."[82]

In the mid-1990s Donner helped launch *Gravitas*, a magazine focused on Canadian foreign and trade policy.[83] It's also provided financing for dozens of books, articles and foreign policy focused research and speaking projects.

While a new director took a hard right turn in the early 1990s, Donner has long funded establishment foreign policy initiatives. Created by US steel magnate William Henry Donner in 1950, the foundation influenced coverage of former Prime Minister Lester Pearson's legacy. It put up $15,000 ($90,000 today) to hire writing help for Pearson's one thousand page memoirs, which was completed after his death.[84] A protégé of prominent diplomat John Holmes and president of the pro-NATO Atlantic Council of Canada, Gerald Wright was vice-president of the Donner foundation between 1972 and 1987.[85] During this period it dedicated substantial resources to foreign policy initiatives.[86]

Canadian Global Affairs Institute

The military identified the Canadian Defence and Foreign Affairs Institute, now Canadian Global Affairs Institute (CGAI), under the rubric of "defence-related organization and defence and foreign policy think tanks."[87] CGAI claims to be the "only think tank focused on Canada's international engagement in all its forms — diplomacy, the military, aid and trade security."[88] The University of Pennsylvania's 2013 survey of go-to think tanks ranked it among the top five think tanks in Canada.[89]

The Calgary-based institute promoted aggressive foreign policy positions. It called for Ottawa to set up a foreign spy service — think CIA, M-16, Mossad etc. — and commissioned a survey claiming most "Canadians are willing to send troops into danger even if it leads to deaths and injuries as long as they believe in the military's goals."[90] In the midst of a wave of criticism towards General Dynamics's sale of Light Armoured Vehicles to Saudi Arabia, institute fellow David Perry published a *Globe and Mail* opinion titled "Without foreign sales, Canada's defence industry would not survive."[91] To disseminate its views the charitable organization publishes reports and books. Its spokespeople, including Tom Flanagan and Jack Granatstein, regularly write and comment for major news outlets.

Beyond the media work most think tanks pursue, the institute expends considerable effort influencing the media. Since 2002 the institute has operated an annual military journalism course run with the University of Calgary's Centre for Military and Strategic Studies. A dozen Canadian journalism students receive scholarships to the 10-day program, which includes a media-military theory component and visits to armed forces units.[92] The stated objective of the course is "to enhance the military education of future Canadian journalists who will report on Canadian military activities."[93] But that description obscures the political objective. In an article titled "A student's look inside the military journalism course" Lola Fakinlede writes: "Between the excitement of shooting guns, driving in tanks, eating pre-packed lunches, investigating the insides of coyotes and leopards — armoured vehicles not animals — and visiting the messes, we were learning how the military operates. ... Being able to see the human faces behind the uniform, being able to talk to them like regular people, being able to see them start losing the suspicion in their eyes and really start talking candidly to me — that was incredible."[94]

Captain David Williams was forthright concerning the broader political objective of the program. In 2010 he wrote, "the intent of this annual visit has always been to foster a familiarity and mutual understanding between the CF and the future media, two entities which require a symbiotic relationship in order to function."[95]

Along with the Conference of Defence Associations, the institute gives out the annual Ross Munro Media Award recognizing a "journalist who has made a significant contribution to understanding defence and security issues."[96] The winner receives a handsome statuette, a gala dinner attended by Ottawa VIPs and a $2,500 prize.[97] The political objective of the award is to reinforce the militarist culture among reporters who cover the subject.

Journalist training, the Ross Munro award and institute reports/commentators are a positive way of shaping the discussion of military matters. But, the institute also employs a stick. In detailing an attack against colleague Lee Berthiaume, *Ottawa Citizen* military reporter David Pugliese pointed out that it's "not uncommon for the site [CDFAI's 3Ds Blog] to launch personal attacks on journalists covering defence issues. It seems some CDFAI 'fellows' don't like journalists who ask the government or the Department of National Defence too many probing questions. … Last year I had one of the CDFAI 'fellows' write one of the editors at the Citizen to complain about my lack of professionalism on a particular issue. … the smear attempt was all done behind my back but I found out about it. That little stunt backfired big time when I showed the Citizen editor that the CDFAI 'fellow' had fabricated his claims about me."[98]

While it may not have succeeded in this instance, online criticism and complaints to journalists' superiors do have an impact. If pursued consistently this type of 'flack' drives journalists to avoid topics or be more cautious when covering an issue.

A Propaganda System

While not forthcoming on its finances, the institute received some military backing. DND's Security and Defence Forum provided funding to individuals who pursued a year-long internship with the institute.[99] CGAI also held numerous joint symposiums with DND, NATO and NORAD.[100]

The institute received financial support from large arms contractors such as General Dynamics and Lockheed Martin Canada, as well as Com Dev, ENMAX, SMART Technologies, the Defense News Media Group and Canadian Council of Chief Executives.[101]

In 2015 CGAI's eight directors included the CEO of IAMGOLD Steve Letwin, Royal Bank Financial Group executive Robert B. Hamilton, former Canadian Brigadier General Robert S. Millar, senior partner in the Calgary office of Bennett Jones LLP and ATCO director Bob Booth.[102] Previous board members include Perrin Beatty, president of the Canadian Chamber of Commerce, as well as former defence minister and head of CBC.[103]

The Legion

Incorporated by an act of Parliament, the Canadian Legion of the British Empire Services League was formed in 1926. Renamed in 1960, the Royal Canadian Legion claimed 300,000 members and 1,400 Branches in 2016.[104]

From the get-go it was designed to counter more critical veteran organizations. In *The Vimy Trap: or, How We Learned To Stop Worrying and Love the Great War*, Ian McKay and Jamie Swift write, "benefiting from government recognition, the Legion slowly supplanted its rivals. It was consciously designed as [a] body that would soothe the veterans temper and moderate their demands."[105]

The Legion is best known for its annual Remembrance Day red poppy campaign. Originally sponsored by the Department of Soldiers Civil Re-establishment in 1922, today about 20 million poppies are sold in the lead-up to November 11.[106] But, poppies abound year-round since the Legion partnered with the Royal Canadian Mint to produce millions of 25-cent coins with a red poppy on them.[107]

Remembrance Day poppies were inspired by the 1915 poem "In Flanders Fields" by Canadian army officer John McCrae.[108] The pro-war poem calls on Canadians "take up our quarrel with the foe" and was used during the First World War to promote war bonds and recruit soldiers.[109]

Today poppies commemorate Canadians who have died at war. Not being commemorated are the Afghans or Libyans killed by Canadians in the 2000s or the Iraqis and Serbians killed in the 1990s or the Koreans killed in the 1950s or the Russians, South Africans, Sudanese and others killed before that. By focusing exclusively on 'our' side Remembrance Day poppies reinforce a sense that Canada's cause is righteous.

The Legion works with various groups. It is part of the Conference of Defence Associations (CDA) and was an initial sponsor (with CDA and DND) of the Canadian Institute for Strategic Studies.[110] More than a half dozen military museums are located at or affiliated with Legion branches across the country.[111] In cooperation with the Canadian War Museum the Legion supports the Lest We Forget Project, which introduces students to World War I and II archives.[112]

In the mid-2000s the Legion battled Canadian War Museum historians over an exhibition about the WWII allied bomber offensive. After shaping its development, the Legion objected to a small part of a multifaceted exhibit, which questioned "the efficacy and the morality of the ... massive bombing of Germany's industrial and civilian targets."[113] With the museum refusing to give the veterans an effective veto over its exhibit, *Legion Magazine* called for a boycott.[114] The Legion's campaign led to hearings by the Senate Subcommittee on Veterans Affairs and a new display that glossed over a bombing campaign explicitly designed to destroy German cities.[115] It also led to the director of the museum, Joe Guerts, resigning.[116]

A number of Legion initiatives target schoolchildren. It runs annual poem, art and essay contests to foster "the tradition of Remembrance" among the young. Winners have presented their work on CBC-TV.[117] The Legion offers teachers a Canadian military history teaching guide and books for students such as *The Story of Remembrance Day: Why we wear a poppy*. With Historica Canada (Dominion Institute) the Legion participates in The Memory Project, which brings veterans to schools.[118]

The Legion takes its media work seriously. Its magazine has been published since the organization was established. At its 1927 convention the Legion decided, notes an official history, to "organize public relations activities that would include a speakers bureau and a publicity liaison at Dominion headquarters."[119] Media training and a Legion public relations manual are available to branches.

As part of its media strategy, the Legion offers speakers to news outlets and organizes media events. As Mallory Schwartz points out in *War on the Air: CBC-TV and Canada's Military, 1952-1992*, the Legion worked closely with the CBC on Remembrance Day broadcasts. At times they suggested changes to the public broadcaster's coverage and produced Remembrance Day content for TV.[120]

The Legion has provided other programming to the public broadcaster.[121] With Veterans Affairs and Crawley Films Canada, the Legion produced a tribute to veterans titled *The Long Silence*, which aired on CBC in 1955.[122] Into the 1960s, notes Schwartz, CBC had "intimate" relations with the Legion.[123]

The Legion also successfully pressured the CBC. It participated in a campaign to block the three-part series *The Valour and the Horror* from being rebroadcast or distributed to schools. The 1992 CBC series claimed Canadian soldiers committed unprosecuted war crimes during World War II and that the British-led bomber command killed 600,000 German civilians. The veterans groups' campaign led to a Senate inquiry, CRTC hearing and lawsuit, as well as a commitment from CBC to not rebroadcast *The Valour and the Horror* without amendments.[124]

While its core political mandate is improving veterans' services, the Legion has long advocated militarism and a reactionary worldview. In the early 1930s it pushed for military build-up and its 1950 convention called for "total preparedness".[125] In 1983 its president, Dave Capperauld, supported US cruise missiles tests in Alberta and into the early 1990s the Legion took "an uncompromising stand on the importance of maintaining a strong Canadian military presence in Europe through NATO, and by supporting the United States build-up of advanced nuclear weapons."[126]

The Legion has also espoused a racist, paranoid and pro-Empire worldview. In the years after World War II it called for the expulsion of Canadians of Japanese origin and ideological screening for German immigrants.[127] A decade before WWII, reports *Branching Out: the story of the Royal Canadian Legion*, "Manitoba Command unanimously endorsed a resolution to ban communist activities, and provincial president Ralph Webb ... warned that children were being taught to spit on the Union Jack in Manitoba schools."[128]

Long after the end of the Cold War the organization remains concerned about "subversives". In 2016 Legion members had to sign a statement that begins: "I hereby solemnly declare that I am not a member of, nor affiliated with, any group, party or sect whose interests conflict with the avowed purposes of the Legion, and I do not, and will not, support any organization advocating the overthrow of our government by force or which advocates, encourages or participates in subversive action or propaganda."[129]

While mostly funded through membership fees, the Legion has benefited from government support. The Governor General, head of the Canadian Forces, is the Legion's Grand Patron and numerous prime ministers and defence ministers have addressed its conventions.[130] An early Legion president stepped down to become deputy minister of defence and numerous legionnaires have been appointed to the federal cabinet.[131]

The federal government has donated hundreds of thousands of dollars to different Legion initiatives.[132] It has also worked closely with the Veteran Affairs-funded Last Post Fund and Veterans Affairs-run Vetcraft, which made the Legion's poppies for 75 years. In 1927 the Legion was granted a monopoly over poppy distribution.[133]

4. The Academic Connection

While love of sport, civic pride and camaraderie are promoted as the point of supporting "our" team, professional hockey is, at its core, driven by money and profit. But it is not just the team owners, players and others directly employed by the squad who have a financial stake in on-ice and box office success. Broadcasters, restaurants, bars, retailers, advertising agencies etc. all have an economic self-interest in convincing us to support the Habs, Leafs or Nuckleheads and the NHL in general.

In a similar way, Canadian foreign policy rhetoric about the Responsibility to Protect, defending democracy, fighting terror etc. can mask what's really driving policy. To a large extent, the point of Canadian foreign-policy is to support "our" corporations and capitalism in general. This helps explain why business interests fund academic centres and think tanks that shape public opinion about this country's international affairs.

Munk Centre

A mining magnate who has an important personal stake in a particular foreign policy financed the international affairs school at Canada's leading university. And the right wing ideologue structured the donation to maximize his influence over the school.

Beginning in 1997 Barrick Gold founder and chairman Peter Munk provided $6.4 million to rename the University of Toronto International Studies Department the Munk Centre for International Studies.[1] As part of the accord, the university agreed the centre would "rank with the University's highest priorities for the allocation of its other funding, including its own internal resources."[2]

The contract stipulated that the centre would receive advice from Barrick's international advisory board, which included former

Prime Minister Brian Mulroney and US President George Bush.[3] Barrick's board would "provide such assistance and resources as the board in its discretion considers appropriate, and the Council (of the Centre) will be receptive thereof."[4] To increase the likelihood that its advice would be heeded, Munk offered his money in instalments. With the money doled out over a decade, Munk could withdraw the cash if dissatisfied with the direction of the centre.[5]

Signed without consulting the university's Academic Board, the agreement was only obtained through an access to information request. It made no mention of protecting academic freedom. An outcry from the university Faculty Association prompted modest revisions to the agreement.[6]

In a 1997 editorial celebrating the donation *The Northern Miner* linked Munk's venture to Canada's growing international mining presence. The industry paper wrote: "International studies are increasingly important now that almost every business sector in North America is looking to foreign markets for growth and expansion opportunities. The mining industry, including its supply-and-service sector, is no exception. Canadian companies are now exploring in almost every mineral-rich country in the world. And, as most have learned, this requires the ability to conduct business across cultural and ethnic lines with grace and sensitivity."[7]

Happy with the centre's direction, Munk put up an additional $5 million in 2006.[8] In 2010 he contributed tens of millions of dollars more to expand the international studies department into a full-blown school.[9]

While presented as a disinterested 'philanthropist', Munk had significant personal interest in Canadian foreign policy. Operating mines on six continents, Barrick benefited from the Canadian aid agency's controversial move to strengthen the ties between mining companies and non-governmental organizations. In 2011 CIDA invested $500,000 in a World Vision Canada/Barrick Gold project.[10]

"In Peru," noted the aid agency, "CIDA is supporting World Vision Canada, in a program that will increase the income and standard of living of 1,000 families affected by mining operations."[11] World Vision and Barrick combined to match CIDA's donation.[12] In response Miguel Palacin, the head of a Peruvian indigenous organization, sent a letter to World Vision, Barrick and CIDA claiming that "no 'social works' carried out with the mining companies can compensate for the damage done" by mining operations.[13] For his part, the former coordinator of Common Frontiers-Canada, Rick Arnold, described the NGO initiative as "a pacification program, and not a development project."[14]

Barrick also benefited from Canadian diplomatic support, including visits by the prime minister. In 2007 Stephen Harper met Barrick officials in Tanzania days after the company claimed a strike at one of its Tanzanian mines was illegal and looked to replace a thousand striking miners. Four months earlier Barrick gained important support for its Pascua Lama operations, which spurred large-scale protests, during Harper's trip to Chile. The prime minister visited the company's Chilean office and said "Barrick follows Canadian standards of corporate social responsibility."[15]

Barrick operates some of the most controversial mining projects in the world. As such, the Toronto-based company aggressively opposed moves to withhold diplomatic and financial support to Canadian companies found responsible for significant abuses abroad. In 2008 Barrick opposed the recommendations of a business/civil society mining roundtable launched by the previous Liberal government, and two years later the company registered seven lobbyists to block Liberal MP John McKay's private members bill C 300 (An Act Respecting Corporate Accountability for the Activities of Mining, Oil or Gas Corporations in Developing Countries). After the bill was narrowly defeated Munk wrote a letter published in the *Toronto Star* "celebrating those MPs who had the courage" to side with Canada's massive mining industry lobby and vote against C 300.[16]

Munk espouses far-right political views. In 1997 he publicly praised dictator Augusto Pinochet for "transforming Chile from a wealth-destroying socialist state to a capital-friendly model that is being copied around the world" while two years later the *Canadian Jewish News* reported on a donation Munk made to an Israeli university and a speech in which he "suggested that Israel's survival is dependent on maintaining its technological superiority over the Arabs."[17] In 2006 he attacked leftist Bolivian president Evo Morales and the next year wrote a letter to the *Financial Times* comparing Venezuelan president Hugo Chavez to Hitler.[18] In a 2011 *Globe and Mail* interview Munk dismissed criticism of Barrick's security force in Papua New Guinea by claiming "gang rape is a cultural habit" in that country while he responded to a 2014 *Economist* question about whether "Indigenous groups appear to have a lot more say and power in resource development these days" by saying "globally it's a real problem. It's a major, major problem. Why? Because human rights and NGOs and young students are idealistic, like we all were, and the underdog gets their support."[19]

A little over a decade after setting up the Munk Centre for International Studies Peter Munk put up $35 million to establish the Munk School of Global Affairs. In exchange for the biggest donation in the 150-year-old institution's history, the University of Toronto administration committed to channelling $39 million from its endowment to the Munk School and the Ontario and federal governments chipped in $50 million (as well as a $16 million tax credit to Peter Munk for his $35 million donation).[20] Former president of Science for Peace Judith Deutsch explained, "'private public partnership' is really the taxpayer footing most of the bill with no say about the direction of its programs."[21]

Munk sought to maximize his influence over the School of Global Affairs. According to the donor agreement, the Munk School's director is to report annually to a board set up by Munk's family and

$15 million of Munk's $35 million donation was to be paid only if the school fulfilled the accord.[22] "The determination of whether the University has achieved the Objective shall be solely that of the Donor and ... shall be conclusive and binding on the University," reads the agreement between the Munk Foundation and university.[23]

The donor agreement guaranteed the Canadian International Council (CIC) a quarter of the school's spacious new building.[24] But the CIC, which included Peter Munk and representatives from Goldcorp and Scotiabank on its Senate, is not an academic organization. Rather, it's an establishment think tank.[25]

The accord includes a number of other decidedly non-academic requirements. Incredibly, the agreement says, "the main entrance of the Heritage Mansion will be a formal entrance reserved only for senior staff and visitors to the School and the CIC."[26] Alongside this feudalistic directive, the accord included a more capitalistic requirement. The donor contract devoted $2 million over eight years to branding the school and media outreach.[27]

As is par for the course with these questionable deals, it was signed in secret "without any form of consultation with governors or with the students, faculty and staff."[28] Nor did the university's Academic Board, which is charged with ensuring the direction of academic priorities, see "the agreement prior to its being signed."[29] To conclude the accord the University of Toronto president extended summer executive authority into the fall of 2009.[30] As a result, the Board of Governors, which is formally responsible for the accord, didn't convene to discuss an agreement signed by the upper administration. Coincidentally, four years after U of T President David Naylor signed the Munk contract, Barrick added Naylor, who had no apparent mining expertise, to its list of "independent" directors.[31]

Flush with resources and strategically located in Canada's media capital, the Munk School is influential. In partnership with the Lionel Gelber Foundation and Foreign Policy Magazine the school awarded the Lionel Gelber non-fiction prize for the world's best English-language non-fiction book on foreign affairs.[32] At the Canadian Embassy in Washington it put on an annual Seymour Martin Lipset Lecture on Democracy in the World with the US government's National Endowment for Democracy.[33] The Munk School also partnered with the Canadian Forces College on workshops and the Toronto International Film Festival (TIFF) on a Contemporary World Speakers series.[34] At a half-dozen TIFF screenings each year Munk School speakers participate in post film discussions.

Alongside its namesake, the school sponsored the Munk Debates. Founded in 2008 by Peter Munk's Aurea Foundation, Munk Debates is a biannual forum dealing with major political issues. Past speakers include former British Prime Minister Tony Blair, actress Mia Farrow and former US Secretary of State Henry Kissinger. Long-time Munk School director Janice Stein was part of the nine-person advisory board overseeing the debate series.[35]

During the 2015 federal election Munk Debates held the first-ever Canadian foreign policy leaders debate.[36] Not surprisingly, Canada's status as a global mining superpower wasn't part of the debate. Nor was there any discussion of regulating mining activities abroad or the appropriate level of government "aid" to these profitable private companies.

In 2012 the school launched the Munk Fellowship in Global Journalism to train individuals considered experts in various subject areas to become journalists. Twenty individuals were awarded fellowships to a year-long program run in partnership with the *Globe and Mail*, CBC News, *Toronto Star*, Postmedia and Thomson Reuters.[37] The head of the Munk journalism program, Robert Steiner, is a former vice president of Bell Globemedia, parent of CTV and the *Globe and Mail*.[38]

The school had significant ties to Canada's newspaper of record. Weeks after stepping down as the *Globe*'s editor-in-chief in 2014 John Stackhouse was appointed senior fellow at the Munk School.[39] Stackhouse joined long-standing *Globe* editor-in-chief William Thorsell in this position. In another example of the close ties between the newspaper and Munk School, prominent columnist Margret Wente was appointed to the committee awarding the Lionel Gelber book prize. But, as the *National Post*'s Chris Selley pointed out, this took place a few weeks after the *Globe* columnist was embroiled in a plagiarism scandal.[40] Coincidentally, a year earlier Wente wrote a column headlined "Our World Needs More Peter Munks."

Munk School faculty were often quoted or published in the *Globe and Mail*. For example, soon after becoming the school's new director in 2015, Stephen J. Toope published two long articles about the direction of Canada's international relations.[41]

Highlighting the ties between the school and the *Globe*, Protest Barrick organizer Sakura Saunders pointed to an illogical editorial the paper published on the Toronto-based mining company in 2011. While describing reports of rape by Barrick security forces in Papua New Guinea and killings in Tanzania, the editorial noted how "[Barrick has] developed detailed corporate social responsibility policies, pledging to carry out their activities in an environmentally, socially and economically sustainable manner, and hiring experts and staff to make sure this happens. Last year, Barrick became the first Canadian mining company to sign a global agreement called the Voluntary Principles on Security and Human Rights, which obliges it to investigate and report human-rights abuses at its work sites."[42] Despite the mining company aggressively opposing legislation that would restrict public support for resource corporations responsible for major abuses abroad, the *Globe* editorial concluded, "Barrick and other Canadian miners now deserve praise for their efforts (perhaps overdue) to raise industry standards."[43] Notwithstanding the *Globe*'s claim, Barrick and Canadian mining companies more generally have been accused of human rights or environmental abuses throughout the Global South.

Munk Centre executive director Marketa Evans helped spawn an initiative for NGOs and mining companies, including Barrick, to discuss corporate social responsibility and development issues.[44] Called the Devonshire Initiative, it took its name from Devonshire Place where the Munk School is located and it was hatched. Many mining solidarity activists saw the 2007 Devonshire Initiative as an effort to undermine the government–civil society Roundtable Recommendations, which called for withholding government financial and political support to resource companies found responsible for major abuses abroad.[45]

As mentioned above, in early 2007 a pan-Canadian roundtable launched by the previous Liberal government crossed the country to interview a wide variety of social actors about Canadian mining. The roundtable put forward 27 recommendations to better address the human rights and environmental effects of Canadian companies operating abroad. Even though the Mining Association of Canada helped formulate the 27 recommendations — and tepidly agreed to them — Barrick, the Prospectors and Developers Association of Canada and the Canadian Chamber of Commerce lobbied against the Roundtable Recommendations, notably the possibility of imposing sanctions. After stalling on the issue for two years, the Conservative government rejected the roundtable's proposal to make diplomatic and financial support for resource companies operating overseas contingent upon socially responsible conduct. Instead of implementing the Roundtable Recommendations, the government set up a Corporate Social Responsibility (CSR) counsellor and the Munk School's Marketa Evans was appointed the inaugural CSR counsellor.

The counsellor was tasked with probing complaints about abuses committed by Canadian companies in poor countries. But, the counsellor could not intervene — let alone take any remedial action — without agreement from the company accused of abuse.

Between 2009 and Evans' resignation in 2014 the counsellor only investigated three cases and in two of the three no dialogue process took place since the companies refused to cooperate.[46]

The Munk School backed the government's pro-corporate mining policy and joined the Harper Conservatives' low-level war against Iran. After severing diplomatic ties and designating Iran a state sponsor of terrorism in 2012, Foreign Affairs ploughed $250,000 into the Munk School's Global Dialogue on the Future of Iran.[47] The aim of the initiative was to foment opposition to the regime and help connect dissidents inside and outside Iran. Employing cutting-edge Internet strategies, the Iran Dialogue was launched at a two-day conference kicked off by Foreign Minister John Baird. During her introduction of the foreign minister, Munk School director Janice Stein said, "Minister Baird gets human rights in his DNA... [He has a] deep permanent reflexive commitment to human rights which informs everything he does."[48]

Some Iranian Canadians criticized the 2013 Global Dialogue on Iran. In a letter to Stein, who was awarded an honorary doctorate from Hebrew University "in tribute to her unwavering devotion to Israel", the president of the Iranian Canadian Community Council Niaz Salimi wrote: "Conspicuously absent from the event were experts, academics, political activists, students, bloggers, journalists and members of the Iranian diaspora (including those of the Iranian-Canadian community) whose views on Iran do not fully concur with the positions of the Harper government."[49]

The Munk School was a hub of anti-Iranian activity. A senior research fellow, Mark Dubowitz, was dubbed "The Man Who Fights Iran" by Ynet, Israel's largest English language news site.[50] Alongside his position at the Munk School, Dubowitz was also executive director of the extremist pro-Israel Foundation for Defense of Democracies where he "co-leads The Iran Task Force."[51] In a 2015 Intelligence Squared debate Dubowitz backed the Benjamin

Netanyahu/Republican Party line, arguing against the motion "that Obama's Iran Deal is Good for America".[52]

The Munk School's Citizen Lab, self described as "an interdisciplinary laboratory ... focusing on advanced research and development at the intersection of Information and Communication Technologies (ICTs), human rights, and global security", also targeted Iran. It published *After the Green Movement: Internet Controls in Iran, 2009-2012* and in the summer of 2015 the Citizen Lab detailed hacking of Iranian dissidents. While the Citizen Lab carefully avoided naming a culprit, their press release hyped the matter and a number of media reports implied Iranian authorities were responsible.[53]

With early financial support from the Ford Foundation, Donner Canadian Foundation and Open Society Institute, the Citizen Lab developed software to bypass government censors.[54] The Citizen Lab worked with Voice of America, Radio Free Europe and Radio Farda in Iran to disseminate its Psiphon technology to Iranian dissidents.[55] The Director of the Citizen Lab, Ron Deibert, was a regular at anti-Iranian events. Deibert spoke at a Toronto International Film Festival screening of a movie about the 2009 Green Revolution in Iran and a 2012 *Walrus* article described a "network of local Farsi speakers linked to Deibert and Psiphon."[56]

Expanding the Global Dialogue on the Future of Iran, Foreign Affairs gave the Munk School $9 million in 2015 to establish the Digital Public Square project.[57] The federal support "will enable the Munk School to create our new Digital Public Square, a square designed for citizens who cannot come together physically to exchange ideas about the future of their country," Stein said.[58] The countries cited were Iran, Syria, Iraq and Russia.[59] There was no mention of employing digital technologies to undermine online censorship in equally repressive allies such as Rwanda, Jordan or Saudi Arabia.

In partnering with Peter Munk the University of Toronto has put itself at the service of his hard right ideology. The university has also turned a blind eye to Munk and his company's flagrant hostility to the free exchange of ideas.

Barrick repeatedly sought to stifle its North American critics. (In Tanzania, Papua New Guinea and elsewhere the gold company's critics received worse.) In 2008 Barrick initiated legal action against Alain Deneault, Delphine Abadie and William Sacher as well as the publisher of *Noir Canada — Pillage, corruption et criminalité en Afrique*. Barrick's heavy-handed actions sparked a successful campaign in Québec to lessen corporations' ability to sue for reputational damage through so-called SLAPP suits (Strategic Lawsuits against Public Participation).

When two of Noir Canada's authors attempted to publish an English-language text on "why is Canada home to more than 70% of the world's mining companies?", Barrick's lawyers sent Talonbooks a fax marked "WITH PREJUDICE". They "demanded that you provide the undersigned with a copy of any portion of the manuscript or text of Imperial Canada Inc. that makes direct or indirect reference to Barrick, Sutton Resources Ltd., or to any of their past or present subsidiaries, affiliates, directors or officers no later than by 5:00 p.m. on February 19, 2010."[60] Sent three months before *Imperial Canada Inc.* was scheduled to be released, the lawyer's letter gave the publisher one week to comply.[61] Without the money to fight Barrick in court, the book was postponed.

In 2003 Barrick pursued Jorge Lopehandia for Internet libel in Ontario. The gold company accused the Chilean-Canadian of defaming it and its Chilean subsidiary. In a 2-1 decision the Ontario Superior Court ruled in Barrick's favour, finding that the Internet was different than other media. "The Court of Appeal has determined that somehow or other, chatter on the Internet is more deadly than other forms of libel and they did this, it seems to me, without any evidence," media lawyer Bert Bruser said.[62] In this precedent-setting case, Lopehandia didn't even have a lawyer representing him.[63]

In 2001 Barrick pursued the *Observer* and its parent, Guardian Newspapers, for publishing a report by prominent investigative reporter Greg Palast. (Under Britain's notoriously punitive, wealthy-centric, libel law "the person who brings the suit doesn't have to prove anything" and "a story can be correct in all of its facts, but if a court finds it to be defamatory, the defendant can be held liable."[64]) Munk claimed an article Palast wrote about an incident where 52 small scale Tanzanian miners are alleged to have been buried alive caused him "great embarrassment and distress" and "seriously damaged" his reputation.[65] Unwilling to spend the money to fight the suit, the Guardian settled and as part of the deal Palast, who is American, agreed to remove the article from his US website even though Barrick's suit would have been immediately dismissed in that country.[66]

When Janice Stein appeared at a Munk OUT of U of T organizing meeting, Angela Regnier asked Stein about Barrick's suit against the authors of Noir Canada and publisher Ecosociété. Stein said she was unfamiliar with the case and told Regnier, who was then executive director of the university's undergraduate student union, she would follow up on the matter.[67] A few days later Regnier received an email and phone calls from Barrick's lawyers with vague threats about the Munk OUT of U of T campaign spreading "misinformation".[68]

Canada's most influential global studies program is the brainchild of a mining magnet with a significant personal stake in a particular foreign policy. And the school has been shaped in his hard right image.

Canada's longest standing international affairs think tank and its billionaire patron

Like "competing" newspapers covering the Maple Leafs there is more than one academic think tank covering Canadian foreign policy. While the emphasis of each may differ slightly, the stories told by both are generally similar.

The Canadian Institute of International Affairs (CIIA), now Canadian International Council, has been Canada's leading foreign policy think tank for most of a century. Its 15 branches hold dozens of conferences and seminars annually while head office publishes *International Journal* and *Behind the Headlines*. CIIA has published dozens of books over the years and in 1990 its executive director reported, "one of our most useful, if less well known, functions is as a resource service for the media. In times of crises we are inundated with requests for the names of people who might appear as the expert commentators and resource people on television and radio."[69]

During its first half-century CIIA was a leading voice on international affairs. It initiated a large number of the texts published on Canadian foreign policy in the 1930s, 40s and 50s. In 1946 when CIAA established the *International Journal* and was seeking an initial editor, National Secretary Douglas A. MacLennan wrote a colleague that he sought someone with "executive flair, a pleasing personality, and 'drive'" rather than "a first grade scholar" because "the committee or editorial board will have to pass on any 'dangerous' articles anyway."[70]

Officially formed in 1928, CIIA's stated aim was to promote "an understanding of international questions and problems, particularly in so far as these may relate to Canada and the British Empire."[71] Its first meeting was held at the Ottawa home of Sir Robert Borden, prime minister between 1911 and 1920.[72] Borden was made first president of CIIA and another former prime minister, Arthur Meighen, became vice-president in 1936.[73]

To get a sense of Borden's worldview, he publicly encouraged Canadian businessmen to buy up southern Mexico and sought to annex the British Caribbean colonies after World War I.[74] Borden noted, "the responsibilities of governing subject races would probably

A Propaganda System

exercise a broadening influence upon our people as the dominion thus constituted would closely resemble in its problems and its duties the empire as a whole."[75] But, the prime minister feared that the Caribbean's black population might want to vote, remarking upon "the difficulty of dealing with the coloured population, who would probably be more restless under Canadian law than under British control and would desire and perhaps insist upon representation in Parliament."[76]

On hand to launch CIIA was the owner of six Canadian newspapers, Frederick Southam, as well as *Winnipeg Free Press* editor John W. Dafoe and *Ottawa Citizen* editor Charles Bowman.[77] An Edmonton branch of CIIA was set up three years later by John Imrie, managing director of the *Edmonton Journal*.[78] At the institute's 10th anniversary dinner Prime Minister Mackenzie King addressed the crowd.[79] "The CIIA's early leadership constituted a roster of Canada's business, political, and intellectual elite", explains Priscilla Roberts in *Tweaking the Lion's Tail: Edgar J. Tarr, the Canadian Institute of International Affairs, and the British Empire, 1931–1950*.[80]

CIIA's genesis was in the post-World War I Paris Peace Conference. At the 1919 conference British and US delegates discussed establishing internationally focused institutes. The next year the Royal Institute of International Affairs (RIIA), or Chatham House Study Group, was founded in London and in 1921 the Council on Foreign Relations was set up, notes *Imperial Brain Trust*, "to equip the United States of America for an imperial rule on the world scene."[81]

The driving force behind these international affairs institutes was British historian Lionel Curtis. An "indefatigable proponent of Imperial Federation" and former Colonial Office official in South Africa, Curtis set up a network of semi-secret Round Table Groups in the British Dominions and US.[82] The aim was "to federate the English-speaking world along lines laid down by Cecil Rhodes", the famous British imperialist.[83] The Rhodes Trust and South African mining magnet Sir Abe Bailey financed the Round Table Groups and former British Secretary of State for War Lord Milner promoted the initiative.[84]

Before its official formation CIIA sought to affiliate with RIIA. A number of prominent Canadians were part of Chatham House and the Canadian elite was largely pro-British at the time. "Much of the impetus and funding to" launch CIIA, Roberts writes, "came from Sir Joseph Flavelle, a meatpacking and banking magnate who strongly supported British Imperial unity. Other key Anglophile supporters included Newton W. Rowell, a leading Liberal politician, the wealthy Liberal politician and diplomat, Vincent Massey, and Sir Arthur Currie, commander of Canadian forces on the Western front during the war, who became principal of McGill University in 1920."[85]

A $21,000 ($350,000 today) grant from the Massey Foundation, overseen by ardent anglophile Vincent Massey, allowed CIIA to hire Escott Reid as its first full-time national secretary in 1932.[86] Funds from Sun Life Assurance Company of Canada president John Nelson, who believed the CIIA was "of great significance from the Imperial standpoint", and other corporate supporters provided the means to begin its "first full public education program in the 1930s."[87]

(Though it was created seven years earlier, some consider the League of Nations Society in Canada the CIIA's "popular arm". Many of the CIIA's founders were executive members of the society and institute members publicized views formed during CIIA study groups.[88] The society sponsored speaking tours and radio broadcasts. The Canadian branch also distributed League of Nations publications and published a 16-page monthly called *Interdependence: A Monthly Review of the League of Nations and Foreign Affairs*. In "The Institute's 'Popular Arm': The League of Nations Society in Canada" Donald Page notes: "Everywhere faithful bands of supporters in branches and corporate club affiliates were organizing study groups based on the latest issue of Interdependence, arranging for broadcasts

A Propaganda System

and editorials, placing speakers on public platforms, and providing materials for use in revised school curricula."[89] It took a half-decade to gain traction, but by the mid-1930s the society required a full-time employee and three part-time regional representatives to distribute its information to newspapers.[90] "Numerous editors", Page writes, "took their lead from its [Interdependence] pages."[91] Sun Life Assurance Company, International Nickel Company of Canada (INCO) and the Army and Navy Veterans Association gave the society large donations.[92] But the government had significant leverage over the society's funding. After Minister of Finance Charles Dunning learned of a proposal to raise funds for a campaign to reinvigorate the League of Nations in 1937, the Society's wealthy donors suddenly withdrew. Dunning and Prime Minister Mackenzie King "reacted strongly to this public campaign on behalf of collective security in the belief that it might embarrass not only their own government but also those of the United States and United Kingdom. With a few phone calls Dunning was able to turn off the Montreal businessmen."[93])

CIIA's Winnipeg branch started sponsoring radio broadcasts on international affairs in 1935.[94] Three years later the organization began enlisting newspapers as corporate subscribers in exchange for CIIA publications and other international information.[95] In the early 1940s the head office commissioned essays for the CBC and during this period CIIA official John Holmes reported that his time was largely spent distributing daily and weekly press releases to media outlets.[96] Before and during World War II CIIA helped "build an 'internationalist mood within Canada.'"[97] (Though it proved a socially worthwhile fight, Nazi expansionism's threat to British interests, not opposition to fascism or anti-Semitism, led Ottawa to war. Canadian support for fascism in Spain (and Japan) in the years leading to World War Two should bedevil the notion that Canada joined WWII to combat this perverse political system/ideology.)

During the war External Affairs asked the CIIA Research Committee to look into the shape of the postwar world and nearly 20 professors with direct or indirect ties to the institute worked for the ministry.[98] According to *Think Tank Traditions*, CIIA was "closer to government than any other private organizations" during World War II.[99]

But the institute's ties to External Affairs began before the war and continued thereafter. The institute's first three national secretaries, note Diane Stone and Andrew Denham, "all went into government service and rose to the top of the mandarinate."[100] In a thesis on the CIIA's first two decades Carter Manny writes, "most of Canada's post-war policy makers have been members of the Institute."[101] Conversely, External Affairs officials helped identify "possible candidates for positions on the Institute's staff."[102]

External Affairs also modified CIIA publications. In 1942 CIIA National Secretary John Holmes asked Lester Pearson to comment on *Canada in World Affairs*. Pearson shared the manuscript with three External Affairs colleagues who suggested a number of revisions to the yet to be published book.[103] CIIA did the same with the 1957 issue of *Canada in World Affairs*.[104]

CIIA sometimes published External Affairs work and government officials regularly spoke at their events. In 1951 the institute reprinted a major External Affairs paper on the Korean War and External Affairs officials often wrote for *International Journal* (sometimes under the signature of a CIIA official).[105] At the time the institute openly touted its close ties to External Affairs. A 1950 CIIA brief to a Royal Commission on the Arts noted, "the friendly cooperation of the government, and particularly of the Department of External Affairs, its minister and its officials. This cooperation we have always enjoyed and we should like to take this opportunity of putting on record our thanks and appreciation of the help we have received from past prime ministers, from the present Prime Minister and his cabinet and from the heads of the departments which serve under them."[106]

The CIIA's early powerbrokers generally identified with British imperialism. But its younger members and staff tended to back Washington's worldview. (In the foreign policy literature this divide is generally referred to as "imperialists" vs. "nationalists".) US foundation funding strengthened the hand of the "nationalists". Between 1936 and 1954 the Rockefeller Foundation donated $127,500 ($1 million today) to support CIIA publications and conferences.[107] In *Rockefeller Philanthropy and the Institute of Pacific Relations*, a book about a sister organization of CIIA, Lawrence T. Woods notes: "The CIIA's profile as a respected national institution was significantly dependent upon RF [Rockefeller Foundation] funding prior to, during, and immediately following World War II, and the Foundation was aware of this reliance."[108] The Rockefeller Foundation accounted for as much as half of its budget in the early 1940s.[109]

Alongside Rockefeller money, the Carnegie Corporation supported the establishment of the institute's foreign policy library and public information services in the 1940s and early 50s.[110] During the 1960s the Ford Foundation provided $365,000 ($1 million today), which paid for 18 books, 20 reports and a research secretary.[111] In *Canada's Voice: the Public Life of John Wendell Holmes*, Adam Chapnick writes, "since the Ford money was the major driver of the CIIA's research agenda, and since [CIIA head] Holmes made sure to integrate government representatives into the new projects as often as possible, it largely framed debates about Canadian foreign policy across the country for the next five years."[112]

Set up by US capitalists responsible for significant labour and human rights abuses, the Big 3 foundations were not disinterested organizations. In *The Influence of the Carnegie, Ford and Rockefeller Foundations on American Foreign Policy* Edward H. Berman writes: "The Carnegie, Ford, and Rockefeller foundations have consistently supported the major aims of United States foreign policy, while simultaneously helping to construct an intellectual framework supportive of that policies major tenants."[113]

CIIA also received government grants.[114] Though it sought to avoid overreliance on External Affairs money, financial difficulties prompted a substantial funding request at the start of the 1970s.[115] In 1972 External Affairs began giving the institute $50,000 annually ($150,000 today).[116] Sixteen years later the Department of National Defence initiated a $50,000 a year operating grant, which was on top of the $45,000 the institute received from External Affairs at the time.[117]

But the institute's nonfinancial ties to the government have always been more significant. After nearly two decades at External Affairs, John Holmes returned to lead the institute in 1960. Chapnick notes, "during Pearson's time in office [1963-68] Holmes had unprecedented access to the highest levels of government. He could reach Pearson personally when he was in Ottawa, and the Prime Minister promoted the CIIA while entertaining. Holmes also drafted speeches for Minister of Trade and Commerce Robin Winters."[118]

Upon leaving office external ministers Lester Pearson, Paul Martin Senior and Mitchell Sharp all took up honorary positions with CIIA.[119] In 1999 former foreign minister Barbara McDougall took charge of the institute and many chapters continue to be dominated by retired diplomats.[120] Active Canadian diplomats regularly speak to CIIA meetings, as did Prime Ministers Pierre Trudeau and Jean Chretien.[121]

Alongside Ottawa and US foundations, Canadian capitalists with foreign policy interests also funded CIIA. In 1950 the former president of Monarch Life Insurance Company, Edgar Tarr, left money in his will to help build its international affairs library. A one-time president of CIIA, Tarr "showed deep interest in India and most of all China, where the Monarch Life Assurance Company had extensive interests."[122] Similarly, Toronto-based Brascan, which was known as the "the Canadian octopus" in Brazil since its tentacles reached into so many areas of the country's economy, paid for CIIA "to present a paper dealing with sources of information on relations between Canada and Latin America."[123]

Annual reports I analyzed from the late 1960s to mid-1990s list numerous globally focused corporate sponsors and corporate councilmembers, including Bata Shoes, Toronto Dominion, Bank of Montréal, Bank of Nova Scotia, Brascan, Barrick Gold and Power Corporation.[124] In the 1970s and 80s the presidents of Toronto Dominion, Bell Canada, Gulf Canada and the National Bank of Canada led CIIA fundraising drives.[125]

In 2006 CIIA's operations were subsumed into the Canadian International Council (CIC). With financing from Research In Motion (RIM) co-founder Jim Balsillie, CIIA partnered with the Balsillie-created Centre for International Governance Innovation (CIGI) to establish CIC.

The CIIA library and its publications were maintained while an infusion of cash bolstered local chapters. The new organization also added a major national fellowship program, which is headquartered at the University of Toronto's Munk Centre for Global Affairs.

Balsillie was made founding chair of CIC and the initial vice chairs were former foreign ministers Bill Graham and Perrin Beattie. "The CIC promises to transform the debate about and understanding of Canadian foreign policy," said Balsillie in 2007.[126]

Balsillie put up $1-million in seed funding and launched a fundraising drive in the corporate community. Trying to drum up support for CIC, Balsillie wrote a commentary for the *Globe and Mail Report on Business*, explaining that "in return for their support, contributing business leaders would be offered seats in a CIC corporate senate that would give them influence over the research agenda and priorities of the new council."[127] In another piece for the *National Post* Balsillie wrote: "To create a research base on Canadian foreign policy, I have spearheaded the creation of the Canada-wide Canadian International Council (CIC). The Americans have their powerful Council on Foreign Relations, which offers non-partisan analysis of international issues and integrates business leaders with the best researchers and public policy leaders."[128]

The Council on Foreign Relations publishes the venerable *Foreign Affairs* journal and in-depth studies of major international issues. In *Wall Street's Think Tank: The Council on Foreign Relations and the Empire of Neoliberal Geopolitics, 1976-2014*, Laurence H. Shoup details the organization's role in bringing top government officials, media figures and corporate titans together. Though the Council on Foreign Relations has kept a low profile, "the most influential foreign policy think tank in the US" has played an important role in shaping the current world order.[129] CIGI was an inaugural and sole Canadian member of CFR's Council of Councils, an "international initiative to connect leading foreign policy institutes from around the world."[130]

In 2011–12 the CIC Senate included Balsillie, CEO of Power Corporation André Desmarais, Chair of Barrick Gold Peter Munk, Sun Life Financial CEO Donald Stewart, RBC President Gordon M. Nixon and other corporate figures. In an article critical of the Munk School of Global Affairs, which has formal ties with CIC, professors John Valleau and Paul Hamel described the CIC "as a right-wing 'think tank', comparable in its make-up and ideology to the Canadian Council of Chief Executives (C.C.C.E.) but with a self-interested focus on Canada's posture in foreign policy and trade. The C.I.C. appears to be the creature especially of 18 high-profile Canadian corporations (including for example Scotiabank, the Power Corporation, Research-in-Motion, Goldcorp, Manulife, Magna International and of course Barrick Gold), the CEOs or Presidents of which constitute the C.I.C. Senate. Its Board of Directors combines such people with other influential people such as Perrin Beatty (now CEO of the Canadian Chamber of Commerce), Bill Graham (former foreign minister) and Janice Stein (current director of the Munk School)."[131]

Beyond CIC, Balsillie provided significant support for the study of international affairs. In 2008 *Embassy* called him the "godfather of Canadian international scholarship ... Balsillie has donated over $130 million to launch three new institutions: the Balsillie School of International Affairs; the Centre for International Governance Innovation (CIGI); and the Canada International Council."[132]

Established in 2001, CIGI was dubbed the "most richly endowed policy institute in Canada."[133] The Waterloo, Ontario, based think tank received an initial $20 million from Balsillie and $10 million from Mike Lazaridis, then co-CEOs of RIM. In 2003 the federal government matched the business executives' $30 million contribution (as well as providing Balsillie and Lazaridis with tax credits for their charitable donations). In 2007 the Ontario government matched another $17 million Balsillie grant to CIGI.[134] A $69 million CIGI Campus was launched six years later. It received another $50 million from the federal and provincial governments as well as a large plot of land from the City of Waterloo.[135] Balsillie told *Embassy* he wanted to make CIGI "not unlike the Brookings Institute," on whose international advisory board he sat.[136] (In November 2002 that Washington-based think tank sponsored the Haiti Democracy Project, which was inaugurated by a number of American diplomats and powerful Haitian businessmen to spur opposition to Haiti's elected government, which culminated in the February 2004 coup.[137] In another part of the world, Brookings operated the Saban Center for Middle East Policy, which was funded by billionaire Haim Saban who said his "greatest concern ... is to protect Israel" and that "I would bomb the living daylights out of the sons of bitches [Iran]."[138])

Similar to its US model, CIGI published books, papers, special reports and policy briefs. In 2011 it began co-publishing the annual Canada Among Nations series with the Norman Paterson School of International Affairs. In the opening chapter of the 2013 issue titled *Canada-Africa Relations: Looking Back, Looking Ahead* editors Yiagadeesen Samy and Rohinton P. Medhora (CIGI's president) write: "Even if very ad hoc and reactive, Canada's engagement, whether it was for developmental reasons, peacekeeping, nation building, democracy promotion or human rights, reflected familiar Canadian values. Commercial interests, although present, have never been a defining feature of that relationship." One wonders how the dispossession of First Nations fits their definition of "Canadian values", but leaving this aside, Ottawa has repeatedly demonstrated its indifference to both democracy and human rights in Africa. Additionally, anyone with access to Google can easily find examples of corporations, particularly the mining industry, shaping Canadian policy in African countries.

Balsillie's foreign policy initiatives weren't without controversy. In 2009 the initial executive director of CIGI, John English, was abruptly let go. The official biographer of Prime Ministers Lester Pearson and Pierre Trudeau, English was a former Member of Parliament, special ambassador for landmines, special envoy for the election of Canada to the United Nations Security Council and president of the Canadian Institute of International Affairs. After English was let go, the *Globe and Mail*'s Michael Valpy reported, "Mr. English's departure shocked many in the academic and public service foreign policy communities, none of whom would comment on the record — and one of whom refused to comment even off the record — because their institutions either receive or are eligible to receive funds from CIGI and CIC."[139]

As part of "cleaning house" Balsillie also removed Ramesh Thakur as the inaugural director of the Balsillie School of International Affairs (BSIA), which is a University of Waterloo and Wilfrid Laurier department housed at CIGI campus. One of the principal authors of the Canadian backed Responsibility to

Protect report, Thakur (ever so timidly) resisted CIGI's effort to control BSIA. After Thakur's dismissal the Canadian Association of University Teachers threatened to censure the University of Waterloo and Wilfrid Laurier if they failed to modify governance provisions that flagrantly contravened the most basic notions of academic integrity.[140]

The $33 million accord between CIGI and Wilfrid Laurier/ University of Waterloo modified the universities' governance structures, giving Balsillie's think tank an effective veto over academic matters at BSIA.[141] In an email released after Thakur's dismissal, secretary to and member of the CIGI Board Cosimo Fiorenza wrote, "it's important that CIGI be at the table regarding all of the academic discussions for the BSIA …to ensure that all approved areas of study are consistent with our mandated themes."[142]

As part of its funding agreement, CIGI also demanded to be consulted on "the selection of individuals" appointed to a dozen academic posts at BSIA.[143] A 70-page Canadian Association of University Teachers report complained that "the donor agreement specifies that the universities are obligated to consult with CIGI about which individuals they are considering for appointment as CIGI Research Chairs and Balsillie Fellows."[144]

With CIGI's funding to BSIA released in instalments, Balsillie had a great deal of leverage over BSIA.

Norman Paterson School of International Affairs

The Norman Paterson School of International Affairs (NPSIA) is the oldest global affairs school in Canada. Founded in 1965, the Carleton University graduate program is highly regarded.

NPSIA was established with a $400,000 ($1.5 million today) grant from long-time Senator Norman Paterson, a grain-shipping magnate.[145] During World War II his company provided vessels for Atlantic convoys and Paterson was a major player within the Liberal party. Twice under-secretary of External Affairs and leading architect of post-World War II Canadian foreign policy, Norman Robertson was the school's first director. Unhappy in a diplomatic post in Geneva, External Affairs colleagues secured Robertson the NPSIA position.[146] During his time at Carleton, Robertson continued to be paid as a "Senior Advisor" to External Affairs, overseeing a major review of a department concerned about growing criticism that it was acting as the US' "errand boy" in Vietnam.[147]

The initial chair of Strategic Studies at NPSIA was a former deputy minister of Veterans Affairs and Canada's principal disarmament negotiator between 1960 and 1968.[148] Lieutenant-General Eedson L. M. Burns left government to take up the Carleton post.[149]

Three months after stepping down as prime minister in 1968 Lester Pearson began teaching a seminar on Canadian foreign policy at NPSIA. In a foreword to *Freedom and Change: Essays in Honour of Lester B. Pearson*, Senator Norman Paterson wrote, "the idea of creating a School of International Affairs in Canada and thoughts on how Lester Pearson might spend part of his time after retiring from public life became intimately bound together in my mind."[150]

After two decades with External Affairs, nine years as external minister and five years as prime minister, Pearson did more than any Canadian to back the US Empire. Rather than a "peacekeeper", Pearson should be viewed as a war criminal. (See my *Lester Pearson's Peacekeeping: The Truth May Hurt* for details.)

After Pearson died in 1972 his friends raised funds to establish the Lester B. Pearson Chair of International Affairs at NPSIA.[151] A former Canadian ambassador to Egypt and the USSR, as well as secretary-general of the Commonwealth, Arnold Cantwell Smith, was the first Lester B. Pearson chair.[152]

The close association between NPSIA and Foreign Affairs continues. Former Canadian ambassador to the UN, president of the

Security Council and director of the government created Canadian Institute for International Peace and Security, William Barton gave $3 million to establish a chair at NPSIA in 2008.[153] The inaugural William and Jeanie Barton Chair in International Affairs was Trevor Findlay, a 13-year Australian diplomat and senior fellow at the Centre for International Governance Innovation (CIGI).

The NPSIA faculty includes numerous former Canadian diplomats and establishment figures, including ambassador to Washington Derek Burney, long-time diplomat Colin Robertson and former ambassador to Jordan, Egypt and Israel Michael Dougall Bell.[154] A former director of DND's Directorate of History Norman Hillmer, security analyst Stephanie Carvin and special advisor to the external minister Gerald Wright were also faculty members.[155] From the corporate world, long-time chief executive of the Canadian Council of Chief Executives, Thomas d'Aquino, was also at NPSIA.

In 1984 NPSIA began publishing the annual "Canada Among Nations" series, which has "become a major publication of record on Canada's policies and actions in the world."[156] DND's Military and Strategic Studies Program funded a number of volumes of Canada Among Nations.[157]

Other Academic Institutions

Corporations and the wealthy, as well as GAC and DND, established or strengthened numerous university chairs, programs and departments indirectly related to Canadian foreign policy.

Allied with the West, the Gulf Cooperation Council monarchies funded various Canadian university programs. In 2007 Kuwait dished out $1 million to McGill, U of Ottawa and U of Alberta to expand their Arabic and Islamic studies offerings.[158] In 2010 Saudi Arabia's King Abdullah bin Abdulaziz donated $5.3 million to establish a Chair for Dialogue among Civilizations at the U of Toronto while Qatar gave McGill's Institute of Islamic Studies $1.25 million in 2012.[159]

A subject more directly tied to Canadian foreign policy, Concordia's Will to Intervene (W2I) project received $1.3 million from James M. Stanford, a long-time CEO of Petro Canada and board member of internationally focused electricity firm Fortis and mining firm Vale Inco.[160] According to the official description, W2I seeks to build "domestic political will in Canada and the United States to prevent future mass atrocities."[161] But the architects of W2I don't mean the "political will" to stop Washington from spurring "mass atrocities" à la Iraq, Vietnam, Somalia, Haiti, Korea etc. Human rights rhetoric aside, W2I is an outgrowth of the Canadian government sponsored Responsibility to Protect doctrine, which was used to justify the 2011 NATO war in Libya and 2004 overthrow of Haiti's elected government.[162] While the less sophisticated neoconservatives simply call for a more aggressive military posture, the more liberal supporters of imperialism prefer a high-minded ideological mask to accomplish the same end. W2I is one such tool.

Since 1991 the Jarislowsky Foundation has endowed some 30 chairs focused on various topics, including the "study of democracy", "central banking" and the "Middle East and North Africa".[163] Jarislowsky generally donates between $500,000 and $2 million per chair with the university matching the funds and providing other forms of support.

A US Army counter-intelligence officer during World War II, Stephen Jarislowsky is a Montréal billionaire who sat on the boards of The Daily Telegraph, Swiss Bank Corp and SNC- Lavalin, which was 14% owned by Jarislowsky's investment firm.[164] (Jarislowsky and the controversial global engineering powerhouse funded a Jarislowsky/SNC-Lavalin Research Chair in the Management of International Projects at Université de Montréal's Polytechnique.) A former director of the right wing C.D. Howe Institute, Jarislowsky equated Québec's independence movement to the Nazis and bemoaned a "change in class structure" in the mid-1970s. "The meek are not just inheriting the earth, they are grabbing it ... The 10 per cent of the people with funds to invest are locked out of the democratic process."[165]

To support Israeli expansionism prominent Jewish Canadians endowed Israel Studies programs. Heir to the Seagram liquor fortune, the Bronfmans provided $1.5 million to the University of Toronto to create an Andrea and Charles Bronfman Chair in Israeli Studies.[166] As part of the 1997 agreement the university invested $1 million in the initiative.[167] "Fifty years after its rebirth, the miracle of modern Israel is of broad interest," said Charles Bronfman at the launch.[168]

The Bronfmans are long-standing Israeli nationalists. The family organized weapon shipments to the Hagganah (pre-state Zionist military force) and more recently the Charles R. Bronfman Foundation supported the Libi Fund, which raises money for Israeli soldiers.[169]

With funds from the estate of deceased oilman Sydney Kahanoff, the University of Calgary opened the Kahanoff Chair in Israeli Studies in 2003.[170] Mandated to spend 60% of its funds in Canada and 40% in Israel, the Kahanoff Foundation was led by Shira Herzog, a member of a storied Israeli family and former executive director of the Canada-Israel Committee.[171]

In 2011 multi billionaire David Azrieli gave Concordia $5 million to set up the Azrieli Institute of Israel Studies — the largest donation the Arts and Science Faculty Council ever received.[172] The money funds conferences and fellowships and established the first minor in Israel Studies at a Canadian university.[173]

This wasn't a disinterested, apolitical, donation. The Israeli-Canadian real estate magnate asserted that "I am a Zionist and I love the country" and he was an officer in a largely Anglo-Saxon Hagganah Brigade responsible for a number of massacres during the 1947/48 war in which 750,000 Palestinians were "ethnically cleansed" from their homeland.[174]

The Azrieli Institute has proven a potent advocate for Israel at Concordia. Its director, Csaba Nikolenyi, was part of the Canadian

Academic Friends of Israel and in 2015 the institute hosted the Association for Israel Studies' annual conference.[175] The gathering included speeches by pro-Zionist activist Irwin Cotler and Israeli Ambassador Rafael Barak.[176] After attending the Association for Israel Studies' conference, prominent anti-Palestinian activist Gerald Steinberg described Azrieli's donation as part of a "counterattack" against pro-Palestinian activism at Concordia.[177] The institute is designed to erase Palestinians from their historical connection to their homeland. Its website failed to even mention the word Palestine. In a December 2014 letter to the *Montréal Gazette* Nakina Stratos noted: "Browsing through the website of the Azrieli Institute of Israel Studies, I was not able to find the words 'Palestine' or 'Palestinian people.' How can an institute that teaches about the history of Israel not mention Palestine on its website? This, to me, intersects with the far-right Israeli narrative, which is a total confiscation of Palestinian history, and an attempt to erase the concept of Palestine from the dictionary of the Middle East."[178]

Often operating alongside Israel Studies, Jewish Studies programs are financed by wealthy, politically motivated, individuals. In 2012 Ken and Larry Tanenbaum gave the University of Toronto $5-million for the Anne Tanenbaum Centre for Jewish Studies and helped raise millions of dollars more.[179] Larry Tanenbaum was one of a half-dozen rich right-wing donors that scrapped the hundred-year-old Canadian Jewish Congress in 2011 and replaced it with the Centre for Israel and Jewish Affairs. As the name change suggests, this move represented a shift towards ever greater lobbying in favour of Israeli nationalism.[180]

In 1999 the Bronfmans gave Concordia $1 million for a Jewish Studies program while 13 years later the estate of Simon and Ethel Flegg contributed $1 million to McGill's Jewish Studies department. The money was for an "education initiative in conjunction with McGill Hillel."[181] But, Hillel refuses to associate with Jews (or others) who "delegitimize, demonize, or apply a double standard to Israel; support boycott of, divestment from, or sanctions against the state of Israel."[182]

As outlined in chapters 2 and 3, military funds influence university priorities. The Canadian Forces direct millions of dollars annually to "defence" and "security" studies and tens of millions of dollars to less politicized scientific research.

Canada's aid agency also directs millions of dollars to Canadian universities. They finance joint "development" projects, student internships and international development studies (IDS) associations.

Canadian universities have participated in government-funded aid projects since the 1950s.[183] In 1978 CIDA and the Crown Corporation International Development Research Centre (IDRC) paid to set up the Association of Universities and Colleges of Canada (AUCC) international development office.[184] CIDA had relations with most Canadian universities and colleges, distributing $250 million to universities between 1986 and 2006.[185] In a highly politicized climate, the McGill Office of International Research received $15 million between 1998 and 2013 for a civil society and peace-building program in Israel, Palestine and Jordan while in the early 2000s the University of Calgary won part of an $8 million CIDA project to help rebuild Kosovo's postwar education system.[186]

Canadian aid had both a direct and indirect hand in the creation of IDS programs. Individuals who participated in aid agency funded projects spurred development studies programs and CIDA/IDRC directly financed IDS initiatives. In the introduction to a *Canadian Journal of Development Studies* special issue on Canadian universities and development, editors Leonora Angeles and Peter Boothroyd write, "thanks mostly to grant funding from the Canadian International Development Agency (CIDA) and the International Development Research Centre (IDRC), Canadian academics have been able to engage intensively in development work for over three decades."[187]

Canadian University Services Overseas (CUSO) representatives also launched IDS programs. To create CUSO, the first major non-religious NGO, Keith Spicer claimed to have "convinced everybody who needed to be convinced, from the Prime Minister on down."[188] Spicer described CUSO to Prime Minister Lester Pearson as "a great idea to help Canada save the world." By sending Canadian university students abroad as volunteers, Spicer argued, CUSO would help "to cope with the advancing enemy" (communism).[189] Since receiving a $500,000 government grant in 1965 most of CUSO's money has come from Ottawa and early CUSO volunteers were flown to their destinations in Canadian military aircraft.[190] (See *Paved with Good Intentions: Canada's development NGOs from idealism to imperialism* for a thorough discussion of the role of NGOs in Canadian foreign policy.)

In a history of the so called non-governmental organization Ruth Compton Brouwer writes, "CUSO staff and RV's [returned volunteers] contributed substantially to the establishment of University – level courses and programs related to global issues and the centres for international education and development studies. These are now such ordinary features of Canadian universities that it is difficult to conceive of how novel they were when they began in the 1960s."[191]

Led by CUSO's former West Africa coordinator Don Simpson, University of Western Ontario opened an office of international education in 1969, which "operated in collaboration with CIDA."[192] Similarly, "valued friends of CUSO" instigated IDS programming at the universities of Ottawa and Toronto.[193]

Individuals who worked on other CIDA funded projects established IDS programs elsewhere. The founding chair of Trent's IDS program, David Morrison, led the university's CIDA-funded program in Ecuador and Mexico and continues to work with CIDA funded NGO Horizons of Friendship.[194] Morrison also published a semi-official history of CIDA on behalf of the CIDA funded North-South Institute.

CIDA and IDRC directly funded IDS initiatives. In the late 1960s CIDA sponsored a study with the AUCC to investigate what schools offered development studies courses.[195] According to *IDRC: 40 years of ideas, innovation, and impact*, "early on, it began funding Canadian area and development studies associations, their conferences, journals, and research — gathering and communication activities."[196] The Canadian Association of African Studies, Canadian Association of Latin American and Caribbean Studies, Canadian Asian Studies Association and Canadian Association of Studies in International Development all "received substantial core funding from IDRC, intermittently in the 1970s and 1980s, and continuously since 1990."[197]

In the mid-1990s IDRC sponsored an initiative to enhance undergraduate IDS programs. This led to the creation of the Canadian Consortium for University Programs in International Development Studies (CCUPIDS), which has as its primary objective to "strengthen the position of International Development Studies."[198] CIDA also funded CCUPIDS conferences.[199]

CCUPIDS is a branch of the Canadian Association for the Study of International Development (CASID), which publishes the *Canadian Journal of Development Studies*. It received significant backing from IDRC. In 2015 its president thanked "IDRC for its support of CASID over the past decade and more."[200] As part of one contract, IDRC gave CASID $450,000 between 2012 and 2015.[201] CIDA also collaborated with CASID.[202]

Student initiatives also benefited from Canadian "aid". IDS student project InSight received IDRC's "generous financial support" while *Undercurrent: Canadian Undergraduate Journal of*

Development Studies was set up with IDRC money.[203] Similarly, the International Cooperation Days put on by the Canadian Council for International Co-operation and Canadian Association of International Development Professionals also "benefitted from the generous support of" IDRC.[204]

Significant sums of aid money flow to IDS programs. The website of the McGill Institute for the Study of International Development listed a half-dozen contracts worth more than $600,000 from CIDA, as well as $400,000 in contracts from IDRC and Foreign Affairs.[205] An NGO and CIDA training ground, IDS programs often include internships and volunteer opportunities funded by development aid. The Students for Development Internships is "offered through the AUCC and CIDA, and students are funded to work for up to four months with an NGO anywhere in the world."[206] Queen's Global Development Studies exchange program, for instance, received $270,000 from CIDA in 2011.[207]

Canadian aid directly shaped IDS politics. Half of the respondents to a 2003 survey of 64 IDS scholars reported that CIDA's six development priorities influenced their research focus.[208] A professor or student who aligns their pursuits with those of the aid agency is more likely to find funding or a fellowship. And the aid agency's priorities don't include challenging Canadian foreign policy.

CIDA cherishes the influence it has within academia. In the late 1980s the AUCC tried to develop a more stable source of funding for its international endeavours, but CIDA blocked the move to create a new government agency to fund universities' international partnerships.[209] The aid agency preferred they stay dependent.[210]

Many university officials were reluctant to challenge Canadian support for Indonesia's near-genocide in East Timor. In *Partnership in an Evil Action: Canadian universities, Indonesia, East Timor and the question of international responsibility*, Peter Eglin documents how Canadian academics minimized Indonesian human rights violations in occupied East Timor. Among a number of examples Eglin cites is a 1993 *Canadian Journal of Development Studies* special issue on Indonesia, which included a map with the whole island of Timor, then illegally occupied, as part of Indonesia.[211] Timor was listed as the 27th province as per Indonesia's definition, which was echoed in a 1993 document titled "CIDA Programs in Asia: Indonesia."[212] The editor of the special issue was Harry Cummings, a University of Guelph professor who participated in a major aid project in Indonesia.[213] CIDA directed tens of millions of dollars to Canadian universities for projects in Indonesia, including a $38 million University of Guelph project and $9.1 million initiative between McGill's Institute of Islamic studies and Indonesia's Department of Religious Affairs.[214]

In addition to CIDA, mining companies operating in Indonesia had influence on Canadian campuses. When Carleton's Public Interest Research Group (PIRG) showed the documentary *Buried Alive* in March 1991 Indonesian officials complained to Carleton's president. Afterwards President Robin Farquhar called PIRG's Jane Beauchamp to tell "her the Indonesian government was unhappy about the film" on East Timor. Eglin continues, "Embassy officials were obviously correct in thinking they could expect a sympathetic response from Carleton's president. Perhaps they were influenced by the fact Carleton had just accepted a $750,000 donation from their own biggest Canadian investor, Inco."[215]

Carleton's president was right to be concerned about the mining giant's reaction if he were seen to be sympathetic to critics of Indonesian president General Suharto. When Laurentian University in Sudbury, Ontario, offered mining critic Joan Kuyek an honorary degree in 1995 Inco threatened to withdraw its $3 million grant to the university.[216] A long-time critic of Canadian mining companies, Kuyek was a director at Mining Watch and editor of *Community Rights and Corporate Responsibility*, a book about Canadian resource companies operating abroad.

Internationally focused resource firms have donated tens of millions of dollars to Canadian universities. In 2005 Inco gave $20 million to Memorial University in Newfoundland while two years later a consortium of BC mining companies donated more than $20 million to the University of British Columbia, including $5 million from Goldcorp.[217] In an agreement that tied the university to a mining firm's international operations, Laurentian partnered with the University of Limpopo in South Africa at the request of Ivanhoe Mines. In 2015 the Vancouver-based company put up $2.5 million US for an educational project in the South African province where it operated a controversial platinum mine.[218]

Individual mining executives are even bigger donors to universities. In 2007 Ian Telfer, the former CEO of Goldcorp and then chair of its board of directors, gave $25 million to the University of Ottawa School of Management while Joseph Rotman, a longstanding member of Barrick Gold's board, gave $36 million to the University of Toronto's School of Management over two decades.[219] Rotman also sat on U of T's top decision-making body while another member of Barrick's board, Marshall Cohen, chaired the board of Toronto's other large university, York. (According to a book on the privatization of Canadian universities, "hundreds of public university board members held corporate directorship positions", including many who represent internationally focused mining companies, banks, military firms etc.[220])

Mining magnate Seymour Schulich is the leading private donor to Canadian universities, endowing a dozen Schulich Schools of engineering, business, music etc. across the country. In response to a Canadian Association of University Teachers' report critical of the universities of Waterloo and Wilfrid Laurier for interceding on behalf of the donor to remove Ramesh Thakur as head of the Balsillie School of International Affairs, Schulich told the *Globe and Mail*: "It's great to be academically free if there's no consequences to your credo, your stance. If there's no cost, you can stand on principle and jump up and down about any number of things."[221]

The federal government also funded university mining initiatives. As part of its multifaceted support to Canada's international extractive sector, the Stephen Harper government commissioned the Canadian International Institute for Extractive Industries and Development (CIIEID), a university hosted think tank, to provide mining related services to developing countries. In 2012 Ottawa committed $25 million over five years to an institute jointly housed by the University of British Columbia, Simon Fraser University and Université de Montréal. A number of mining companies also pledged millions of dollars to support CIIEID programming.

In June 2013 then International Development Minister Julian Fantino told a Mining Association of Canada meeting that CIIEID "will be your biggest and best ambassador."[222] Drawing from the minister's statement, Mining Watch concluded: "CIIEID will promote extractive industry growth, not poverty reduction."[223]

***

GAC, DND and the wealthy have funded a slew of academic initiatives related to foreign policy. These programs generally advance their worldview. But they also effectively weaken other domains. Universities allocate resources partly based on a department's ability to draw resources and no one funds chairs focused on Canadian imperialism, the Haitian revolution, NATO violence etc.

On foreign policy, academia is broadly subservient to state and corporate power. One reason for this is that leading international affairs scholars often move between university, government and institutes in the pay of the wealthy or DND/GAC. Founding director of the University of Ottawa Centre for International Policy Studies, Roland Paris became a senior adviser to Prime Minister Justin Trudeau in 2015. Previously, Paris had been a member of a major NATO panel tasked with developing recommendations to strengthen the alliance and was one of two Canadian members of the "Agenda Working Group" for the militarist US-based Halifax International Security Forum.[224] (Long time Munk School of Global Affairs Director, Janice Stein, was the other.) President of CIDA from 2008-2013, Margaret Biggs joined Queens' School of Policy Studies and Department of Political Studies afterwards.[225] In 2016 she was made chair of the International Development Research Centre.

Norman Paterson School of International Affairs faculty member Gerald Wright was vice president of the Donner Canadian foundation between 1972 and 1987.[226] A protégé of prominent diplomat John Holmes, Wright oversaw a House of Commons study on Canada's international relations and served as special advisor to the external minister. He has also had positions with the pro-NATO Atlantic Council of Canada and Atlantic Treaty Association, as well as the Canadian Institute for International Peace and Security and Canadian International Council. The above examples are a small sample of a broader trend.

The back and forth among academia, government and DND/GAC/corporate funded think tanks certainly limits criticism. It's hard to criticize former or future colleagues and if a government or institute position is a possibility it is professionally dangerous to aggressively challenge Canadian foreign policy.

A Propaganda System

5. 'Arms Length' Institutions

> *"Let me take this opportunity, on behalf of the Canadian peace researchers, to convey our heartfelt appreciation to the last Liberal government for its initiative, and to the Opposition parties — The Progressive Conservative Party and The New Democratic Party — for their sincerity and cooperation in helping the establishment of the Institute."*[1]
>
> **Canadian Institute of International Peace and Security founder M. V. Naidu**

A friend once ran a website for fans of the Canadiens. A local newspaper paid him to maintain it and advertising was sold to cover the costs. Many fans preferred to get their Habs' fix through an "arms length" institution — one that appeared to be independent of the team, even if the essential point of the website was to cheer on their Canadiens. Fans liked having a forum where they could criticize players not living up to their potential, get insider information and engage in all things red, white and blue. But in reality, the website was close to the team. It had to be in order to maintain access to the players, coaches and management.

Similar organizations exist in the world of Canadian international affairs. The most important are discussed below:

Canadian Institute for International Peace and Security

In 1984 the federal government passed "An Act to Establish the Canadian Institute for International Peace and Security." Under the legislation CIIPS was obliged to carry out research proposed by the "designated" minister.[2]

Associated with peace researchers, CIIPS was run by former External Affairs and military officials. Its first chair was William

Barton who worked at External Affairs for three decades, including a stint as Canadian ambassador to the UN.[3] The organization's founding director was Brigadier-General George Gray Bell, who spent three decades in the military, and its initial executive director was Geoffrey Pearson, son of Lester Pearson.[4] A former ambassador to the Soviet Union and Mongolia, Geoffrey Pearson wrote, "I have been identified with the government most of my life."[5]

CIIPS published a magazine, background papers and organized media roundtables. It also published books and the executive director prepared an annual summary and critique of Canadian foreign policy. Additionally, CIIPS produced fact sheets and teachers handbooks for a high school audience.[6]

Between 1985 and 1992 CIIPS doled out 618 research grants worth $5.5 million to NGOs and individuals.[7] They also funded and organized a number of conferences.

While the institute generally reflected the liberal end of the dominant foreign policy discussion, CIIPS coordinator of research Mark Heller supported Canadian participation in the first Gulf War.[8] The organization also aligned itself with Canadian policy in other ways. Geoffrey Pearson described the motivation for organizing a conference on Canada–Caribbean relations: "I thought that Canada ought to pay more attention to the ... British Caribbean countries, where we had traditional interests and potentially important influence."[9] But Canada's "traditional interests" in the British Caribbean have often been characterized as "imperialistic". Canadian banks and insurance companies have dominated the English Caribbean's financial sector for more than a century and prominent Canadians repeatedly sought to annex these territories.

In 1992 Brian Mulroney's government disbanded CIIPS. While some suggested the decision was a response to policy prescriptions the government didn't like, Ottawa claimed its decision was strictly financial. The government's official explanation gives a good sense of how they viewed the institute. "It will cost the government $2.5 million less annually, because instead of having the Canadian Institute for International Peace and Security, we will have officials within the Department of External Affairs doing the same job."[10]

International Development Research Centre

In 1970 Parliament passed the International Development Research Centre Act. The Crown Corporation was mandated "to initiate, encourage, support and conduct research into the problems of the developing regions of the world and into the means for applying and adapting scientific, technical, and other knowledge to the economic and social advancement of those regions."[11]

Before establishing the IDRC Canadian officials canvassed leaders of the World Bank, International Monetary Fund, USAID, Brookings Institution, as well as the Carnegie, Ford and Rockefeller foundations.[12] The Ottawa-based organization's initial president was David Hopper, a Ford Foundation official, and former Prime Minister Lester Pearson was the first chair of its board.[13] Since its founding, the federal government has appointed the majority of its board and has been the source of most of the organization's $300 million budget.[14] IDRC reports to Parliament through the foreign minister.[15]

IDRC funds development journalism prizes and international development studies programs at universities (see chapter 4).[16] More significantly, it publishes studies, reports, articles and books. Looking through hundreds of titles listed on its website, none appeared critical of Canadian foreign policy. In a chapter critical of so-called "democracy promotion" during the war in Afghanistan, Anthony Fenton and John Elmer write: "Closely involved in the creation of the R2P [responsibility to protect] doctrine, the IDRC, since 9/11, has deepened its focus on democracy promotion. A Crown corporation, the IDRC functions as an arm's length foreign policy tool of the Canadian state. With the coming to power of the

Harper Conservatives, the IDRC added a commitment to 'a whole new field of endeavour: helping to rebuild democratic institutions in Afghanistan'. ... IDRC has also played an important legitimacy — and consensus building role for the Afghanistan war domestically."[17]

In the early 1990s IDRC explicitly aligned itself with Canadian objectives in the Middle East. Alongside CIDA, it financed the Expert and Advisory Services Fund, which was established to support Canada's role in an international "peace process" weighted in favour of Israeli expansionism.[18]

While many tout its independence in directing international research funding, IDRC acceded to the Harper Conservative's effort to defund organizations supporting the Palestinian cause. In 2010 IDRC abruptly terminated two grants worth $800,000 to MADA al-Carmel, the Haifa based Arab Center for Applied Social Research.[19] A long-standing partner of IDRC, MADA's contract was cancelled after extremist pro-Israel group NGO Monitor raised the matter.

North-South Institute

The North-South Institute was established in 1976. The first Canadian policy research organization dedicated to "international development", NSI's motto was "Research For a Fairer World".

NSI was largely set up by CIDA. In 1975 CIDA officials brought together a number of academics as well as individuals from the Privy Council and the government's Parliamentary Centre for Foreign Affairs and Foreign Trade.[20] The meeting called for the development of an institution similar to the US Overseas Development Council or UK Overseas Development Institute.[21]

Set up seven years earlier, the Overseas Development Council received half of its budget from the Rockefeller and Ford foundations and most of the rest from US companies with significant operations in the Global South.[22] Established in 1960, the UK's Overseas Development Institute performed consultancy work for the government's Department for International Development and was funded by the Ford Foundation.[23]

NSI received its initial funding from CIDA, International Development Research Centre and Donner Canadian Foundation.[24] NSI's founding executive director was Bernard Wood, deputy director of the Parliamentary Centre for Foreign Affairs and Foreign Trade and former Department of Industry, Trade and Commerce official.[25] (The Parliamentary Centre for Foreign Affairs and Foreign Trade was the brainchild of a long-time member of the Canadian foreign service and was funded by the government.[26]) During more than a decade as head of NSI, Wood was a special advisor to Canadian delegations to the UN General Assembly and personal representative of the prime minister to Commonwealth bodies.[27]

In a semi-official history of CIDA, NSI research fellow David R. Morrison points out that NSI was set up largely to deal with "criticism" of an expanding aid agency, which was "undermining public support for international development."[28] CIDA's aim in establishing NSI was to spur research in support of "aid" and, by extension, an interventionist foreign policy in the US-dominated post-World War II international order.

The broad rationale for extending foreign aid was laid out at a 1968 seminar for the newly established Canadian International Development Agency. This day-long event was devoted to discussing a paper titled "Canada's Purpose in Extending Foreign Assistance" written by University of Toronto Professor Steven Triantis. Foreign aid, Triantis argued, "may be used to induce the underdeveloped countries to accept the international status quo or change it in our favour."[29] Aid provided an opportunity "to lead them to rational political and economic developments and a better understanding of our interests and problems of mutual concern." Triantis discussed the appeal of a "'Sunday School mentality' which 'appears' noble and unselfish and can serve in pushing into the background other motives ... [that] might be difficult to discuss publicly."[30] A 1969 CIDA background paper, expanding on Triantis' views, summarized the rationale for Canadian aid: "To establish within recipient countries those political attitudes or commitments, military alliances or military bases that would assist Canada or Canada's western allies to maintain a reasonably stable and secure international political system. Through this objective, Canada's aid programs would serve not only to help increase Canada's influence within the developing world, but also within the western alliance."[31]

Canadian aid was driven by economic interests as well. With most aid "tied" to the purchase of Canadian products and services, the aid program was an outlet for surplus commodities and contracts for Canadian exporters. The government may call it foreign aid, but a central aim of CIDA was to help Canadian companies expand abroad.

NSI conducted the first significant review of CIDA's international programs in 1980. Morrison writes, "the Institute signed an agreement with CIDA for access to documentation on condition that final drafts would be submitted to a liaison committee that 'would read and if necessary provide a formal written response to the drafts.'"[32]

At the same time as it reviewed CIDA's programs, NSI publicly criticized cuts to the aid agency's budget. Their criticism provides a window into the institute's political outlook. A 1989 NSI-Canadian Council for International Cooperation statement denounced aid cuts "when many Third World countries were struggling to cope with crippling debts and sharply reduced living standards, and were taking steps to introduce painful reforms on the understanding that rich countries like Canada would support their initiatives with increased financial resources."[33] "Painful reforms" was a reference to structural adjustment policies the World Bank and International Monetary Fund imposed with devastating impacts on countries' health and education sectors. Rather than criticize Canadian (including CIDA's) support for structural adjustment programs, NSI effectively called for more "aid" to soften their impacts ("adjustment with a human face", was the term used by some).

I scanned the description of 134 NSI reports in Concordia University's collection and read a dozen of them. My conclusion is that NSI represented the liberal, "developmentalist" wing of the dominant foreign policy discussion. Rarely did the institute investigate the structural forces driving Canadian policy or express moral outrage at decisions taken.

NSI's investigations generally reflected the focus of the sitting government. The institute promoted the Liberal government sponsored Responsibility to Protect (R2P) doctrine, which asserts that where gross human rights abuses occur it is the duty of the international community to intervene, over and above considerations of state sovereignty. In the midst of the government's mid-2000s push to have the UN adopt R2P, NSI published at least two reports on the subject and held a roundtable titled "Delivering on the Responsibility to Protect in Africa".[34]

On paper this Canadian-promoted doctrine is a good idea, unless one considers national borders, usually created through colonial violence, sacrosanct. But who decides when gross human rights abuses are occurring? Was the US responsible for gross human rights abuses in Iraq? Even though credible reports found that the 2003 US invasion and subsequent occupation led to hundreds of thousands of Iraqi deaths, leading R2P proponents never called on the international community to intervene in Washington. Rather than a tool to improve international human rights standards, R2P was used by the powerful against the weak. In the early 2000s Liberal government officials cited R2P to oust Haiti's elected government, which led to thousands of deaths.[35] Many commentators/ex-politicians also invoked R2P to justify NATO's 2011 bombing of Libya.[36] During that war Canadian-commanded NATO fighter jets dropped thousands of bombs in a bid to secure regime change in the oil-rich nation.[37]

In a bid to maintain its funding from a government hostile to any mention of a "fairer world", NSI took up the Stephen Harper government's extractivist cause in Africa. In 2013 the institute hosted a conference on African natural resource management opened by Conservative Party MP and chair of the House of Commons' Foreign Affairs and International Development Committee, Dean Allison. The event was sponsored by mining companies Teck and Kinross, as well as the Department of Foreign Affairs, Trade and Development and Export Development Corporation.[38] In an article titled "Popularizing new neo-colonial governance processes for African minerals? An analysis of Canada's North-South Institute's 'Governing Natural Resources for Africa's Development' conference" Paula Butler and Evans Rubara write: "Notably absent from the conference were well-known academics with long experience and expertise on African mining, and representatives of leading civil society organizations such as Third World Network-Africa, Mining Watch Canada, etc. Moreover, there was no formal representation from any communities in African countries where Canadian mining or exploration is occurring. In fact, only 18 of the 187 attendees at the conference were from African countries."[39]

The Canadian and Tanzanian academics further explain: "Significantly, there was a deafening silence throughout the conference with regard to South Africa's mining regime (with its Mining Charter, 'Black Economic Empowerment' quotas, veto powers of communities vis-à-vis new mine developments, etc.) in comparison with Tanzania, which was touted throughout the conference as the darling of Western advisors on African mining policy. (No mention of course of the aggressive role played by Canadian mining companies, Canadian lawyers and Canadian diplomats to establish the pro-foreign-investor content of Tanzanian mining codes since the mid-1990s.) There were no critical voices from African governments. Panellists seemed to have been very carefully selected to reinforce the emerging dominant policy prescriptions for African mining."[40]

Throughout its existence NSI depended on CIDA for most of its core funding. Even after the Harper Conservatives began to cut government support, NSI still received more than half its budget from Canadian aid.[41] The rest largely came from mining companies, other G7 governments and US foundations such as the Bill and Melinda Gates Foundation.[42] A 2002 NSI paper titled "Aboriginal Peoples and Mining in Canada: Consultation, Participation and Prospects for Change" said it "was supported through contributions from Syncrude Canada, Rio Algom (now BHP Billiton) and Falconbridge to The North-South Institute's Corporate Social Responsibility Program."[43]

NSI shut down in 2014 after the Harper government refused to renew any of its funding. In response, the organization marshalled powerful allies to its cause. In a *Globe and Mail* opinion piece titled "North-South Institute: We've lost a Canadian asset" former Prime Ministers Paul Martin and Joe Clark, as well as former NDP leader Ed Broadbent, criticized the government's move. All had been members of the NSI board.

Rights and Democracy

Created by an act of Parliament in 1989, the International Centre for Human Rights and Democratic Development, also known as Rights and Democracy (R&D) was the Canadian government's "arms-length" human rights organization. R&D was funded almost entirely by the federal government.

The Montréal-based organization was partly modeled after the US National Endowment for Democracy, which performed work the CIA had previously done covertly. Allen Weinstein, who helped establish the National Endowment for Democracy and became its first president, told the *Washington Post* in 1991: "A lot of what we do today was done covertly 25 years ago by the CIA."[44]

I was first introduced to R&D after returning from a December 2004 trip to meet victims of the coup in Haiti. Members of Montréal's Haitian's community picketed an R&D press conference given by Danielle Magloire, a member of the "Council of the Wise" that appointed Gérard Latortue as interim prime minister after the elected government was overthrown. A blatant violation of Haiti's constitution, the US, France and Canada created the "Council of the Wise" after the coup. In mid-July 2005 Magloire issued a statement on behalf of the seven-member council saying that any media that gives voice to "bandits" (code for Aristide supporters) should be shut down. She also asserted that Aristide's Lavalas party should be banned from upcoming elections.[45] Magloire, who headed up an R&D initiative in Haiti, was brought to Montréal to provide a "progressive", "feminist", justification for the coup.

At the urging of the federal government R&D joined the campaign to destabilize Haiti's elected government. Six months before the coup, R&D released a report that described Haiti's pro-coup Group of 184 as "grassroots" and a "promising civil society movement."[46] The truth was that the Group of 184 was spawned and funded by the International Republican Institute (funded by the US government) and headed by Haiti's leading sweatshop owner, Andy Apaid. Apaid had been active in right-wing Haitian politics for many years and, like former Group of 184 spokesperson Charles Henry Baker, Apaid was white.

In an extreme case of siding with Ottawa, R&D smeared a study released in the *Lancet* medical journal detailing widespread human rights violations in the 22 months after Aristide's ouster. After the report received front-page coverage in the *Montréal Gazette* and *National Post*, with quotes from Haiti Action Montréal adding political context, R&D worked strenuously to discredit a study that estimated 8,000 were killed and 35,000 raped in Port au Prince. (While the *Lancet* numbers were high, investigations by the Institute for Justice and Democracy in Haiti, University of Miami, Harvard University, National Lawyers Guild etc. all documented significant persecution of Aristide sympathizers after the coup.) The organization sent emails to various journalists in which they claimed a co-author of the *Lancet* report was biased. Additionally, Nicholas Galetti, in charge of R&D's Haiti file, was quoted in the *Globe and Mail* claiming the peer-reviewed study was "based on flawed methodology."[47] (After an investigation the prestigious health journal later reaffirmed the study.)

Haiti wasn't the only country in which R&D aligned itself with Ottawa. The group defended the war in Afghanistan. Echoing the official description of the Canadian mission, R&D "urged the Security Council to increase the peacekeeping forces to at least 30,000 and to deploy peace troops throughout the country with instructions to disarm warring factions." In 2002 R&D's Women's Rights Fund for Afghanistan opened an office in Kabul with $500,000 from CIDA. Vancouver researcher Harsha Walia explained the one-sided nature of the Women's Rights Fund: "A 'non-partisan' Afghanistan backgrounder on the website of the Fund highlights only the historic abuse of women by the Taliban and characterizes the current period as one of 'ongoing conflict' without any mention of foreign forces in the country."[48]

The federal government gave R&D more than $5 million for its Afghan work.[49] Some of this was channelled to other groups, such as Canadian Women for Women in Afghanistan, which used feminism to justify imperialism. In a January 2009 *Ottawa Citizen* commentary headlined "The cultural relativists can't excuse evil" Lauryn Oates, president of Canadian Women for Women in Afghanistan, argued against those opposing Canada's mission in Afghanistan.[50] An earlier piece by Oates in the *Globe and Mail* was headlined, "Don't share a table with the Taliban."[51]

Established and funded almost entirely by the federal government, R&D took its cues from Ottawa. But, Stephen Harper's government demanded total obedience and in 2013 they shut down R&D.

Canada's International Communications apparatus, media aid and NGOs

At the end of World War II Canada was the world's second biggest creditor nation and had one of the biggest armies. Since that time Ottawa has been well positioned to disseminate Canada's views to the world. Through Radio Canada International, Canadian studies programs, cultural initiatives and diplomatic infrastructure Ottawa has promoted its worldview.

Since 1945 the CBC International Service (now Radio Canada International) has beamed radio abroad. Its programming has reflected "Canadian foreign policy commitments and interests."[52] Initially focused on Eastern Bloc countries, the International Service was part of "the psychological war against communism", according to external minister Lester Pearson.[53] But, the "Voice of Canada" also produced programs for Latin American, African and Caribbean countries.

The CBC International Service ran a program titled the "Canadian Viewpoint on International Events" and responded to criticism of Canada's international policies.[54] Describing the International Service to a Standing Committee on External Affairs, its head Jean Désy said, "if there is an attack directed against Canada at some international gathering, we will avail ourselves the opportunity to correct the accusations made against us."[55]

External Affairs had close ties to CBC International Service.[56] Early on the department was given a copy of the scripts used by commentators and its funding came directly from External Affairs into the 1990s.[57]

A Propaganda System

In 1952 Jean Désy was appointed director of the service even though the External Affairs official didn't have any broadcasting experience.[58] According to one account, Desy "ruthlessly 'purged' the service of all suspicion of leftist bias."[59]

The renamed Radio Canada International (RCI) has always consulted with Foreign Affairs to determine broadcast languages.[60] To fill a mid-1990s budget hole, RCI received $6 million from Foreign Affairs, $6 million from Canadian Heritage and $4 million from CIDA and DND combined.[61] Down from its high point, between 2000 and 2012 Ottawa spent about $12 million annually on RCI.[62]

Alongside RCI, External Affairs began funding Canadian studies programs in 1975.[63] Six years later the International Council for Canadian Studies was established with federal government funds.[64] Ottawa provides about $5 million annually to international universities to study Canada.[65] Relations with foreign academics are managed by diplomats in the field.[66] Canadian diplomats also oversee international cultural programs. Foreign Affairs spends about $5 million annually on its Arts and Cultural Industries Promotion Program.[67]

Diplomats make the case for Canada more directly. In 2007 Foreign Affairs had 10,000 personnel at headquarters and over 270 embassies, high commissions, consular offices and trade offices, promoting this country's international positions.[68] In *Branding Canada* Evan, Potter writes, "ambassadors spend large portions of their working days giving speeches to local business audiences, universities, and service clubs, in support of strategic communication objectives. There are also other information programs, such as sponsoring and hosting seminars ... as well as publishing mission newsletters and managing the mission website. In addition, all G8 foreign ministries have some form of foreign visitors program, which they use to invite targeted foreign opinion leaders."[69]

In 2009 there were 21 full-time public affairs positions at the Canadian Embassy in Washington.[70] (This doesn't include the ambassador's public affairs work or that of the military personnel.) A government summary notes, "Public Affairs produces highly-focused and targeted information and advocacy materials and also purchases sophisticated data that is used by the Embassy in Washington and by Canada's Consulates General to support Canada's U.S.-wide advocacy efforts. Public Affairs uses the full range of new media tools (including, for example, websites, Facebook and Twitter) in order to connect with targeted audiences."[71]

As early as 1879 the High Commission in London advertised Canada in Britain. It distributed pamphlets and posters and had the only reference library of a colony in the English capital.[72] Canadian officials organized tours of Canada for British journalists and arranged for the Ministry of the Interior to send articles to the British press. At the turn of the 19th century a Canadian official in Cardiff, William L. Griffith, wrote for newspapers and magazines such as the *Western Mail* and *Young Wales*.[73]

Canada's extensive diplomatic apparatus, as well as funding for Canadian studies, cultural programs and RCI, shape Canadians' attitudes towards their country's place in the world. The generally pro-Canada information they produce flows back into this country through travelers, immigrants, academics, media etc.

Alongside the government's international communications apparatus, the Canadian aid agency has doled out tens of millions of dollars on other media initiatives. CIDA funded a slew of journalist fellowships that generated aid-related stories and linked journalists to Canadian officials. The aid agency supported a Canadian Newspaper Association fellowship to send journalists to Ecuador, Aga Khan Foundation Canada/Canadian Association of Journalists Fellowships for International Development Reporting, Canadian Association of Journalists/Jack Webster Foundation Fellowship, University of Ottawa Bill McWhinney Memorial Scholarship for International Development Journalism and a Langara college

A Propaganda System

Journalism Development Scholarship.[74] It also offered eight $6,000 fellowships annually for members of the Fédération professionnelle des journalistes du Québec, notes CIDA, "to report to the Canadian public on the realities lived in developing countries benefiting from Canadian public aid."[75] To promote a Canadian documentary on international development, CIDA sponsored the Deborah Fletcher Award of Excellence in Filmmaking in international development. The selected filmmaker received $10,000 to produce a new documentary.[76]

Between 2005 and 2008 CIDA spent at least $47.5 million on the "promotion of development awareness."[77] According to a 2013 *J-Source* investigation titled "Some journalists and news organizations took government funding to produce work: is that a problem?", more than $3.5 million went to articles, photos, film and radio reports about CIDA projects.[78] Much of the government-funded reporting appeared in major media outlets. But, a CIDA spokesperson told *J-Source*, the aid agency "didn't pay directly for journalists' salaries" and only "supported media activities that had as goal the promotion of development awareness with the Canadian public."[79] One journalist, Kim Brunhuber, received $13,000 to produce "six television news pieces that highlight the contribution of Canadians to several unique development projects" to be shown on CTV outlets.[80] While failing to say whether Brunhuber's work appeared on the station, CTV spokesperson Rene Dupuis said another documentary it aired "clearly credited that the program had been produced with the support of the Government of Canada through CIDA."[81]

During the war in Afghanistan CIDA operated a number of media projects. A number of CIDA-backed NGOs sent journalists to Afghanistan and the aid agency had a contract with Montréal's *Le Devoir* to "[remind] readers of the central role that Afghanistan plays in CIDA's international assistance program."[82]

In another highly politicized context, CIDA put up $2 million for a "Media and Democratic Development in Haiti" project overseen by Montréal-based Réseau Liberté and Alternatives.[83] As part of the mid-2000s project, Réseau Liberté (RL) supported media outlets that were part of L'Association Nationale des Médias Haïtiens (ANMH), which officially joined the Group of 184 that campaigned to oust elected President Jean-Bertrand Aristide.

RL sent Canadian (mostly Québec) journalists to "train" their Haitian counterparts for a month. In an article titled "Embedding CBC Reporters in Haiti's Elitist Media" Richard Sanders writes: "If RL's Canadian journalists did not already harbour anti-Aristide sentiments before their intensive 'coaching' experiences, they would certainly risk absorbing such political predilections after being submerged in the propaganda campaigns of Haiti's elite media. ... RL journalists would likely return home from Haiti armed with newly implanted political biases that could then be spread liberally among their colleagues in the media and hence to the broader Canadian public."[84]

A number of leading Québec reporters interned with ANMH media outlets. Assistant program director for Radio Canada news, Guy Filion was one of them. Even though ANMH outlets barred Haiti's elected president from its airwaves in the lead-up to the coup, Filion described those who "formed the ANMH" as "pro- Haitian and they are pro neutral journalistic people ... as much as it can be said in this country."[85] Filion also praised the media's coverage of the 2006 election in which Haiti's most popular political party, Aristide's Lavalas, was excluded.[86] In a coded reference to Aristide supporters, Filion noted, "even thugs from [large slum neighbourhood] Cité Soleil were giving interviews on television!"[87]

RL also worked closely with "virulently anti-Aristide reporter" Nancy Roc who commented regularly on Québec media.[88] Living between Montréal and Port-au-Prince, she hosted a program produced by RL and Télé Québec and coordinated a major teleconferencing project whose partners included RL.[89] (When I challenged panellists at an August 2005 Alternatives conference titled "Haiti: A democracy to construct" for failing to mention the coup or bloodshed, Roc called me a "Chimères", a purported pro-Aristide thug.)

A smaller part of CIDA's "Media and Democratic development in Haiti" project went to Alternatives. The Montréal-based NGO created a "Media in Haiti" website and paid for online Haitian media outlet AlterPresse, which aggressively opposed Lavalas. During the 2007 Québec Social Forum AlterPresse editor Rene Colbert told me there was no coup in 2004 since Aristide was never elected (not even the George W. Bush administration made this claim).

Ignorant of their government funding and position on Haiti at the time, I submitted an article to *Journal d'Alternatives* about visiting prominent political prisoner Annette "So Ann" Auguste and a young journalist whose aunt was killed by police searching for him after the coup (he worked at a children's radio station set up by Lavalas). The article was accepted and translated, but never published in the CIDA-funded monthly inserted in *Le Devoir*. Presumably, somebody who better understood Canada's role in Haiti, and the likely reaction of *Journal d'Alternatives*' government benefactors, spiked it.

What the supposedly left-wing Alternatives published about Haiti was shocking. In June 2005 the individual in charge of its Haiti portfolio wrote an article that demonized the residents of impoverished neighbourhoods targeted for repression by the installed government. In particular, François L'Écuyer denounced community activists Samba Boukman and Ronald St. Jean, who I'd met, as "notorious criminals."[90] This was exceedingly dangerous in an environment where the victims of police operations were routinely labeled "bandits" and "criminals" after they were killed.

Seven months earlier L'Ecuyer published a front-page article headlined "The Militarization of Peace in Haiti", claiming "Chimères, gangs loyal to and armed by President Aristide," launched "Operation

Baghdad" to destabilize the country.[91] Echoing the propaganda disseminated by the George W. Bush administration, it claimed the exiled president was profiting politically from violence.

Although Alternatives printed numerous articles about Haiti during this period, their reporting omitted any mention of political prisoners, violent repression of Lavalas activists, or basic facts about the coup.

Independent or not?

Non-Governmental Organizations are sometimes considered critics of Canadian foreign policy. But NGOs are not well placed to challenge Ottawa.

Reliance on government aid and charitable status hampers their political independence. So does the back and forth between individuals working for CIDA and NGOs. It's hard to criticize former or future colleagues and if a position with the aid agency is a possibility it is professionally dangerous to publicly challenge Canadian foreign policy.

On top of failing to join the struggle, government-funded NGOs often undermine critical political forces. Government funds empower state sanctioned NGOs to maintain organizational structures and to offer internships/jobs to internationalist minded individuals willing to focus on charity work abroad rather than challenging Canada's contribution to global impoverishment.

During a spring 2016 Québec Solidaire "citizens circle" I caught a firsthand glimpse of this subtle dynamic at play. Part of a process of formulating the left provincial party's international positions, the two other speakers invited to lead the discussion were from Oxfam Québec and AQOCI, Québec's NGO umbrella organization. While the Québec Solidaire discussion paper referred to "imperialism" and the need for an independent Québec to withdraw from NATO, the two NGO speakers focused on increasing federal government aid, setting up a Québec aid organization and the "do more" NGO mantra. Canadian state and corporate policies contributing to global impoverishment were all but ignored.

Not particularly active on the subject, the organizers of the "citizens circle" reached out to organizations they were familiar with (I was added on by a friend concerned with the political direction of the discussion). With most of its $30 million budget coming from Global Affairs Canada and other government sources, Oxfam Québec has chapters at CEGEPS (colleges) and universities across the province.[92] Government funds allow Oxfam to maintain its institutional structure, which draws internationalist minded youth into their orbit. While it opens many young peoples' eyes to global inequity, Oxfam Québec simultaneously takes up political space that would often be filled by those more critical of Canadian foreign policy.

While its funding crowds out oppositional forces indirectly, sometimes CIDA directly co-opts NGOs. After leaving her position as head of CIDA in Afghanistan, Nipa Banerjee explained that Canadian aid was used to gain NGO support for the war there. "Our government thinks they are getting public support and [NGO support] for their mission if they fund NGO programs," she told the *Globe and Mail*.[93]

In 2007 CIDA gave Peace Build $575,000, which was on top of money from Foreign Affairs and the government-run International Development Research Centre.[94] Largely focused on Afghanistan, Peace Build was a newly created network of NGOs viewed as a moderate counterweight to the more activist-oriented (and financially independent) Canadian Peace Alliance, which opposed Canada's occupation of Afghanistan.[95] Peace Build founder Peggy Mason was a former Canadian diplomat.[96]

Two decades earlier CIDA encouraged the creation of a new NGO to undercut criticism of Canadian complicity with apartheid

South Africa. In a history of the aid agency Cranford Pratt explains, "CIDA secured creation of the South African Education Trust Fund because it did not think the strong NGOs already active vis-à-vis South Africa sufficiently sensitive to Canadian foreign policy concerns."[97]

At the same time as it pushed to undercut South African focused NGOs, CIDA sought to set up an alternative development education organization. While Futures Secretariat ultimately failed to take off, the Canadian Council for International Cooperation and other NGOs saw it as "an effort to undercut their own 'dev ed' [development education] work," which was critical of Canadian policy.[98]

Aid officials have also slashed funding to organizations that criticize Canadian foreign policy. In the late 1970s SUCO, CUSO's French language equivalent began to critique Canadian corporate ties with apartheid South Africa, Israel's treatment of Palestinians and other politically sensitive subjects. CIDA responded to the political turn by pushing institutional reforms and eventually chopped all financial support to the group in 1984. SUCO's annual budget dropped from $6 million to $400,000 and staff levels fell from 45 employees to 4, leading to the collapse of the organization.[99]

CIDA delivered another blow to NGOs critical of Canadian foreign policy when it cut funding for the Development Education Animateur Program (DEAP). Dating to the early 1970s, DEAP's development education centres featured a wide array of hard-to-find educational material about development and the Third World. As CIDA conceived it, development education would educate the public about the social and economic problems faced by the Third World while simultaneously explaining how Canadian aid helped overcome these problems. To CIDA's chagrin, development education departments at CUSO, the Canadian Council for International Cooperation and other NGOs became a source of sustained criticism of Canada's conduct on the world stage. As a result, CIDA worked to undermine the program by placing detailed controls on what NGO development education centres could do with their funds. In *CUSO and Liberation Movements in Southern Africa,* Christopher Neal writes, "CIDA specified, for example, that CUSO could not use CIDA funds to criticize Canadian foreign policy or to draw parallels between struggles against oppression in developing countries and struggles by powerless groups in Canada."[100] With these moves failing to stop criticism from development education centres, CIDA pulled the plug on the entire Development Education Animateur Program in 1995.[101]

During Stephen Harper's reign the government severed aid to a number of NGOs that refused to toe its line on Palestine and (to a lesser extent) international mining. In 2009 CIDA chopped $7 million from Kairos, a Christian aid organization that had received government money for 35 years.[102] During a December 2009 visit to Israel immigration minister Jason Kenney said Canada "defunded organizations, most recently like Kairos, who are taking a leadership role" in campaigns to boycott Israel (while sympathetic to Palestinians Kairos Canada, unlike the unaffiliated Kairos Palestine, did not endorse the boycott, divestment and sanctions campaign).[103] Palestinian advocacy was also the reason Ottawa failed to renew its funding to Montréal-based Alternatives, which received most of its budget from the federal government. Shortly after the Canadian Council for International Cooperation publicly complained that the government had created a "chill" in the NGO community by adopting "the politics of punishment ... towards those whose public views run at cross purposes to the government," its $1.7 million CIDA grant was cut, which forced it to lay off two thirds of its staff.[104]

He who pays the piper, calls the tune.

A Propaganda System

6. Owning the Media

In professional hockey, the dominant media are willing participants and at times prime drivers of the propaganda bus that visits every neighbourhood to make sure we support our team in its noble quest for Lord Stanley's Cup.

The relationship between sports departments at newspapers or TV stations and team PR departments is usually close. Reporters rely on the team for access to players and coaches. Reporters often fly on team-chartered flights. Trying to be too independent or overly critical of the team will generally result in problems for a reporter.

Once again there are parallels in the world of international affairs.

Less than the full picture

The corporate media (and CBC) permit only a narrow spectrum of opinion regarding Canadian foreign policy. The dominant media's refusal to report critical information about this country's foreign policy can be startling.

On January 31, 2003, Prime Minister Jean Chrétien's Liberal government organized the "Ottawa Initiative on Haiti" to discuss that country's future. No Haitian officials were invited to this two-day assembly where high-level US, Canadian and French officials discussed removing Haiti's elected president, re-creating the dreaded army and putting the country under a Kosovo-like UN trusteeship.[1] Thirteen months after the Ottawa Initiative on Haiti meeting, President Jean-Bertrand Aristide and most other elected officials were pushed out and a quasi UN trusteeship had begun. Since that time the Haitian National Police has been heavily militarized and steps have been taken towards recreating the military.

A Propaganda System

Prominent journalist Michel Vastel brought the gathering to public attention in the March 15, 2003, issue of *l'Actualité*, Québec's equivalent to *Maclean's* magazine, in an article titled "Haiti put under U.N. Tutelage?"[2] Yet, since the coup the dominant Canadian media has refused to investigate the Ottawa Initiative or even mention the meeting. A mid-2016 Canadian Newsstand search of major daily papers found not one single English language report about the meeting (except for mentions by myself and two other Haiti solidarity activists in opinion pieces). The dominant Canadian media has ignored the Ottawa Initiative even though information about the meeting is easily accessible online and solidarity activists across the country referenced it repeatedly.

The refusal to investigate the Ottawa Initiative on Haiti represents an extreme example of media bias, but it's far from the only one. Since 2008 Canada has concluded and/or signed more than a dozen Foreign Investment Promotion and Protection Agreements (FIPAs) with African countries. FIPA treaties include an Investor State Dispute Settlement mechanism that gives corporations the right to sue governments — in private, investor-friendly tribunals — for pursuing policies that interfere with their profit making. As such, they undermine Africans' ability to democratically determine economic policy. (Since few African companies invest in Canada it's unlikely Ottawa will be sued or pressured to modify policy because of a FIPA.)

FIPAs are primarily about protecting Canadian mining firms from popular discontent. After two decades of privatization and loosened restrictions on foreign investment, mining companies operating in Africa fear a reversal of these policies. The ability to sue a government in an international tribunal for lost profits partially alleviates those fears.

In another sign of how they undercut democracy, FIPAs are generally locked in for 16 years. So an African government that signs an investment accord with Ottawa constrains future governments' ability to shift direction.

In the most egregious example of a FIPA undermining electoral democracy, Ottawa signed a FIPA with the transition administration that took over after President Blaise Compaoré's 27-year reign was ended. Burkina Faso was represented at the April 2015 FIPA signing ceremony in Ottawa by Prime Minister Yacouba Isaac Zida, who was deputy commander of the presidential guard when Compaoré was ousted by popular protest six months earlier. While the West African nation's caretaker government was supposed to move aside after an election planned for later that year, the FIPA cannot be fully repealed for 16 years.

I was unable to find a single criticism of an African FIPA in a major Canadian news outlet. Even when Ottawa signed the long-lasting FIPA with the interim, military-dominated regime in Burkina Faso, the media ignored it. Four major dailies refused to publish a tame opinion piece I submitted about this flagrant disregard for electoral democracy.

In another startling example of media bias in favour of "righteous Canada", criticism of Senator Romeo Dallaire's actions in Rwanda have been almost entirely ignored by the Canadian media even though his commander published a book criticizing the Canadian general's bias in favour of the Rwandan Patriotic Front (RPF). In his 2005 book *Le Patron de Dallaire Parle* (The Boss of Dallaire Speaks), Jacques-Roger Booh Booh, a former Cameroon foreign minister and overall head of the United Nations mission in Rwanda, claims Dallaire had little interest in the violence unleashed by the RPF despite reports of summary executions in areas controlled by them. A Ugandan-spawned force, RPF soldiers were regularly seen in Dallaire's office, with the Canadian commander describing the Rwandan army's position in Kigali. This prompted Booh Booh to wonder if Dallaire "also shared UNAMIR [UN mission in

Rwanda] military secrets with the RPF when he invited them to work in his offices."[3] Finally, Booh Booh says Dallaire turned a blind eye to RPF weapons coming across the border from Uganda and he believes the UN forces may have even transported weapons directly to the RPF.[4] Dallaire, Booh Booh concludes, "abandoned his role as head of the military to play a political role. He violated the neutrality principle of UNAMIR by becoming an objective ally of one of the parties in the conflict."[5]

A Canadian Newsstand search found only three mentions of *Le Patron de Dallaire Parle*. (A *National Post* review headlined "Allegations called 'ridiculous': UN boss attacks general," an *Ottawa Citizen* piece headlined "There are many sides to the Rwanda saga" and a letter by an associate of Dallaire). Other critical assessments of Dallaire's actions in Rwanda have fared no better, including *Rwanda and the New Scramble for Africa* and *Enduring Lies: The Rwandan Genocide in the Propaganda System, 20 Years Later* in which Edward Herman and David Peterson "suggest that Dallaire should be regarded as a war criminal for positively facilitating the actual mass killings of April-July [1994], rather than taken as a hero for giving allegedly disregarded warnings that might have stopped them."[6] On the other hand, a Canadian Newsstand search of "Romeo Dallaire Rwanda" elicited over 6,000 articles that generally provide a positive portrayal of Dallaire. Similarly, a search for mention of Dallaire's 2003 book *Shake Hands with the Devil* elicited 1,700 articles.

I submitted an expanded version of the above information as an article to *Maisonneuve* magazine. The editor responded, "it's fascinating subject matter. Daniel and I have a few follow-up questions. Mostly, we're curious about how you'd go about reporting the story. You mention Jacques-Roger Booh Booh's 2005 book, *Le Patron de Dallaire Parle*, but we'd like to know what other sources you have available. Are there primary sources that you've accessed or could access? Sources other than *Le Patron de Dallaire Parle*?"

I mentioned *Enduring Lies* and the *New Scramble for Africa* in my response, but they refused to publish the article and I've yet to see them take up the issue.

Even when dissidents' claims are proven by leading reporters through access to information requests, the result is often sent down the memory hole. Internal government documents unearthed by foreign policy journalist Lee Berthiaume about Canada's $300 million, five-year aid program to the Palestinians is a prime example. "There have been increasing references in the past months during high-level bilateral meetings with the Israelis about the importance and value they place on Canada's assistance to the Palestinian Authority, most notably in security/justice reform," read a November 2012 note signed by CIDA president Margaret Biggs.[7] "The Israelis have noted the importance of Canada's contribution to the relative stability achieved through extensive security co-operation between Israel and the Palestinian Authority."[8] The heavily censored note suggests the goal of Canadian "aid" was to protect a corrupt Mahmoud Abbas led Palestinian Authority, whose electoral mandate expired four years earlier, from popular backlash. Biggs explained that "the emergence of popular protests on the Palestinian street against the Palestinian Authority is worrying and the Israelis have been imploring the international donor community to continue to support the Palestinian Authority."[9]

Berthiaume effectively confirmed that Canadian aid money was used to train a Palestinian security force to serve as an arm of Israel's occupation. While Berthiaume's article was reported in a number of Postmedia papers, there was no commentary in a major paper or follow-up stories about Biggs' internal note or Operation PROTEUS, Canada's effort to build a Palestinian security force under the US military's direction (with the exception of stories in small town papers covering individual police or soldiers leaving for the mission).

A Propaganda System

Two years before Berthiaume's revelation I emailed *Globe and Mail* Middle East correspondent Patrick Martin about Canada's aid/military mission to support Israel's occupation of the West Bank. I wrote, "Hi Pat, not sure if you saw [Conservative Minister] Peter Kent's comment on Operation PROTEUS, Canada's military mission in the West Bank. In a recent interview with the Jerusalem Post Kent dubbed PROTEUS Canada's 'second largest deployment after Afghanistan' and said it receives 'most of the money' from a five-year $300 million Canadian aid program to the Palestinians. It's an issue that has barely been discussed and I thought it might interest you. Below is a piece I recently wrote partly on it." Martin responded, "it's a good idea", but at press time the *Globe* had yet to publish anything on Operation PROTEUS or Biggs' comment that Canadian aid to the Palestinian Authority was designed to suppress "popular protest" by a people suffering under a 50-year illegal occupation.

The dominant media also ignored a Canadian Press report that confirmed Haiti solidarity activists' claims about Ottawa's response to the 2010 earthquake that rocked Port-au-Prince. While most Canadians worried about uncovering those trapped, getting survivors water and connecting family members, officials in Ottawa were concerned about something else. According to internal documents examined by CP, Canadian decision-makers feared a post-earthquake power vacuum could lead to a "popular uprising". One briefing note marked "Secret" explained, "political fragility has increased the risks of a popular uprising, and has fed the rumour that ex-president Jean-Bertrand Aristide, currently in exile in South Africa, wants to organize a return to power."[10] The documents also explain the importance of strengthening the Haitian authorities ability "to contain the risks of a popular uprising."[11] To police Haiti's traumatized and suffering population 2,000 Canadian troops were deployed (alongside 10,000 US soldiers).[12] At the same time the half dozen Heavy Urban Search and Rescue Teams in cities across the country were readied but never deployed because, reported the *Toronto Sun*, foreign minister Lawrence Cannon "opted to send Canadian Armed Forces instead."[13]

The files uncovered by CP go to the heart (or lack thereof) of Canadian foreign policy decision-making. Almost always strategic thinking, not compassion, motivates policy. One is hard-pressed to find an instance where compassion was more warranted, and Heavy Urban Search and Rescue Teams more needed, than post-earthquake Haiti. Yet, an August 2016 Canadian Newsstand search found only the *Kamloops Daily News* ran CP's initial report in its paper and there was not a single mention of the internal document afterwards. Down the memory hole this explosive information went.

A stark contrast exists between how Canadian policy in Haiti was portrayed in the dominant media versus left media outlets. Dozens of articles, reports, theses, documentaries and books detailed Canada's violent, antidemocratic, policy in that country in the mid-2000s. But only tidbits of the story were reported in the corporate media. Left vs. corporate media coverage of the Canadian mining industry is also stark. Since the early 2000s progressive media outlets have published hundreds of articles detailing conflicts, ecological destruction and human rights violations at Canadian-owned mines around the world. Yet only a tiny proportion of these stories have found their way into major Canadian media outlets.

In a Masters thesis titled "Extracting an Ounce of Truth: Mainstream media coverage of Canadian mining neoliberalism" Sheena Cameron details the *Globe and Mail* and *Toronto Star*'s biased coverage of Bill C-300, which would have restricted public support for resource companies found responsible for significant human rights or environmental abuses abroad. According to Cameron, in the lead-up to the 2010 House of Commons vote, both papers "relied on official sources and did not provide background information about specific infractions from the mining companies to back up the

A Propaganda System

accusations from dissidents."[14] Cameron continues, "there were no articles, except in the alternative independent media, which admitted the flaws with Bill C-300 in its inability to place criminal sanctions on those in violation of the standards. Yet, most of the criticisms over the bill came from the mining industry and consistently purported that the bill would damage their competitive advantage, subject its members to unfair accusations and create legal vulnerability."[15]

With 1,300 projects across the globe, Canadian mining firms dominate resource extraction in many countries.[16] Pick almost any country in the global south — from Papua New Guinea to Ghana, Ecuador to the Philippines — and you will find a Canadian-run mine that has caused environmental devastation or been the scene of violent confrontations. But, the corporate media largely ignores this.

A common form of bias is for media outlets to focus on the misdeeds of enemies and ignore those of allies. Indonesian violence in East Timor provides a stark example. *In Complicity: Human Rights and Canadian Foreign Policy: The Case of East Timor*, Sharon Scharfe compares the *Globe and Mail*'s coverage of Cambodia and East Timor, which both saw similar levels of mass killings in the late 1970s.[17] She found that the Khmer Rouge's atrocities in Cambodia were widely reported while Indonesia's killings in East Timor were downplayed.[18] Between November 1, 1977, and August 31, 1993, the *Globe and Mail* published 12 times as many major articles on Cambodia as East Timor (751 to 63).[19] The coverage of Cambodia detailed widespread killings and sometimes even exaggerated the horror, while the stories about East Timor tended to present Jakarta's (generally false) version of events.

Wilfrid Laurier professor Jeffery Klaehn came to similar conclusions. Author of a 2005 article titled "Corporate Hegemony: a critical assessment of the Globe and Mail's news coverage of near genocide in occupied East Timor, 1975 – 1980" Klaehn writes: "Globe and Mail coverage reduced significantly after Indonesia invaded and dropped to almost nil as the atrocities reached their peak throughout 1978/79. The absolute low volume of news coverage effectively concealed (1) Indonesia's near genocidal aggression and (2) Canada's diplomatic and material contributions from public view."[20]

Prior to the December 7 Indonesian invasion, the *Globe* published 29 articles on East Timor in 1975.[21] The paper ran seven more articles that year after the invasion and "a one-paragraph article on January 5 and a two-paragraph piece on January 16 reporting on the invasion. This was the extent of its coverage of the invasion throughout the entire year of 1976. Four additional articles on East Timor were published during 1976, three of which reported on its annexation. It published one article on East Timor in 1977 — a single-paragraph article on March 1, which was headlined 'Australians Charge 100,000 Killings'. Throughout the next 16 months there was no additional coverage of East Timor published in the G&M. On 9 October 1978, the newspaper published an investigative piece by Mick Lowe, headlined '60,000 Have Died in Unseen War'. Throughout 1979, it published three small articles on East Timor. This was the extent of the G&M news coverage of the crucial invasion period."[22]

Other Canadian papers' coverage was even worse. In a search of the news database Klaehn didn't find anything in the *Calgary Herald*, *Montréal Gazette* or *Winnipeg Free Press* about East Timor between the Indonesian invasion and 1980.[23] The *Toronto Star* published a single article the day after the invasion, which gave prominence to the Indonesian foreign minister's claims.[24]

Who owns the news?

Various factors explain the media's biased international coverage. Most importantly, a small number of mega corporations own most of Canada's media. These firms are integrated with the leading internationally focused Canadian companies and depend on other large corporations for advertising revenue. Less dependent on advertising, CBC relies on government funds and has long been close to the foreign policy establishment.

Drawn into a symbiotic relationship with powerful sources of information, media firms rely on easily accessible international information, which is largely generated by GAC, DND and globally focused corporations. Further shaping coverage, international correspondents often take their cue from the foreign policy establishment and a great deal of the international news Canadian media disseminates is produced by US sources. Finally, DND, GAC and major corporations have the power to punish journalists and media outlets that upset them.

A small number of large corporations dominate Canadian media. In 2016 four companies controlled over 90% of all paid English language daily newspaper circulation and a half dozen firms controlled almost all TV and radio. While worse today, a 1969 Senate committee investigating media concentration found Canadian "information" services were dominated by "an extremely privileged group of businessmen."[25] At the time three newspaper chains controlled nearly half of English Canada's daily newspapers.[26]

The proprietor's worldview is generally transmitted into the newsroom in a general way, but on occasion evidence has come to light of owners directly shaping international coverage. Founder of the Canada-China Business Council, Paul Desmarais used his Québec papers to criticize Stephen Harper's anti-China policy. In an article titled "Tory China card riles Power [Corporation]" the *Globe and Mail Report on Business* pointed out how Desmarais-controlled *La Presse* ran a series of articles critical of Canada–China relations. A toughly worded November 2006 editorial argued, "the development of China's economy and relations with the outside world have a better chance of moving the dictatorship towards democracy than sermons. Especially if the latter come from the mouth of a government leader whose reign — the Chinese surely know — might be short."[27]

After buying a dozen dailies in 2000 Izzy Asper pushed the CanWest newspaper chain to adopt extremist pro-Israel positions. When *Montréal Gazette* publisher Michael Goldbloom suddenly resigned in 2001 the *Globe and Mail* reported "sources at The Gazette confirmed yesterday that senior editors at the paper were told earlier that month to run a strongly worded, pro-Israel editorial on a Saturday op-ed page", which was written by the head office in Winnipeg and was accompanied by a no rebuttal order.[28] The CanWest editorial demanded Ottawa support Israel even as Israeli government ministers called for the assassination of PLO head Yasser Arafat after 15 Israelis were killed. "Canada must recognize the incredible restraint shown by the Israeli government under the circumstances. ... Howsoever the Israeli government chooses to respond to this barbaric atrocity should have the unequivocal support of the Canadian government without the usual hand-wringing criticism about 'excessive force.' Nothing is excessive in the face of an enemy sworn to your annihilation."[29]

In 2004 the CanWest head office was caught directing papers to edit Reuters stories to denigrate Palestinians. "The message that was passed down to the copy desk was to change 'militant' to 'terrorist' when talking about armed Palestinians," Charles Shannon, a *Montréal Gazette* copy editor, told *The Nation*.[30] "One definite edict that came down was that there should be no criticism of Israel."[31]

(One Reuters story was changed from "the al-Aqsa Martyrs Brigades, which has been involved in a four-year-old revolt against Israeli occupation in Gaza and the West Bank" to "the al-Aqsa Martyrs Brigades, a terrorist group that has been involved in a four-year-old campaign of violence against Israel.")[32]

While the Gazette's publisher officially resigned, owners unsatisfied with international coverage have sometimes removed an editor. *Time* magazine described an example of this at the Southam-owned *Ottawa Citizen* in the spring of 1955. "When [editor Charles

James] Woodsworth came out against the rearmament of West Germany, publisher [Robert] Southam got fed up. ... [and] quietly sacked his editor."[33]

The relationships of media owners to corporate Canada in general also shape international coverage. In *Conflicts of Interest: Canada and the Third World*, Eleanor O'Donnell writes, "the corporate elite that controls Canada's media is linked to other power elites" through common "social circles" and "class backgrounds."[34] Media representatives are directors of financial, resource and other internationally focused Canadian firms. In a late 1980s study University of Windsor communications professor James Winter found that English Canada's two major newspaper chains Southam and Thompson had directors on the board of Toronto Dominion and "each of the five major banks is accessible to Thompson either through direct or indirect [board] interlocks."[35]

Media outlets also have ties to Canada's global mining industry. In *Extracting an ounce of truth: Mainstream media coverage of Canadian mining neoliberalism*, Sheena Cameron writes, "many of the board members of Canadian mining companies also sit on the boards of some of these media corporations or are involved in broadcasting with smaller media companies."[36] The director of BCE's board, for instance, sat on the Rio Tinto board.[37] Before his position at BCE, Robert E. Brown led military contractors CAE and Bombardier and two other top BCE representatives were board members at Bombardier.[38] In mid-2016 Postmedia director Robert Steacy was also a CIBC director while the Thomson Reuters board included long-time CEO of TD Bank Ed Clark, and Thomas Jenkins, a director at internationally focused Manulife Financial.[39]

Media leaders and foreign-focused corporations also collaborate through lobby organizations. In 2009/10 the Canadian Council of Chief Executives included the head of media companies Corus, Rogers and BCE, as well as global mining firms Barrick Gold,

Rio Tinto Alcan and Teck Resources.[40] Similarly, the Chief Financial Officer of the Year selection committee included two board members from Goldcorp and one from BCE as well as sponsorship from BCE and the recipient of the 2010 award was David Garofalo, an executive from mining company Agnico-Eagle.[41]

Through lobbying organizations and corporate boards, media representatives develop ties to internationally focused firms. These relations influence individual opinions about military spending, government support for mining companies abroad, etc., which trickles into the newsroom.

In addition, profit-oriented media companies must remain on good terms with the corporations responsible for the bulk of their revenue. Ads represent the bulk of newspaper, magazine, radio and TV revenue. This gives the corporate class another important lever to bend coverage to their worldview.

With significant international operations, Canadian banks are large advertisers. So are the government, oil sector and insurance industry, which have important international concerns.[42] Auto companies are far and away the largest advertisers and as I, and Bianca Mugyenyi, detail in *Stop Signs: Cars and Capitalism on the Road to Economic, Social and Ecological Decay,* they've repeatedly withdrawn ads to protest news coverage. Between its establishment in 1950 and its sale in 2003 General Motors Defence was often Canada's largest arms maker.[43] (In a history of the CBC, Knowlton Nash writes, "General Motors often demanded and sometimes got script changes on the drama series 'General Motors presents' — so often, in fact, that the insider nickname for the show was 'General Motors prevents.' When the CBC refused to remove a hanging scene in 'Shadow of a Pale Horse,' GM withdrew its commercials."[44])

While CBC is reliant on ads for a quarter of its budget, the crown corporation is not profit oriented or owned by leading capitalists.[45] But, CBC has other foreign policy entanglements.

A Propaganda System

Without a mandatory license fee, CBC's funding fluctuates based on the government of the day. The government also appoints its board of directors and at the start of 2016 eight of ten CBC board members had donated to the Conservative party.[46]

Since launching in the late 1930s the public broadcaster has had close ties to the foreign policy establishment. (In fact, the initiators of the public broadcaster got together at the Canadian Institute for International Affairs.[47]) CBC's initial nine-person board included a general (Victor Odlum), colonel (Wilfred Bovey) and foreign policy advisor (Leonard Brockington).[48]

The close ties between the public broadcaster and foreign policy decision-makers was reflected in coverage. In the build-up to World War II, CBC radio commentator George Ferguson angered Prime Minister Mackenzie King by criticizing British Prime Minister Neville Chamberlain's appeasement policy. Not long thereafter, Ferguson was removed from the air.[49] Three years into WWII King polled Canadians about reversing his commitment to forsake conscription. During the plebiscite CBC "allow[ed] only those in favour of voting yes to present their point of view on the national airwaves."[50]

External Affairs' close relations with CBC continued after WWII. For the next 13 years CBC was led by Arnold Davidson Dunton, general manager of the government Wartime Information Board (see chapter 7).[51] During the quarter century after the war External Affairs' responsibility for CBC International Service gave the department a formal entry point into the public broadcaster.[52] Additionally, CBC provided special nightly broadcasts for External Affairs to distribute to Canadian diplomatic missions abroad.[53]

Throughout the 1950s CBC participated in civil defence tests and its representatives attended National Defence College courses in Kingston.[54] During the 1950–53 Korean War CBC provided radio recordings to destroyers, Station Radio Maple Leaf and other outlets accessed by Canadian soldiers.[55] In 1956 DND opened Radio Canadian Army Europe in Germany. It was managed by CBC staff on loan to the military and lasted for a decade and half.[56]

The public broadcaster's close ties to the military made it highly deferential, according to Mallory Schwartz in *War on the Air: CBC-TV and Canada's Military, 1952-1992*. "When CBC-TV produced programs that raised controversial questions about defence policy, the forces or military history, it did so with considerable care. Caution was partly a result of the special relationship between the CBC and those bodies charged with the defence of Canada."[57]

CBC worked closely with military PR and even showed military-produced content. A Director of Naval Information proposed the 1958 CBC program *Challenge From the Sea* while CBC-TV broadcast a 38-minute DND and Veterans Affairs supported war commemoration on Remembrance Day 1965.[58] In *A Christmas Letter*, a Canadian Forces/NFB produced film aired on CBC Christmas day 1960, Defence Minister Douglas Harkness notes: "As party to the North Atlantic Treaty Organization, we are strongly committed to protecting the rights and freedoms of ourselves and our allies. ... Canada, through the United Nations, has also accepted the role of peacemaker in the Middle East along the troubled zone between Israel and Egypt; in Asia, where Canada is a member of the Truce Commission in Laos; and now in the Congo, where a new African state struggles to find its way to nationhood. ... I am sure we can all agree that the splendid efforts being made by these men and women will help lead to a world at peace with itself."[59]

CBC's ties to DND and External Affairs sometimes translated into formal censorship. When External Affairs Undersecretary Norman Robertson learned whom the public broadcaster planned to dispatch to cover the United Nations founding conference in mid-1945, the government had the "politically unreliable" individuals sidelined.[60] After broadcasting *The Homeless Ones* in 1958 Deputy

A Propaganda System

Federal Civil Defence Co-ordinator Major-General George S. Hatton requested the film's withdrawal from the National Film Board Library and the public broadcaster cancelled its planned rebroadcast.[61] Hatton insisted the CBC clear all content on civil defence with his staff.[62]

In *When Television was Young: Primetime Canada 1952-1967*, Paul Rutherford describes the "suppression" of a report by correspondent "(René) Levesque that Lester Pearson, then minister of external affairs visiting Russia, had been savaged by Soviet leader Khrushchev, because the news reflected badly on the government and on Canada."[63] During Pearson's time as prime minister CBC refused to broadcast Dick Ballentine's 1964 film "Mr. Pearson".[64] It was not broadcast until Pearson left office in 1968 and there was a change at the helm of CBC.[65]

The public broadcaster's independence from DND/External Affairs may have increased over the years. But, since its inception the government has appointed CBC's board and provided most of its funds.

PR spin versus news

Government ties, ownership structure, relations with other corporations and advertising dependence all shape foreign policy coverage. Additionally, the institutions with the resources to produce regular press releases and events are better positioned to influence foreign policy coverage. DND and GAC employ hundreds of PR personnel to fulfill media outlets' need for accessible stories.

Over the past few decades the number of professional journalists has stagnated while the stock of PR professionals has grown. According to Statistics Canada, the ratio of PR professionals to paid journalists reached 4.1 in 2011.[66] The ratio is greater in foreign affairs. The number of professional journalists focused on military and international affairs likely equals several dozen while

GAC and DND employ hundreds of communications professionals and internationally focused corporations many more.

In 2009 Foreign Affairs employed 115 Information Services officers while a 2006 CIDA report said there were 144 positions in its Communications Branch.[67] According to a 2011 DND report, its Public Affairs department had 286 staff.[68] Hundreds of other GAC and DND officials devote some time to PR work and the ministries provide media training to thousands of employees.[69]

International solidarity groups have a fraction of the PR resources available to GAC while peace groups can't produce even a sliver of the military's media output. DND's PR capacities are probably a hundred times greater than all Canadian antiwar and disarmament groups combined. (See chapter 2 for more on military PR)

In addition to their means of producing newsworthy events, large bureaucracies such as DND and GAC are considered "credible" sources of information. As such, their claims demand less scrutiny/investigative expense than those of antiwar groups or dissidents. Sourcing information from valued news creators such as DND and GAC becomes ever more important as newsrooms shrink.

Thousands of internationally focused Canadian corporations spend tens, even hundreds, of millions of dollars every year on PR operations. Their work also influences opinion about Canada's international role. Most Canadian companies operating abroad employ PR personnel and some of the large ones have entire departments. With 50,000 employees worldwide, Montréal-based private security firm GardaWorld says its "communications department provides journalists and editors with assistance in referencing background information, setting up interviews with executives and experts, securing press materials, and checking facts."[70]

According to its 2015 annual financial report, Barrick Gold spent $76 million on "community relations" in 2014 and $62 million in 2015.[71] Whatever proportion of that money could properly be described as PR is almost certainly more than the budgets of all the organizations challenging Canadian mining abuses abroad combined. And 1,300 other Canadian mining firms operate internationally.[72]

While most mining PR focuses on investor relations, some of it takes a highly politicized form. At the Standing Committee on Foreign Affairs and International Development debate on Bill C-300 former Argentine environment minister Romina Picolotti testified she was "physically threatened" and her "staff was bought" after pursuing environmental concerns about a project run by the world's largest gold producer. (C-300 would have withheld some diplomatic and financial support from Canadian resource companies found responsible for significant abuses abroad.) In response, Barrick Gold's executive vice-president of communications Vince Borg called Picolotti's allegations "nonsense", bemoaning how "some individuals have not been made to substantiate even their wildest allegations about the Canadian mining industry and Barrick Gold."[73]

In an effort to defeat growing opposition to its mine in Ecuador, Corriente Resources backed an indigenous delegation to Ottawa to denounce watchdog group Mining Watch.[74] During the delegation's October 2007 visit, a mining industry public relations firm, Kokopell, organized a presentation titled "The Business of Poverty" that blamed anti-mining groups for profiting from Ecuador's poverty.[75] A few months after the delegation's visit, the Vancouver-based mining firm released a press release entitled "Responsible Mining Activities Supported by Major Ecuadorian Indigenous Association." The release explained: "CONFENIAE, an association representing approximately 220,000 people from all 16 indigenous nationalities of the Ecuadorian Amazon, held a Special Assembly on Thursday, November 29th in Puyo, Ecuador. During the Special Assembly, the CONFENIAE leadership overwhelmingly voted in favour of a resolution supporting the responsible mining activities of EcuaCorriente S.A. (Corriente) in the Zamora Chinchipe and Morona Santiago Provinces of Ecuador, as part of their goal to eradicate indigenous poverty in the region."[76]

But, it turns out, the indigenous representatives Corriente brought to Ottawa were paid by the company.[77] Already expelled from the organizations they claimed to represent, one of them had been publicly denounced as early as 1998.[78] A communiqué by the legitimate CONFENIAE explained: "The mining and oil companies and others that have invaded our territories in Amazonia have organized a campaign by a false CONFENIAE, lead by José Aviles, who is sending out communiqués in the international arena, to confuse public institutions, governments, and international cooperation organizations about what is happening in the Ecuadorian Amazonia. The indigenous Mafia lies in the most shameless and condemnable way, usurping the name of the CONFENIAE ... they are not ashamed to send communiqués prepared in the public relations offices of the mining companies, affirming such ridiculous things as that mineral exploitation provides education, hospitals, and culture to our communities."[79]

Alongside company specific PR, industry associations and regionally-based corporate lobby groups pursue similar efforts. The Mining Association of Canada and Prospectors and Developers Association of Canada publicly defend Canada's controversial mining sector. While devoting most of their efforts to private lobbying, they also comment in the media and organize conferences.

So do mining-industry-dominated regional corporate lobby groups such as the Canadian Council on Africa or Canadian Council of the Americas. Led by Barrick Gold, Kinross, ScotiaBank, KPMG and SNC Lavalin, the Canadian Council of the Americas organizes talks, comments in the media and publishes reports such as its 2015 "Canada in the Hemisphere Perspective Paper".[80]

The Canadian Association of Defence and Security Industries (CADSI) fulfills a similar function for Canadian arms manufacturers.

In 2014 CADSI president Tim Page told the press that arms control measures should be relaxed and celebrated a $15 billion Light Armoured Vehicle sale to Saudi Arabia as a "good day for Canada."[81] While they backed controversial arms deals and loosened restrictions on weapons sales, CADSI also promoted a "scary" worldview. "Social media powerful tool for terrorists, expert warns panel discussion on counter-terrorism at CADSI conference," noted a 2015 *Ottawa Citizen* headline.[82] The article quoted former director of counter-terrorism for the Canadian Security Intelligence Service, Ray Boisvert, predicting decades of politically motivated religious violence empowered by technology.

Many of CADSI's 1,000 members are also part of the Canadian Manufacturers & Exporters, Council of Chief Executives, Canadian Chamber of Commerce or Aerospace Industries Association of Canada. These groups also promote militarism and a pro-US foreign policy, though rarely do they speak in favour of military retrenchment or withdrawing from military alliances.

With military contracts representing nearly a fifth of the Canadian aerospace sector, the Aerospace Industries Association of Canada called on Ottawa to purchase Lockheed Martin's controversial F-35 jet in the 2010s.[83] In the mid-1980s Aerospace Industry president, retired air force Lieutenant-General Kenneth E. Lewis, publicly campaigned in favour of Ronald Reagan's so-called "Star Wars" or Strategic Defense Initiative, which ramped up Cold War tensions.[84]

The Canadian Manufacturers and Exporters also promoted arms sales. Its spokesperson, Derek Lothian, responded to criticism of a $15 billion Light Armoured Vehicle deal with Saudi Arabia by saying the monarchy has been "a long-time ally of both Canada and the United States."[85]

Representing 190,000 businesses, the Canadian Chamber of Commerce publicly backed Reagan's 1980s "Star Wars".[86] They also promoted Ballistic Missile Defence. (It's called "missile defence" because it's designed to defend US missiles when they use them in offensive wars.) When Prime Minister Paul Martin bowed to public pressure and officially removed Canada from the project, Chamber President Nancy Hughes Anthony complained. "It is naive to think that the BMD decision will not somehow have negative economic consequences," said Anthony.

To obfuscate their (ruling) class-conscious politics and profit-oriented objectives, corporations' back charitable initiatives. For example, Barrick Gold boasts about funding health clinics, water projects, scholarships etc. as part of its "corporate social responsibility" agenda. With former CEO Peter Munk claiming "corporate social responsibility is part of our DNA", the Toronto company set up a CSR advisory board in 2012.[87] It includes high profile individuals such as former Canadian diplomat Robert Fowler. But, Barrick's projects in Tanzania, the Dominican Republic, Papua New Guinea and Chile have spurred substantial environmental and human rights abuses. Between 2005 and 2016 Barrick-paid security operatives killed dozens of villagers at, or in close proximity, to its North Mara mine in Tanzania.[88]

After Haiti suffered a terrible earthquake in 2010, *Maclean's* listed Gildan Activewear among its "Top 50 Socially Responsible Corporations". The magazine reported that the Montréal-based company "donated more than $570,000 through the Gildan Haiti Relief and Reconstruction Fund. The money helped fund food deliveries, medicine, diapers, tents and financial support to Gildan's employees, their families, and contractors of the company's Haitian manufacturing facility."[89] One of the largest blank T-shirt makers in the world, Gildan employed thousands (directly and indirectly) in Port-au-Prince's assembly sector. A notoriously anti-union employer, Gildan CEO Glenn Chamandy boasted to the *Globe and Mail* in 2005 that its labour costs in Haiti are "cheaper than in China."[90] The

Canadian firm also worked closely with right-wing businessman Andy Apaid, who led the Group 184 domestic opposition that pushed to overthrow Haiti's elected government in 2004 (at the start of 2003 Aristide's government increased the minimum wage from 36 gourdes ($1) a day to 70 gourdes). Gildan workers in Port-au-Prince obviously don't have the resources to compete with the apparel company's PR machine. Nor do anti-sweatshop or Haiti solidarity groups in Canada.

The PR capacities of internationally focused corporations, as well as DND and GAC, partly explain pro-power foreign coverage.

Another factor shaping coverage is the Canadian media's reliance on US news outlets for international stories.[91] In *Canada and the New American Empire*, Jacqueline and Tareq Ismael write, "the Canadian media relies heavily on its American counterparts for acquiring and reporting news, as well as on global newswire services like the British Reuters, the French Agence France Presse and the American Associated Press and United Press International. These four news agencies account for more than 80% of international news."[92]

In a seminal 1980 UNESCO report the US, British and French newswires were harshly criticized for their coverage of the Third World.[93] To this day they still emphasize the North's perspective on international affairs. In the 2013 article "The World According to (Thomson) Reuters" John Jirik describes "the structural asymmetry" in the "international news ecosystem", which "reflect the history and relative power of different players within the system and historically has privileged the interests of the United States and Western Europe."[94]

Embedded journalism

News agencies and international correspondents face pressure to slant coverage in favour of their home country and powerful allied states. The *Toronto Star*'s Jack Cahill, "one of the best Canadian foreign correspondents of the 1970s," writes: "There is little doubt, however, that some US foreign correspondents depend almost entirely on their embassies, and thus indirectly the CIA, for their information. It is, after all, the natural thing to be attracted to the truth as propounded by one's own countrymen in the Embassy offices, at the official briefings, and on the cocktail circuit. It's this information, with its American slant on world affairs, that eventually fills much of Canada's and the Western world's news space."[95]

At times journalist–CIA ties are quite close. A 1976 US Senate Intelligence Committee documented CIA agents writing Associated Press stories and the spy agency conducted journalism training.[96] In a 1980 book Cahill describes bunking with a CIA agent during the 1975 US pull-out from Saigon and notes he was "debriefed by American intelligence and it had never occurred to me not to tell them everything I knew."[97]

Other leading foreign correspondents reported close ties to the US and Canadian military establishments. A CBC TV correspondent for four decades, David Halton said: "I found it easier (and generally safer) covering a war with regular army units, as opposed to reporting independently. In Vietnam, for example, the U.S. Army provided reporters with fairly accurate information about situations at the fronts you wanted to visit, and transportation to get there. Ditto with the Canadian ICCS [International Commission of Control and Supervision] force I deployed to Vietnam with."[98] (The "Five O'Clock Follies" was the sobriquet other journalists gave to the daily US military press briefings in Saigon.)[99]

The Canadian military often transported correspondents abroad. During the early 1960s UN mission in the Congo three CBC reporters traveled to the newly independent central African nation aboard a Royal Canadian Air Force aircraft. After receiving military administered inoculations, Mallory Schwartz reports, "they were closely tied to [Canadian] Army Signals, which was their only means of communicating with the CBC."[100]

On air CBC TV's Norman DePoe lauded the Canadian peacekeeper's work as "something to be proud of."[101] Schwartz describes the Congo correspondents "reports" as "wholly positive about the role Canada was playing in the Congo", even though Canadian soldiers undermined elected independence leader Patrice Lumumba.[102]

A number of commentators have highlighted the political impact of military sponsored trips. In *Turning Around a Supertanker: media-military relations in Canada in the CNN age,* Daniel Hurley writes, "correspondents were not likely to ask hard questions of people who were offering them free flights to Germany" to visit Canadian bases there.[103] In his diary of the mid-1990s Somalia Commission of Inquiry Peter Desbarats made a similar observation. "Some journalists, truly ignorant of military affairs, were happy to trade junkets overseas for glowing reports about Canada's gallant peacekeepers."[104]

During the 2001–14 war in Afghanistan the federal government reportedly paid for journalists to visit the country. Canadian Press envoy Jonathan Montpetit explained, "my understanding of these junkets is that Ottawa picked up the tab for the flight over as well as costs in-theatre, then basically gave the journos a highlight tour of what Canada was doing in Afghanistan."[105]

The diplomatic apparatus and aid agency also sponsored correspondents' work. During a period in the mid-2000s when she wrote for the *Globe and Mail* and CBC, Madeleine Drohan conducted Canadian embassy, High Commission and Foreign Affairs sponsored media workshops in Zambia, Tanzania, Kenya and elsewhere (she taught journalist ethics).[106] At the time Drohan also sat on the board of the government-funded Partnership Africa Canada and North South Institute (see chapter 4).[107]

While some journalists have financial ties to policymakers, almost all correspondents developed ties to the foreign service.

The Canadian Embassy in Moscow, for instance, organized weekly briefings for Canadian reporters in the city and regularly invited them to parties.[108] "The Canadian government", Cahill reports, "can be good to foreign correspondents if it thinks they are reliable and I had two passports, one for general purposes and one for difficult countries."[109]

Correspondents often take their cues from diplomats in the field. Cahill writes that he found Canadian embassies "more reliable" while long time *Globe and Mail* development reporter John Stackhouse acknowledges "Canadian political officers" in Indonesia for their "valuable insights" into the country under Suharto.[110] In *Out of Poverty*, Stackhouse also thanks "the Canadian diplomatic missions in Accra, Abidjan and Bamako [for their] ... invaluable service in arranging interviews and field trips."[111]

In "Covering the coup: Canadian news reporting, journalists, and sources in the 2004 Haiti crisis" York Masters student Isabel Macdonald concludes that the reporters dispatched to Port-au-Prince largely took their cues from official Canada. "My interviews revealed that journalists' contacts with people working in the Canadian foreign policy establishment appear to have played a particularly important role in helping journalists to identify appropriate 'legitimate' sources."[112]

CBC reporter Neil Macdonald told Isabel Macdonald his most trusted sources for background information in Haiti came from Canadian diplomatic circles, notably CIDA where his cousins worked.[113] Macdonald also said he consulted the Canadian Ambassador in Port-au-Prince to determine the most credible human rights advocate in Haiti. Ambassador Kenneth Cook directed him to Pierre Espérance, a coup backer who fabricated a "massacre" used to justify imprisoning the constitutional prime minister and interior minister.[114] (When pressed for physical evidence Espérance actually said the 50 bodies "might have been eaten by wild dogs."[115])

A Propaganda System

A mid-1980s study by communications professor Robert Hackett found a similar dynamic with reporters covering foreign affairs from the home front. After interviewing 20 journalists "specialized in reporting or analyzing the peace and security field" from major papers and the CBC, Hackett writes: "Some of the correspondents interviewed largely defined their beat as comprising the government's policy on defence and external affairs, and its reaction to international developments. Given that definition, the most appropriate sources are the Prime Minister's Office (PMO) and the two relevant government departments, defence and external affairs."[116]

Extremely close ties between the military and media during World War II shaped international coverage for decades. Famed war correspondent and military propagandist Ross Munro later became publisher of the *Edmonton Journal*, *Vancouver Province*, *Winnipeg Tribune* and *Montréal Gazette*.[117] Military press officials also led media outlets after the war. Charged with establishing the Canadian Forces "public relations and press service" during World War II, afterwards Major Richard Malone became president of FP Publications, the largest newspaper chain in the country.[118]

Long-time dean of the Parliamentary Press Gallery and World War II veteran, Doug Fisher explained: "Many of the heavyweights in journalism had been war correspondents, like Charles Lynch and Greg Clark. They had an immense respect and interest for the military, which really lasted a long time. [Clark] always seemed to be going hunting or fishing with generals or brigadiers."[119]

Toronto Sun founding editor Peter Worthington echoed this opinion. A veteran of World War II and Korea, the long-time international correspondent pointed out how "the media was filled with people who'd been soldiers, sailors, airmen or something and had a visceral understanding of the mentality and could assess it."[120]

According to a number of accounts, the "very good" relations between the military and press lasted into the 1980s.[121] Staunch militarist David Bercuson noted how "half the [reporters] that were writing for the media were good buddies of the military. So the story rarely got out and if it did, it was sugarcoated."[122] In *Turning Around a Supertanker: media-military relations in Canada in the CNN age,* Daniel Hurley cites an incident in Cyprus that went unreported possibly due to the close ties between the press and military. A member of the 1968 UN mission, Johnny Carson beat and killed a Turkish-Cypriot police officer who interrupted a drunken search for alcohol. A military tribunal demoted the sergeant for disorderly conduct, but Carson was never charged with manslaughter and later regained his rank. The story went unreported until Carson made it public three decades later.[123]

During World War II the Canadian Press' ties with the military were particularly close. CP "cemented" itself as Canada's national news service during the war. "To accomplish this," Gene Allen writes in a history of the organization, "CP cultivated unprecedentedly close relations with Canada's military authorities — who had reasons of their own for wanting extensive coverage of the national war effort — and thereby moved some distance away from traditional notions of journalistic independence."[124] In an extreme example, CP recruited a Canadian Forces public relations officer who led reporters into battle zones. Bill Boss remained with the same unit but began reporting for the news service.[125]

CP was established during the First World War. A predecessor newswire disseminated Associated Press stories in Canada but the war spurred criticism of the US news agency, which did not cheerlead British/Canadian policy loud enough for some (Washington had yet to join the fighting). "In effect, an arm of the British Foreign Ministry", Reuters offered Canadian newspapers free wire copy during the war.[126] But the British press agency would only deliver the service to Ottawa. If the federal government "wanted to ensure that this pro-war imperial news service was distributed effectively across the country", it had to subsidize a telegraph connection to the West Coast.[127] To support CP the federal government put up $50,000 ($800, 000 in today's dollars) a year, which lasted for six years.[128]

Funding for the West Coast telegraph was considered a way to "bind the nation together".[129] To justify the subsidy William A. Buchanan, Liberal MP and publisher of the *Lethbridge Herald*, emphasized "the large foreign population in the west and the national importance of assimilating them" through "a national Canadian, British and world service of news."[130]

Nationalism remains an important media frame and the dominant media often promotes an "our team" worldview. "As a war correspondent in the 1990s", former CP reporter Stephen Ward describes facing nationalist pressures. Ward writes, "I came under pressure to be patriotic when reporting on Canadian soldiers or peacekeepers in the former Yugoslavia and elsewhere [Iraq] ... I should not embarrass Canada by reporting on mistakes in the field; I should not quote soldiers puzzled about their mission; I should do 'feel-good' pieces about soldiers watching hockey via satellite in warring Bosnia."[131]

Flack from the flacks

Like most institutions, media outlets respond to pressure and criticism. But, it's the DND, GAC, large corporations and their associates that have the means to punish media outlets. 'Flack' mostly consists of letters to the editor and op-eds or emails and phone calls to reporters. Sometimes it may lead to a call to an editor or owner or a critical press release. Occasionally, a publication has been sued or had its distribution or revenue streams targeted for its foreign coverage. (And hanging in the background of a major flack campaign is the possibility a media outlet could lose its government support or license.)

In October 2014 Bloomberg reported on community opposition to a $1.5 billion Ivanhoe mine in South Africa. The

Vancouver company responded with a release saying Bloomberg "did not accurately and fairly" represent the circumstances of its Platreef mine.[132] The company claimed the story "failed to acknowledge the extensive criminal past of its apparent principal source of information, Aubrey Langa, whom Bloomberg identified simply as a community advisor."[133]

Two months later, the *Globe and Mail Report on Business* described Ivanhoe's use of "court injunctions, ultimatums to government, and digging up dirt on opponents" during a two-decade-long effort to establish its South African operations.[134] The company responded by publishing an open letter to the "attention" of *Report on Business* editor Paul Waldie and the Globe's Africa correspondent Geoffrey York. Ivanhoe spent thousands of dollars to distribute the 1,900 word statement to Marketwire and other outlets.

Mining firms have also sought to suppress discussion of their international abuses. As discussed in chapter 5, Barrick sued media outlets and commentators for criticizing their operations in Tanzania and Chile. In 2008 Barrick and Banro sued the publisher and authors of *Noir Canada — Pillage, corruption et criminalité en Afrique* for $11 million.[135] When two of Noir Canada's authors attempted to publish an English-language text on "why is Canada home to more than 70% of the world's mining companies?", Barrick's lawyers "demanded that you provide the undersigned with a copy of any portion of the manuscript or text of Imperial Canada Inc. that makes direct or indirect reference to Barrick, Sutton Resources Ltd., or to any of their past or present subsidiaries, affiliates, directors or officers no later than by 5:00 p.m. on February 19, 2010."[136]

Honest Reporting Canada is devoted entirely to Israel apologist flack. The registered charity monitors the media and engages its supporters to respond to news outlets that fail to toe its pro-Israel line. HRC attacked when a (single) daily paper reviewed my *Canada and Israel: Building Apartheid.* In the lead-up to the 2010

London launch, University of Western Ontario professor David Heap submitted a positive review to his local paper. Two weeks later the *London Free Press* published HRC head Mike Fegelman's response. He claimed it was "professionally unethical for Heap to not disclose his highly partisan stance on the Mideast file" when reviewing *Canada and Israel*.[137] Half the article was spent criticizing Heap's activism and in the second part Fegelman claimed I "tacitly support funding terror groups" and called on people to "peacefully disrupt ... Jewish community meetings."[138]

When I attended Concordia University in the early 2000s I saw more extreme pro-Israel flack. At the start of the 2001 school year the Concordia Student Union published a pro-Palestinian, pro-queer and anti-capitalist student handbook titled *Uprising*. Three weeks after 9/11 the Executive Director of B'nai Brith, Frank Dimant, held a press conference where he asked, "is this a blueprint for Osama bin Laden's youth program in North America?"[139] In the midst of a media storm over the student handbook the *Montréal Gazette* quoted a company spokesperson that advertised in the handbook saying I'll "think twice about doing an ad with you [CSU]" next year.[140]

Dependence on advertising gives companies leverage over media institutions. So does control over distribution.

At the end of 2010 Vancouver-based *Adbusters* juxtaposed photos of the World War II Warsaw Ghetto with images of Gaza. In response Canadian Jewish Congress CEO Bernie Farber urged people to complain to stores selling the magazine.[141] A week later Shoppers Drug Mart told *Adbusters* it would no longer sell its magazine.[142]

The military also throws its weight around with the media. In fall 2015 *Ottawa Citizen* military reporter David Pugliese revealed Canada's top soldier's call for the "weaponization of public affairs."[143] New Chief of Defence Staff Jon Vance proposed a plan to induce positive coverage and deter critical reporting. Journalists producing unflattering stories about the military were to be the target of phone calls to their boss, letters to the editor and other 'flack' designed to undercut their credibility in the eyes of readers and their employers.

While the "weaponization of public affairs" slogan was novel, Pugliese pointed out that "Vance isn't the first to attempt to bring pesky journalists to heel. It was quite common for officials working for then Defence Minister Peter MacKay to phone editors of various publications to complain about reporters."[144]

In the late 1980s Gwynne Dyer co-produced a documentary/book project titled The Defence of Canada. In his book *Canada in the Great Power Game: 1914–2014*, the former board member of the Royal Military College says DND created a speakers bureau to respond to its argument that Ottawa's alliances and overseas commitments were unnecessary for security and often contrary to the country's interests. Dyer writes, "there was a concerted howl of rage from the Canadian military history establishment, who condemned it down to the last man."[145] The book did well but the second edition was not published.[146] Similarly, the television series received good numbers but the public broadcaster failed to run the scheduled second run "even though the CBC had already paid for it."[147]

After CBC showed *The Valour and the Horror* in 1992 the chairman of the National Council of Veterans Associations and CEO of the War Amps, Cliff Chadderton, launched a campaign to block the three-part series from being rebroadcast or distributed to schools. The series claimed Canadian soldiers committed unprosecuted war crimes during World War II and that the British led bomber command killed 600,000 German civilians as part of a top-secret campaign to weaken public morale (even the bombers, flying at night, were largely unaware of their true mission). In response to the pressure, CBC Ombudsman William Morgan asked DND historian Sydney F. Wise to prepare a report on *The Valour and Horror*. The veterans' campaign also led to a Senate inquiry, a CRTC hearing and a lawsuit.[148] CBC said it would not rebroadcast *The Valour and the Horror* without amendments.[149]

The military also tried to shutter critical media. In *Unembedded: Two Decades of Maverick War Reporting*, Scott Taylor describes the military's effort to kneecap *Esprit de Corps*, which aimed "to contribute to the esprit de corps that has made the Canadian military one of the finest professional armed forces in the world."[150] To gain access to Air Canada military charters in the late 1980s, the magazine was to obtain DND "approval for all editorial content prior to publication."[151] But, in 1991 *Esprit de Corps* criticized the appointment of Marcel Masse as defence minister and interviewed Vice Admiral Chuck Thomas after he resigned as vice chief of defence. In response DND directed Air Canada to stop carrying *Esprit de Corps*. The airline sent the magazine a note saying, "due to concerns over editorial content, the Department of National Defence has ordered Air Canada to cease distribution of *Esprit de Corps* aboard military charter flights."[152]

Almost entirely distributed in-flight at the time, DND's move would have crippled the magazine. The CF only backed down after *Esprit de Corps* went public and then privately threatened to reveal a possible conflict of interest between Chief of Defence Staff John de Chastelain and *Canadian Defence Quarterly*.[153]

When *Esprit de Corps* helped expose the military's attempt to cover up the 1993 killings in Somalia, the CF again targeted the magazine. Taylor writes, "memos were sent to the CANEX military retail stores, ordering them to cease the sale of our publication; the copies we had donated through the Royal Canadian Legion were to be burned, according to the official directive from National Defence Headquarters."[154] Even more debilitating for the magazine, DND asked *Esprit de Corps* defence clients to "cancel their advertising contracts."[155]

Fear of flack partly explains the pro-power bias in international coverage. Angering powerful individuals and institutions often has costs, a reality most reporters and news outlets have internalized.

Objectivity

The structural forces shaping foreign policy discussion are deeply ingrained. Individuals who rise to positions of influence within major media outlets have generally internalized the aforementioned structural biases and dominant worldview (those who haven't must be discrete and/or incredibly hard-working/skilled). In *Manufacturing Consent: The Political Economy of the Mass Media*, Edward Herman and Noam Chomsky write: "The elite domination of the media and marginalization of dissidents that results from the operation of these filters occurs so naturally that media news people, frequently operating with complete integrity and goodwill, are able to convince themselves that they choose and interpret the news 'objectively' and on the basis of professional news values. Within the limits of the filter constraints they often are objective; the constraints are so powerful, and are built into the system in such a fundamental way, that alternative bases of news choices are hardly imaginable."[156]

This analysis is as good as any I've come across about the Canadian media's coverage of foreign affairs.

A Propaganda System

7. Case Studies — Propaganda During War

"The first casualty of war is truth."
US Senator Hiram Johnson

During the playoffs the propaganda machine goes into overdrive. Teams go to great lengths to hide injuries or tactical considerations. All the parts of the propaganda system work together to "push our team over the top". TV stations increase their hours of coverage; newspapers run supplements paid for by advertisers clamouring to bask in some of the team's glow; bars and restaurants expand their opening hours to take advantage of the profit making opportunities. It is the best time to see the propaganda system at work.

In international affairs wars offer a similar opportunity. While the tactics have varied based on technologies, balance of power and type of conflict, the government has pursued extensive information control during wars. There was formal censorship during World War I, WWII and the Korean War. In recent air wars, the military largely shut the media out while in Afghanistan they brought reporters close.[1] The justifications given for deploying Canadian troops abroad have often been transparently false. Government officials generally claim some humanitarian rationale to mask wars motivated by geostrategic and corporate interests. Blatant manipulation of public opinion becomes the order of the day. This becomes especially clear the farther back in history we look.

Boer war

Between 1899 and 1902 more than 7,000 Canadians fought to strengthen Britain's position in southern Africa. About 200,000 Boer were rounded up and sent to concentration camps in a war largely driven by mining interests. Twenty-eight thousand (mostly children) died of disease, starvation and exposure in these camps.[2] Another 100,000 Black Africans were held in concentration camps but the British didn't keep statistics so we don't know how many died.[3]

To justify the war British officials criticized Boer treatment of Blacks. In *Painting the Map Red: Canada and the South African War, 1899-1902,* Carman Miller notes the self-serving nature of this claim. "Although imperialists had made much of the Boer maltreatment of the Blacks, the British did little after the war to remedy their injustices." In fact, the war reinforced white/British dominance over the region's Indigenous population. The peace agreement with the Boer included a guarantee that Black Africans would not be granted the right to vote before the two defeated republics gained independence and, of course, they would not gain full civil rights until the end of apartheid nine decades later.

Cecil Rhodes and other British mining interests shaped the international discussion of southern Africa. Newspapers received copy from Capetown and Johannesburg papers run by Rhodes and others "who own or control the diamond mines at Kimberley."[4] The Rhodes-financed South Africa Association promoted anti-Boer and pro-war sentiment in Canada. Its representative J. Davis Allen convinced *Montréal Star* editor Hugh Graham to telegram 6,000 politicians, clergyman, military leaders and other notables to ask their opinion about Canada joining the war. Pierre Berton writes, "the prepaid (and often prewritten) answers appeared daily in Graham's newspaper, creating the illusion of a massive wave of support."[5]

Pro-empire media pushed a government attentive to antiwar sentiment among Francophone Quebeckers to participate. The most widely read newspaper at the time, the *Montréal Star* described "Canada's duty in the Transvaal" and compared Prime Minister Wilfred Laurier to Boer leader Paul Kruger because of his initial reluctance to send Canadians to war.[6] Once he decided to participate Laurier sought to pressure Francophone media to support his position. The prime minister wrote a long letter to the editor of Québec City's *Le Soleil,* which included an article to publish. "Here is the attitude you should take," Laurier informed his friend Ernest Pacaud. *Le Soleil* fulfilled the prime minister's request as did Montréal's *La Presse.*[7]

A year into the fighting, the government commissioned Steven Leacock to promote the war. The famous author and McGill professor toured the empire as an "imperial missionary."[8]

Seven journalists accompanied the initial deployment of Canadian soldiers to South Africa.[9] The British deterred colonial journalists from covering the fighting by controlling correspondents' licenses. In at least one instance Prime Minister Laurier arranged for a sympathetic reporter to acquire a license to cover the war.[10]

In *Breaking the News by Following the Rules*, Kate Barker notes, "Canadian reporters only filed stories that showed Dominion troops in the best, most heroic light. They ignored reports of Canadians having a reputation for shooting rather than taking prisoners, for example."[11]

With British censors blocking them from witnessing the fighting, Canadian correspondents' stories were generally filed from headquarters.[12] In one embarrassing episode, Richard Smith wrote that Canadian soldiers "covered themselves with glory" and accomplished "a great deed that will live in history" by blowing up the Boer supply lines to the sea.[13] Smith must have written the story before the assault on the Komatipoort railway bridge was to begin since it was abandoned when the Boer caught wind of the mission.[14]

The line between soldier and journalist was not always clear.[15] The *Montréal Herald* "engaged 11 sub correspondents among the Canadian contingent. These soldiers were paid to send back letters to private addresses, to be handed over to the paper for publication."[16] *Ottawa Citizen* editor E. W. D. 'Dinky' Morrison enlisted and sent letters to the *Citizen* and *Hamilton Spectator* while the *Toronto Globe*'s correspondent was the former editor of the *Canadian Military Gazette* and lieutenant in the volunteers Frederick Hamilton.[17] Most famously, British lieutenant Winston Churchill was also a special correspondent for London's *Morning Post*.[18]

WWI

A century after it began, many still believe Canada fought against tyranny during World War I. But Germany had universal (male) suffrage and Ottawa was allied with the brutal Russian Czar.

During the war Ottawa worked hard to control the message. Only a small number of Canadian reporters were allowed access to a trench line that barely moved for three years.[19] British and French allies controlled the fighting zone and threatened to shoot journalists who approached without permission.[20] Author of *Propaganda and Censorship during Canada's Great War,* Jeffrey Keshen writes, "to obtain access to battle zones, some publishers wrote authorities that patriotism, not the desire for sensationalism and newspaper sales, would guide their reporters."[21]

Canadian war coverage was largely produced or overseen by Canadian-raised British newspaper baron William Maxwell Aitken (later Lord Beaverbrook). Given the rank of lieutenant-colonel, Aitken ran Canada's War Records Office in London. His office wrote inspiring tales of a war that left millions, including 60,000 Canadian, young men dead. With 60 researchers, cameramen and support staff, the War Records Office mostly based their stories on military press releases and statements by generals.[22] In *The Fog of War*, Mark Bourrie writes, "Aitken was eyewitness to very little. He rarely went near the front, and simply wrote press releases based on memos from military intelligence agents."[23]

Aitken even glorified a disastrous battle in St. Eloi, Belgium where 1,400 Canadians were accidentally killed by allied fire.[24]

A Propaganda System

According to army newspaper *The Maple Leaf*, Aitken is "considered the father of today's Public Affairs Branch."[25]

Many artists, cinematographers and photographers were hired to depict Canadians fighting. Canada's official war art program created almost 1,000 works of art.[26] On the home front the government produced war posters to recruit soldiers and rally public opinion. They also organized a speakers bureau of "'five minute men' who inspired patriotic support for Canada's war effort."[27]

Alongside its propaganda efforts, the government aggressively repressed information about a war with no clear and compelling purpose other than rivalry between up-and-coming Germany and the imperial powers of the day, Britain and France. Bourrie writes, "no one could publicly criticize the Army or Navy. People were not allowed to advocate a negotiated peace and, eventually could not even discuss the reasons for the war or suggest the Allies were partially to blame for it. The government, along with most newspaper and magazine owners, flooded propaganda into the marketplace of ideas. Censorship created the illusion that these official ideas were the only version of reality."[28]

At the beginning of the conflict Robert Borden's government passed the War Measures Act. Hundreds of pacifists and antiwar activists were arrested under it.[29] The War Measures Act allowed "censorship and control and suppression of publications, writings, maps, plans, photographs, communication and means of communication."[30] A June 1915 order-in-council established a Chief Press Censor's Office empowered to prohibit media. With the approval of the Secretary of State, Chief Censor Colonel Ernest Chambers was authorized to block any news sources "assisting or encouraging the enemy, or preventing, embarrassing or hindering the successful prosecution of the war."[31] A September 1918 Order in Council empowered the censor to shutter all publications in an "enemy language."[32]

To encourage compliance, early in the war the Censor's Office sent 1,500 news distributors instructions outlining acceptable commentary.[33] Unsure of what was kosher, many outlets asked the censor to screen letters and other articles. In one instance Chambers blocked a letter to the *Monetary Times* (Toronto) from a private who wrote that "the man who said war was hell did not know anything about it, for it [was] far worse."[34]

At its high point 120 postal employees helped the Censor's Office keep an eye out for "unpatriotic" materials.[35] The posties were empowered to open suspicious letters — generally those not in English or French — and report their contents.

Chambers quashed a number of films, plays and records.[36] "In the last months of the war," notes Bourrie, "the censors began poking through record stores and demanded catalogues from the major US record companies. Thirty-four records were banned, all of them foreign language songs."[37] Chambers also suppressed numerous articles, books and movies available in Britain. His rationale was that the British public could better handle unpleasant news since they were more likely to have heard stories from the front and air raids drove home the consequences of losing the war. Physically and intellectually distant from the fighting, Canadians' commitment was said to be based more on idealistic sentiment.[38] As such, learning about the horrors of the conflict was more likely to dissuade Canadians from supporting the war.

Chambers banned two popular temperance books by Arthur Mees — *The Fiddlers* and *The Parasite* — and popular British war movie *The Battle of the Somme* was only allowed to be shown after footage of dead allied soldiers was removed. Almost 13% of the film was excised.[39]

Beyond individual books, films and records, the Censor's Office banned 253 news sources.[40] The vast majority of them were from the US, which stayed neutral until late in the conflict. The censored publications were generally in foreign languages and a good number of them promoted some variant of Marxism.[41] With the War Measures Act remaining in force until January 1920, the censor banned dozens of socialist reviews after the Armistice was signed in November 1918.[42]

WWII

"Many Canadians, especially in Québec, believed the horror stories about the Nazis were cut from the same cloth as Britain's First World War propaganda", explains Bourrie. "For many, it took the end of the war revelations of Hitler's Final Solution to show there was, indeed, a wolf this time."[43]

During their first few years in office many Canadian papers reported sympathetically on the Nazis. The *Toronto Globe*, *Toronto Evening Telegram* and *Montréal Gazette* published articles by an individual who "admired Hitler's record of achievement", which included jailing and killing socialists and communists as well as Roma and Jews.[44] The tide turned as the Nazis ran up against British interests. When London made its intentions clear, the Canadian media beat the war drums. But, Ottawa wasn't willing to rely on a patriotic press. During the war they set up PR organizations at the Canadian Military Headquarters in London, National Defence Headquarters in Ottawa and thirteen military district headquarters across the country.[45] By 1945 hundreds of media relations personnel produced press releases, articles, radio, newsreel, photos and films. They also briefed journalists, provided material to the CBC and coordinated with their allied counterparts.[46]

At the start of the war a photographic section was set up at Canadian Military Headquarters in London and in September 1941 the Canadian Army Film and Photo Unit was officially formed.[47] It shot over 60,000 still photos, 1.5 million feet of film, 2,000 edited film stories and a dozen feature documentaries to prop up morale and stimulate recruitment.[48] According to the commissioner of the

Canadian Government Motion Picture Bureau, Frank Badgley, the objective of the Film and Photo Unit was "to provide informational and inspirational material."[49]

Based in Ottawa, the Wartime Information Board (WIB) sought to convince the public of the righteousness of the conflict.[50] It produced pamphlets, a monthly publication called *Canada at War* and pioneered systematic public opinion polling.[51]

The WIB worked closely with the National Film Board of Canada (NFB), which was established in 1939 to promote the war effort.[52] Head of both the NFB and WIB for half the conflict, John Grierson called for "a totalitarian war for the population's minds."[53] The NFB supplied theatres with newsreel and short features dramatizing the war effort. It swelled to 800 employees and produced numerous war films, including the six-part *Canada Carries On*.[54] The principal newsreader on CBC radio's national news, Lorne Greene, narrated several NFB war films.[55]

In a long history of the public broadcaster Knowlton Nash describes how the recently created "CBC also went to war. More than ever before or since, during the war years the CBC became almost an arm of government."[56] The military, other government agencies and the Canadian Legion produced a significant amount of CBC programming.[57] According to the "CBC War Effort" pamphlet, the public broadcaster's aim was "to inspire the nation as a whole and every individual to greater effort. To put everyone in the proper frame of mind to accept willingly the inevitable sacrifices involved in the war effort."[58]

More significant than CBC, Canadian Press was the main source of news copy during the war. It "acquiesced to all censorship requirements", notes Kate Barker, "providing the country with a diet of soft features rather than hard war news stories."[59]

A number of military public relations officers (PROs) were trained journalists. *In Breaking the News by Following the Rules:*

Canadian War Correspondents in World War Two Continued a Tradition of Bending to Authority, Kate Barker notes, "the fact that the Canadian Army employed so many former journalists as PROs contributed to the collegial atmosphere between the Army and the correspondents, further blurring the lines between the military and the Fourth Estate."[60]

Effectively part of the military, Canadian war correspondents were subject to military discipline. The 1943 correspondents regulation booklet said they must "comply with any orders received from superior authority and to conform with the requirements of the Army Act or the Air Force Act, as applicable to a person holding status as an officer, while subject to military or air force law."[61]

Some correspondents acted as official state propagandists. After CBC correspondent Ross Munro survived the disastrous 1942 raid at Dieppe, he was hired by the Wartime Information Board to tell Canadians about the "heroic" attack. During a speech in Montréal Munro presented himself as an eyewitness to the exploits of the French Canadian regiment largely wiped out during the raid. But, Munro landed with another Regiment three kilometers away.[62] Béatrice Richard asks, "how could he claim to have witnessed the French Canadians in action? In essence, Munro became a propagandist working on behalf of the war effort and his story mirrored the Army's press releases."[63]

Even after the war, Munro continued to peddle the military leadership's self-serving description of the disastrous invasion at Dieppe. In *Gauntlet to Overlord: The Story of the Canadian Army*, he claimed, "lessons were learned at Dieppe ... which gave the Allied command the key to invasion."[64] Today, the Conference of Defence Associations and Canadian Global Affairs Institute give out a Ross Munro Media Award to recognize a "journalist who has made a significant contribution to understanding defence and security issues."[65]

While the media's pro-war bias made it largely unnecessary to suppress information, the government gave itself that stick. The Defence of Canada Regulations stated: "No person shall a) spread reports or make statements intended or likely to cause disaffection as to His Majesty or to interfere with the success of His Majesty's forces or of the forces of any allied or associated Powers or to prejudice His Majesty's relations with foreign powers; b) spread reports or make statements intended or likely to prejudice the recruiting, training, discipline, or administration of any of His Majesty's forces; or c) spread reports or make statements intended or likely to be prejudicial to the safety of the State or the efficient prosecution of the war."[66]

At its high point the DND Directorate of Censorship oversaw nearly 1,000 employees who mostly opened mail.[67] More than 45 million letters and packages were opened during the war.[68]

A dozen publications were banned during WWII and at least three corporate dailies — *Vancouver Sun*, *Le Droit* and *Le Soleil* — were fined for breaching censorship regulations.[69] Many books were also banned and a number of dissidents jailed.[70]

Korea

After the Communists took control of China in 1949 the US tried to encircle the country. They supported Chiang Kai-shek in Taiwan, built military bases in Japan, backed a right-wing dictator in Thailand and sought to "establish a pro-Western state" in Vietnam.[71] The success of China's nationalist revolution also spurred the 1950-53 Korean War in which eight Canadian warships and 27,000 Canadian troops intervened in what was essentially a civil war. US–led UN forces were largely responsible for a war that left as many as four million dead.

Canadian newspapers described North Koreans as "communists", "bandits", "dogs", and "evildoers".[72] Displaying a mix of racism and Cold War hysteria, a *Globe and Mail* headline noted:

"Mongol Hordes Spearhead Drive: Reds Rip Gaping Hole in UN Line, Pour South."[73] Another *Globe* story called North Korean forces crossing the 38th parallel a "challenge to our civilization" while the *Calgary Herald* wrote they "don't imagine that many Occidental's care very deeply about what happens to Korea and the Koreans" but Canadians needed to be "cold-blooded and admit that we are fighting for nothing more and nothing less" than our "national survival."[74]

Driven by Cold War hysteria and ever-present nationalism, the press cheered on the Korean War. The small number of reporters who traveled to the region mostly relied on communiqués from the US-led UN headquarters in Tokyo.[75] Few reporters traveled to the front.

Journalists in Korea operated under strict censorship. Soon after the war began the UN force warned that "unwarranted criticism of command decisions or of the conduct of Allied soldiers on the battlefield will not be tolerated."[76] Six months into the war the UN command produced censorship criteria, which further restricted journalists. Reporters were not permitted to discuss casualties or allied air power, nor employ the word "retreat" to describe the UN's ejection from North Korea.[77] In effect, they weren't allowed to criticize UN forces. Any attempt to bypass the censors or defy the rules in other ways could result in court-martial or removal from the theatre. In the first ten months of the war at least 17 journalists were expelled.[78]

In early 1951 there were only two Canadian reporters in Korea.[79] As such, most Canadian coverage of the Korean War came from US wire services.

On March 17, 1951, three Canadian soldiers raped and murdered two South Korean women and savagely beat allied Korean soldiers who intervened. After locals complained, Canadian Press reporter Bill Boss learned about the crime, which included a Canadian throwing a grenade.[80] But, Boss' story was intercepted by UN officials in Tokyo and forwarded to Canadian Army Headquarters, which squashed it.[81]

A lieutenant during World War II and son of a Canadian Colonel, Boss was attacked for his reporting.[82] Boss "was subjected to a campaign of vilification from United Nations public relations officers. He was called 'subversive' and an abortive attempt was made to oust him from the Korean theatre."[83]

On another occasion Canada's external minister complained UN censorship was not more robust. Lester Pearson was angry when the *New York Times* reported on a North Korean village hit by US napalm. The story noted, "the inhabitants throughout the village and in the fields were caught and killed and kept the exact postures they had held when the napalm struck … There must be almost two hundred dead in the tiny hamlet."[84]

In a letter to the Canadian ambassador in Washington, Hume Wrong, Pearson wondered how the article might affect public opinion and complained about it passing censors. He wrote, "such military action was possibly 'inevitable' but surely we do not have to give publicity to such things all over the world. Wouldn't you think the censorship which is now in force could stop this kind of reporting?"[85] Wrong agreed with his boss, but there's no indication of whether he discussed the matter with US authorities.

Government officials also pressured the media to suppress information. In response to gory radio reports, Defence Minister Brooke Claxton asked CBC Chairman Arnold Davidson Dunton, who had been general manager of the WWII Wartime Information Board, "to advise radio stations to prioritize propriety" (socially proper behaviour).[86]

After the outbreak of a series of diseases at the start of 1952, China and North Korea accused the US of using biological weapons. Though the claims have neither been conclusively substantiated or disproven — some internal documents are still restricted — in *Orienting Canada*, John Price details Ottawa's authoritarian response to the accusations, some of which were made at the time by Canadian peace groups. When the *Ottawa Citizen* revealed that British, Canadian, and US military scientists had recently met in Ottawa to discuss biological warfare, Pearson wrote the paper's owner to complain and squash the story elsewhere. Price writes: "In reaction to a 2 May Ottawa Citizen article revealing that tri-national meetings of military scientists to discuss biological warfare were being held in Ottawa and other Canadian cities, [External Affairs Deputy Under-Secretary Escott] Reid noted that Pearson felt that such articles played into the hands of communist propagandists and that he now felt he had to write to Mr. Southam (owner of the Citizen) to complain. Omar Solandt, head of the Defence Research Board, reported Reid, had told Pearson at a meeting to discuss the fallout from the accusation, that 'as soon as he heard of the story he had taken measures to see that it was not carried further and had it killed in the Ottawa Journal and over the CP wires.' On the grounds of national security, the truth about Canadian involvement in biological warfare preparations remained hidden."[87]

In addition to squashing information about Canada's role in developing biological weapons, Pearson misled the public about what the government knew of possible germ warfare in Korea. While publicly highlighting a report that exonerated the US, Pearson concealed a more informed External Affairs analysis suggesting biological weapons could have been used. Price explains, "to avoid revealing the nature of the biological warfare program and Canadian collaboration, which would have lent credence to the charges levelled by the Chinese and Korean governments, the Canadian government attempted to discredit the peace movement."[88]

They bitterly denounced Canadian Peace Congress chairman James Endicott. Pearson called Endicott, who had been a college friend, a "red stooge" and the "bait on the end of a Red hook".[89] Pearson even called for individuals to destroy the Peace Congress from the inside. The external minister publically applauded

50 engineering students who swamped a membership meeting of the University of Toronto Peace Congress branch. He proclaimed: "If more Canadians were to show something of this high spirited crusading zeal, we would very soon hear little of the Canadian Peace Congress and its works. We would simply take it over."[90]

Government attacks spurred media and public hostility.[91] A number of public venues refused to rent their space to the Peace Congress and Endicott's Toronto home was firebombed during a large Peace Congress meeting.[92]

Persian Gulf War

Canada deployed three naval vessels, 26 CF-18 aircraft and 4,000 personnel to the Middle East.[93] Canadians also oversaw a military headquarters in Bahrain.

To justify Canadian participation in the 1991 war Prime Minister Brian Mulroney echoed claims, orchestrated by a Washington PR firm working for the Kuwaiti monarchy, that Iraqi troops stole incubators leaving babies "to die on the cold floor" of a Kuwaiti hospital.[94] Canadian officials also went along with the George H. W. Bush administration's lie that hundreds of thousands of Iraqi troops were amassed on the Saudi border, preparing to invade.[95]

During the prewar build-up the Pentagon set up a press "pool" supervised by public affairs officers "who kept a close watch on their charges."[96] Some major media outlets were excluded from the pool and stories were often censored. In one instance censors cleared an article by *Los Angeles Times* reporter Douglas Jehl only to decide the story was contrary to their "best interests and ordered him out of the press pool."[97] In a *Vancouver Sun* article headlined "CF-18 mission reports under strict censorship" Tim Harper wrote: "Reporters in the gulf have been given strict rules about what they can and cannot report. Reports are cleared by military authorities and some must be approved by national censors in countries such as Israel and Saudi Arabia."[98]

As part of its promotion of Canada's war effort, DND sponsored academics to visit Canadian troops in the Persian Gulf.[99] They also bent over backwards to garner coverage. In one instance, two Sea King helicopters were dispatched to Bahrain to bring reporter Scott Taylor aboard *HMCS Huron*.[100] Aboard *HMCS Athabascan* on Christmas, Ian MacLeod's editor wanted a story about the day's celebration for the Boxing Day *Ottawa Citizen*. Unable to file his story due to satellite problems caused by an unstable connection, the lieutenant commander ordered the bridge to steer a straight course, which diverted the vessel from its patrol zone and prompted an American inquiry.[101]

Wanting press but fearing the result, the military restricted what journalists aboard naval vessels could write.[102] Ostensibly for operational security reasons, reporters had to sign a waiver allowing military personnel to review stories filed aboard ships.[103] When the *Globe and Mail*'s Paul Koring wrote about sailors' fears and desire to return home, a Public Affairs Officer (PAO) asked him to edit the story, saying "you're going to affect the morale of the families back home and ... our morale."[104] Koring waited until he was ashore to file the story and was later blocked from a cocktail party aboard *HMCS Athabaskan*.[105]

During a sojourn at sea CBC Halifax reporter Rob Gordon overheard a conversation about a secret exercise. Set to leave the ship the next day he could have published the story without the military's approval, but navy officials dissuaded him from doing so. Gordon explained why he conceded: "You had to take it [the military position] into account, because if you didn't play ball with them, you weren't going to get out to a ship the next day, or suddenly it would be very difficult to interview somebody. They had all the cards."[106]

In the lead-up to the first Gulf War a number of papers reported a rumour that body bags were thrown on the lawn of a soldier in Victoria. Presumed to be the work of antiwar activists, it probably never happened.[107] Bob Bergen investigated the matter in a PhD thesis, but was unable to confirm the story.[108] That didn't stop the military from citing the purported incident to restrict information about Canadian fighter jets.

Somalia

In 1993 Project Censored Canada found the potential for extracting oil in Somalia the most under-reported news story that year.[109] A 1991 World Bank/United Nations Development Program study pointed to significant hydrocarbons in the country's north and in January 1993 the *Los Angeles Times* reported that it had obtained documents revealing that President Siad Barre had given four major US oil companies — Chevron, Amoco, Conoco, and Phillips — exploration rights over two-thirds of the country. The paper reported, "far beneath the surface of the tragic drama of Somalia, four major U.S. oil companies are quietly sitting on a prospective fortune in exclusive concessions to explore and exploit tens of millions of acres of the Somali countryside. That land, in the opinion of geologists and industry sources, could yield significant amounts of oil and natural gas if the U.S.-led military mission can restore peace to the impoverished east African nation."[110]

Somalia became a scandal for the Canadian military. During their 1992/93 deployment Canadian soldiers murdered a number of Somalis. In the worst incident a handful of soldiers tortured 16-year-old Shidane Arone to death while dozens of other Canadians heard his screams.[111] The top brass attempted to cover up the killings and, once it came to light, shifted blame to lower ranks. And, as mentioned above, *Esprit de Corps* played an important role in exposing the cover-up and the CF responded by targeting the military magazine.

As part of its cover-up, CF officials illegally doctored documents concerning the brutal murder of Arone. As part of an investigation into the March 1993 slayings in Somalia, CBC reporter

Michael McAuliffe requested briefing notes for officers dealing with the media. DND was caught hiding documents, wildly inflating the cost of releasing them and altering files. At the 1995-97 inquiry into the killings in Somalia, Chief of Defence Staff Jean Boyle admitted the CF deliberately violated the spirit of access to information rules, while a colonel and commander were convicted by a military court of altering documents requested under that legislation.[112] *Dishonoured Legacy: The Lessons of the Somalia Affair: Report of the Commission of Inquiry Into the Deployment of Canadian Forces to Somalia* described DND's "unacceptable hostility toward the goals and requirements of access to information legislation."[113]

Officials even thumbed their nose at the official inquiry set up to look into a cover-up reaching to the upper echelons of the CF/DND. *Dishonoured Legacy* notes: "Document disclosure remained incomplete throughout the life of the Inquiry. It took the form of a slow trickle of information rather than an efficient handing over of material. Key documents were missing, altered, and even destroyed. Some came to our attention only by happenstance ... Some key documents were disclosed officially only after their existence was confirmed before the Inquiry by others. ... Finally, faced with altered Somalia-related documents, missing and destroyed field logs, and a missing National Defence Operations Centre computer hard drive, we were compelled to embark on a series of hearings devoted entirely to the issue of disclosure of documents by DND and the Canadian Forces through DND's Directorate General of Public Affairs, as well as to the issue of compliance with our orders for the production of documents."[114]

Yugoslavia

During the Yugoslav wars Canadian forces participated in both UN and NATO missions. On September 15/16, 1993, Canadian soldiers exchanged heavy fire with Croatian troops in the Medak

Pocket in what's now Croatia. In the Balkans to intercede between warring Croats and Serbs, the Canadians killed as many as 27 Croatian soldiers.[115] But, both Ottawa and Zagreb sought to deny the fighting. The Croatians didn't want the world knowing its forces attacked United Nations Protection Force (UNPROFOR) soldiers who stood their ground against efforts to cleanse the area of Serb civilians.[116] Canadian officials didn't want to weaken the Croatian position since Washington and Berlin actively backed Zagreb's effort to break up the former Yugoslavia.[117] (The fighting would almost certainly have received attention if Serbian forces had attacked Canadian troops overseeing a negotiated withdrawal and left behind dozens of dead civilians.)

In the annals of Canadian history, our soldiers' actions in Medak Pocket represent a noble use of force. But, Ottawa prioritized Western geopolitical objectives over publicizing the soldiers' good deeds. The story didn't come to public attention until three years later and the 2nd Battalion wasn't officially commended for their actions in Medak Pocket until 2002.[118]

In July 1994 Canadian soldiers were again targeted by hostile non-Serb forces. Bosnian Muslim militiamen fired on them and in the battle two of them were killed. Similar to the Medak Pocket, Scott Taylor writes, "the Canadian government never officially acknowledged the killing of two Muslims — and the Muslims never complained."[119]

An image-conscious DND failed to gather proper records of UNPROFOR casualties.[120] Confused by the lack of accurate records, editor of the army's *Garrison* newspaper Captain Bob Kennedy published a Canadian casualty list. A few days after he gave an interview about Canadian casualties in the Balkans, the head of Public Affairs advised Kennedy "his services were no longer required" and he was dismissed from the military.[121]

In the last stage of the break-up of the former Yugoslavia, 18 Canadian fighter jets participated in NATO's 78-day bombing of

Serbia in the spring of 1999.[122] The CF 18s dropped 530 bombs in 682 sorties — approximately 10 percent of NATO's bombing runs.[123] Hundreds died during NATO's bombing and hundreds of thousands were displaced in a war that contravened international law.[124]

Prominent British war historian Alistair Horne called the 1999 Kosovo war "the most secret campaign in living memory. The public was served up a feast of meaningless, deceitful words and images about the state of the operation. It was only revealed months later that the Kosovo Liberation Army had, in fact, been trained by the US Central intelligence Agency, had provoked the Serbs into committing atrocities, and had not been disarmed by NATO troops, despite assurances to the contrary. Pilots had, in fact, targeted civilians. And a handful of bodies were discovered in mass graves, nowhere near the 500,000 ethnic Albanians that were supposedly murdered by the Serbs."[125]

NATO justified its bombing of Serbia as a humanitarian intervention to save Albanian Kosovars. Three weeks into the bombing Foreign Minister Lloyd Axworthy said, "we cannot stand by while an entire population is displaced, people were killed, villages are burned and looted, and the population is denied its basic rights because it does not belong to the 'right' ethnic group"[126] But, contrary to the government's characterization of the campaign, NATO's bombing of Yugoslavia spurred the ethnic cleansing they claimed to be curbing. The exodus of Albanians from Kosovo began two days after NATO airstrikes commenced.[127] Taylor writes, "the second objective of NATO's air campaign had been the prevention of a humanitarian crisis in Kosovo. In fact, the bombing had triggered a Serbian offensive and a massive exodus of Albanians. In a deft manoeuvre, NATO spin doctors then proclaimed that their air attacks were now necessary to halt a humanitarian crisis."[128]

CBC TV produced a major story about an Albanian girl who said her sister was raped and killed by Serbs, which prompted her

A Propaganda System

to join the thuggish Kosovo Liberation Army. Initially broadcast a month before NATO began bombing, CBC replayed the story the day the bombing started.[129] It was later found to be a complete fabrication.[130]

In *Unembedded: Two Decades of Maverick War Reporting*, Taylor writes about the stiff propaganda he ran up against. He describes an off-air exchange with a radio producer in Canada who dismissed a scene he described of Albanians stoning a bus full of elderly Serbians and mothers with children since they were "probably war criminals" who "did nothing to prevent the atrocities [against Albanians] from taking place." Taylor responded by saying, "you mean in the same way our NATO soldiers stood at the Albanian gauntlet and did nothing to stop the stoning of the Serbs?" to which the producer said, "boy, do you ever need to get home and be deprogrammed."[131]

The CF blocked journalists from filming or accessing Canadian pilots flying out of Aviano, Italy. They also refused to provide footage of their operations. While they tightly controlled information on the ground, the CF sought to project an air of openness in the aftermath of the Somalia scandal (see above). For 79 days in a row a top general gave a press conference in Ottawa detailing developments in Yugoslavia.[132] But, the generals often misled the public. Asked "whether the Canadians had been targeted, whether they were fired upon and whether they fired in return" during a March 24 sortie in which a Yugoslavian MiG-29 was downed, Ray Henault demured.[133] The deputy chief of Defence Staff said: "They were not involved in that operation."[134] But, Canadians actually led the mission and a Canadian barely evaded a Serbian surface-to-air missile.[135] While a Dutch aircraft downed a Yugoslavian MiG-29, a Canadian pilot missed his bombing target, which ought to have raised questions about civilian casualties.[136]

One reason the military cited for restricting information during the bombing campaign was that it could compromise the security of the Armed Forces and their families. Henault said the media couldn't interview pilots bombing Serbia because "we don't want any risk of family harassment or something of that nature, which, again, is part of that domestic risk we face."[137] Military officials claimed they conducted an assessment into risks for pilots and their families, but Bergen points out that a postwar search of DND records failed to uncover any risk assessment.[138] According to Bergen, Chief of Staff for Joint Operations Brigadier-General David "Jurkowski even considered it [domestic risk] hearsay, but used the myth nonetheless as a reason for restricting the information the Canadian Forces provided to Canadians about the Kosovo air war."[139]

Afghanistan

More than 40,000 Canadian troops fought in Afghanistan between 2001 and 2014.[140] At the height of the fighting in Kandahar DND spent considerable resources spinning the war. The CF produced books, articles and movies about the conflict, as well as embedded reporters, trained journalists and sponsored reporters. Additionally, the $2 billion in aid Canada spent in Afghanistan was at least partially a public relations exercise.[141]

A number of books about the war were financed by the CF or written by soldiers and vetted by Public Affairs prior to publication.[142] The CF also vetted a number of documentaries soldiers produced.[143]

Military produced/vetted content influenced discussion of the war. So did DND-sponsored trips for Canadian opinion leaders and journalists.[144]

But, the military focused its efforts on influencing coverage in major media outlets. PR personnel fed journalists the government's line at "operational briefings", explained James Laxer after perusing documents uncovered through access to information. "At what are called 'message events' where journalists are updated on developments in Afghanistan, officials from Foreign Affairs, National

Defence and the Canadian International Development Agency are to present the government line following 'dry runs' to make sure the briefing motivates journalists to adopt what is called the 'desired sound bite'."[145]

Significant energy was devoted to training/influencing the reporters deployed to Afghanistan. The Journalist Familiarization Course prepared reporters to accompany military patrols all the while deepening their affinity with the military. "The purpose of the course is to make you in the media familiar with us and what we do," PAO Major Jean Morissette told the *National Post*. "The better you understand us, the better it is for us."[146]

In a 2007 *Walrus* article about the Journalist Familiarization Course, Semi Chellas wrote: "At Meadford [training grounds] I also learned this: it's hard to be objective when you're hurtling backward through the air. We'd entrusted the soldiers with our safety and in return we'd hoped to impress them with our courage. There was an exhilarating sense that we were all in this together — and it was only nine in the morning on our first day. As we stood around afterwards with our Dixie cups full of watery green refreshment, one reporter remarked that we were quite literally 'drinking the Kool-Aid.' I can only imagine how difficult it would be to stay objective if your life actually depended on the soldiers around you."[147]

When the Pentagon began training reporters in 2003 it provoked outrage. Yet the Journalist Familiarization Course received little attention.

As it prepared journalists for military life, the CF trained its members to manage reporters in the field. At the Canadian Manoeuvre Training Centre (CMTC) in Wainwright, Alberta, the CF established a "media cell" and hired journalism students to play act as "embedded", "unilateral" and Afghan journalists. According to University of Calgary Centre for Military & Strategic Studies professor Bob Bergen, "the primary purpose of the media cell: training soldiers to become comfortable working with and managing the news media."[148] After the "media cell" exercises garnered attention, the CF barred reporters from observing CMTC.[149]

The CF embedding (or in-bedding) program brought reporters into the military's orbit by allowing them to accompany soldiers on patrol and stay on base. "The military does not embed journalists out of a conviction that the public has a right to know what is going on in Afghanistan", noted Carleton journalism professor Allan Thompson. "The military's mandate is to build support for the Afghanistan mission by using the media to show the troops in action, to 'push information.'"[150]

When they arrived on base senior officers were often on hand to meet journalists. Top officers also built a rapport with reporters during meals and other informal settings. Throughout their stay on base PAOs were in constant contact, helping reporters with their work. After a six-month tour in Afghanistan PAO Major Jay Janzen wrote: "By pushing information to the media, the Battalion was also able to exercise some influence over what journalists decided to cover. When an opportunity to cover a mission or event was proactively presented to a reporter, it almost always received coverage."[151]

Alarmed about a growing casualty list and other negative news, in fall 2006, the Prime Minister's Office directed the military to "push" reconstruction stories on embedded journalists. Through an access request the *Globe and Mail* obtained an email from Major Norbert Cyr saying, "the major concern [at Privy Council Office] is whether we are pushing development and [Foreign Affairs] issues with embeds."[152] In an interview with *Jane's Defence Weekly*'s Canadian correspondent, the embedded journalist described what this meant on the ground. "We've been invited on countless village medical outreach visits, ribbon-cutting ceremonies, and similar events."[153]

In addition to covering stories put forward by the military, 'embeds' tended to frame the conflict from the perspective of the troops they accompanied.[154] By eating and sleeping with Canadian soldiers, reporters often developed a psychological attachment, writes Carleton professor Sherry Wasilow, in *Hidden Ties that Bind: The Psychological Bonds of Embedding Have Changed the Very Nature of War Reporting*.[155]

Embedded journalists' sympathy towards Canadian soldiers was reinforced by the Afghans they interviewed. Afghans critical of Canadian policy were unlikely to express themselves openly with soldiers nearby. Scott Taylor asked, "what would you say if the Romanian military occupied your town and a Romanian tank and journalist showed up at your door? You love the government they have installed and want these guys to stay! Of course the locals are smiling when a reporter shows up with an armoured vehicle and an armed patrol."[156]

Public Affairs officials believed the embedding program "improved" coverage. Major Janzen wrote, "the development of rapport and shared experience resulted in better media relations existing between the military and their embedded media than the military and nonembedded journalists."[157] Another PAO told Bob Bergen that embedding led to sympathetic stories as well as longer-term bonds. "Measuring embedding on the basis of press clippings is an error. The real success is the growth of understanding [of the military] in the media."[158]

Although the embedding program gave journalists access to the military, it deterred (or excluded) other forms of reporting. In *The Savage War: the untold battles of Afghanistan*, Murray Brewster writes, "early in the war the Army had a deep, vested interest in keeping the spotlight squarely and tightly focused on itself. The embedding program was weighted toward telling individual soldier stories, not exploring the bigger picture."[159]

The CF determined who could stay at their base and often they refused independent journalists. In the Fédération professionnelle

A Propaganda System

des journalistes du Québec magazine *Trente*, Louise Bourbonnais described being denied access to the base for a film/book project with a CF media official "subtly making me understand that it is difficult to control an independent journalist."[160] Additionally, reporters outside the wire were blocked from accessing military sites or personnel. When reporting from Afghanistan as a "unilateral" Scott Taylor was refused access to the military on a number of occasions. At one point he was told by a soldier "since you're not embedded, you get no access" to film a medical incident at a Canadian camp.[161]

The embedding program restricted journalists to six-week stays at the Kandahar base. The reason, according to Taylor, is "the less time you spend there, the easier it is to get fooled."[162]

Most Canadian journalists who gathered news in Afghanistan did so under the CF Media Embedding Program Ground Rules. As part of the agreement, reporters had to focus primarily on CF and Canadian government activities. A reporter could be expelled for spending "an inordinate amount of time covering non-military activities", which was an attempt to discourage journalists from covering Afghans.[163]

Under the embed agreement the military could also restrict the release of information and images. It allowed the CF to control "any other information the task force commander orders restricted for operational reasons."[164]

"The censorship," noted *Globe and Mail* reporter Geoffrey York, was "tougher and more arbitrary than I had expected."[165] After several extended stays in Afghanistan, Canadian Press reporter Murray Brewster said, "I can't emphasize enough how political this thing [embedding rules] was. It's all about protecting the brand."[166] Another Canadian Press reporter concurred. Bill Graveland noted, "they are really, seriously trying to manage the media."[167]

(Some reporters, of course, embraced the embedding program. Erstwhile Postmedia militarist, Matthew Fisher, boasted he was "embedded more in Afghanistan than any other reporter" while the *Globe and Mail's* Christie Blatchford said it was "fascinating" spending time with the troops.[168])

The military/government closely monitored embedded reporters. In an email the *Globe and Mail* acquired through an access request, PAO Norbert Cyr reported that the Privy Council requested "to know which embeds are in theatre and what they are doing." Information about journalists' stories, questions and the information divulged to them was compiled and circulated to the Ottawa headquarters of Joint Task Force Afghanistan, Foreign Affairs, CIDA, CF Psychological Operations and the Privy Council Office.[169] The CP's Graveland complained about PAOs monitoring his interviews. He described "giant satellite dishes" through which the military "check emails and eavesdrop on telephone calls. They watch everything we do. They know immediately what we've written or what we're saying."[170]

A number of journalists who broke the embedding agreement were subject to "immediate removal" from military facilities.[171] On February 12, 2002, *Toronto Star* reporter Mitch Potter was removed from a base after reporting on JTF2 special-forces night operations as well as the guard towers around a prisoner detention centre.[172] Potter claimed his expulsion was retaliation for criticizing the restrictions placed on journalists.[173]

On a number of occasions the CF reprimanded embeds or suddenly removed them from a base. After reporting on a Chinook helicopter crash he survived, Canadian Press journalist Colin Perkel said he faced "excommunication", which meant the CF refused to take him on patrol or provide him with information.[174] In another instance of the military asserting its power over 'embeds', Christie Blatchford, *Toronto Star* reporter Rosie Dimanno and two other journalists were suddenly removed from a forward operating base by helicopter after a Canadian and US soldier were killed by friendly fire.[175] The military told them it was for their safety, but a *Globe and Mail* access to information requested document suggests an ally, probably US special forces, asked for their removal.[176]

The military relied on special forces partly as a PR strategy. While they likely participated in controversial night-time assassination raids and a JTF2 soldier claimed his commanders "encouraged" war crimes, it's difficult to know the scope of special forces operations. "At the Kandahar airfield", *Shadow Wars* explains, "Canadian military public affairs officers threatened journalists with expulsion from the installation if they dare to write about special forces operating from the base. Some reporters were even told not to look in the direction of the JTF2 compound as they walked by."[177]

Throughout the war special forces were on the ground. "What Canadians don't seem to understand is that ... Special Forces have been on the ground continuously since 2001", noted Murray Brewster. "Even when our battle groups haven't been there, they've been there. It's a huge hole in our understanding of what has gone on in Afghanistan."[178]

The government sought to restrict information at home as well. As the Canadian death toll rose, in April 2006, the government barred journalists from attending the ceremonies where soldiers' bodies were repatriated.[179] Eleven months later the Strategic Joint Staff established a "Tiger Team" to scrutinize access requests, which were already screened through the standard procedure. It was a response to the Military Police Complaint Commission investigation into detainees Canadian troops delivered to Afghan security forces knowing they would likely be abused.[180] Ultimately, the "Tiger Team" dealt with virtually all Afghanistan related access requests. "Any ATI [Access] request for information related to DETAINEES, or Battle Damage Assessments (any report, SOP, SIR, sitrep related to IEDs, Vehicle Damage, casualties, protection, armour enhancements) is to be severed in its entirety less the address group at the top of the

A Propaganda System

correspondence," wrote the Director General of Operations with the Strategic Joint Staff, Brigadier-General Peter Atkinson, in an email to colleagues describing the "Tiger Team".[181] "The rationale for doing so, is that this information if allowed to go into the public domain can be used by our enemies ie the Taliban, to further target and make assessments on their effectiveness against our own troops ... it is based on these issues that the information identified above cannot be released as it puts our troops at greater risk."[182]

The military restricted ever more information as the war progressed. In February 2008 Atkinson told the media: "Your appetite for information serves positive and lawful objectives of our Canadian democracy ... [But] here is an excerpt from an Al-Qaeda training manual with respect to their use of information sources. They identify that an organization must gather as much information as possible about the enemy, in other words about us. Information in their words has two sources: Public sources. Using this public source openly and without resorting to illegal means it is possible to gather at least 80% of the information about the enemy. ... So we need to make their collection efforts as difficult as possible, by denying them 80% of the solution."[183] In other words, the Canadian public should be kept in the dark about its Armed Forces' actions in Afghanistan.

The federal government took extreme measures to suppress information about the military. On December 10, 2009, the opposition parties, which were then in the majority, passed a motion requiring the release of all un-redacted documents concerning Afghan detainees to the parliamentary committee hearing the issue. The Stephen Harper Conservatives refused, which may have violated the constitution and put it in contempt of Parliament. On December 30, 2009, the prime minister "prorogued" (suspended) Parliament to prevent the committee from continuing to probe the issue. Opposition MPs, reported CBC.ca, called this "move an 'almost despotic' attempt to muzzle parliamentarians amid controversy over the Afghan detainees affair."[184]

Libya

Canada played a significant role in the 2011 NATO attack on Libya. A Canadian general led the bombing campaign, seven CF-18 fighter jets participated, two Canadian naval vessels patrolled the Libyan coast and Canadian special forces were likely on the ground. (See my *The Ugly Canadian* for more detail.)

In the lead-up to the NATO intervention, the rebels accused Gaddafi's forces of mass rape, a charge that was repeated by Western media and politicians. Canadian foreign minister John Baird was still repeating the mass rape justification for bombing Libya months after Gaddafi was killed. At the end of 2011 he told CTV: "When you talk about rape as an instrument of war, women being raped in Libya, it's a very uncomfortable issue. Just ignoring it, throwing it under the carpet, it's not an option."[185] But did Gaddafi's forces engage in mass rape? Probably not, according to Human Rights Watch and Amnesty International investigators. Amnesty's senior crisis response adviser Donatella Rovera, who was in Libya for three months after the start of the uprising, said:"We have not found any evidence or a single victim of rape or a doctor who knew about somebody being raped."[186] Liesel Gerntholtz, head of women's rights at Human Rights Watch, concurred. "We have not been able to find evidence [of mass rape]."[187]

One of the main incidents that justified the intervention was the claim that on February 21, 2011, Libyan helicopters and fighter jets fired and dropped bombs on civilians. Without any video proof Qatar's *Al Jazeera* broadcast these accusations, which were picked up by much of the Western media. Some even talked of genocide. During a high profile post-war celebration Prime Minister Stephen Harper repeated a variation of this claim. "The Gaddafi regime responded, unleashing the full fury of the state — police, army and air force — against them, calling all who protested 'germs, rats, scumbags and cockroaches,' and demanded Libya be cleansed 'house by house'. It was an invitation to genocide."[188]

But, what's the evidence for this accusation? Researchers from both the International Crisis Group (ICG) and Amnesty International couldn't find any evidence that Gaddafi's forces fired on civilians from fighter jets or helicopters. In June 2011 the ICG explained: "There are grounds for questioning the more sensational reports that the regime was using its air force to slaughter demonstrators, let alone engaging in anything remotely warranting use of the term 'genocide.'"[189]

Globe and Mail and *Toronto Star* reporters who traveled to the base in Italy where Canadian jets flew from weren't allowed to interview the pilots.[190] Once again, the reason given for restricting media access was protecting pilots and their families. Major Leah Byrne said, "the concern is that not everyone is in favour of this air campaign and what we are doing. Until a thorough threat analysis could be completed it was determined that only the detachment commander would speak to the media. Due to their positions they have an added level of responsibility and with this comes any additional risk that might (or might not) be associated with having their name in public."[191]

But, the military released some photos to get the public in the fighting spirit. At the start of the NATO bombing campaign the CF released onboard video footage of a CF-18 destroying a Libyan weapons depot.[192] After Muammar Gaddafi was killed in October 2011 the government spent $850,000 on a nationally televised celebration for the troops that fought in Libya.[193]

Syria/Iraq

The military was tight-lipped about Canadian Forces fighting in Iraq and Syria. At an October 2014 press event for soldiers departing to the Middle East, PAO Julie Brunet asked photographers at CFB Trenton to delete pictures showing destination stickers with "Kuwait City, Kuwait."[194] Apparently, the military didn't want the public knowing Canadian warplanes operated from a base in Kuwait (though it was already public knowledge).[195]

Reporters complained about limited access to the forces in Kuwait.[196] NATO Association of Canada blogger Kelsey Berg noted, "the media has been barred from entering Canadian air bases in Kuwait, the strategic centre of operation IMPACT. This means that official DND public briefings have been the only source for news on the ongoing combat mission."[197]

To justify restricting photos and interviews of CF members dispatched to the Middle East DND again claimed concern for soldiers and their families' safety.[198] Since the first Gulf War they've repeatedly invoked this rationale to restrict information during air wars. But, as Bob Bergen reveals in *Balkan Rats and Balkan Bats: The art of managing Canada's news media during the Kosovo air war*, it was based on a rumour that antiwar protesters put body bags on the lawn of a Canadian pilot during the 1991 Gulf War.[199] It likely never happened and, revealingly, the military didn't invoke fear of domestic retribution to curtail interviews during the more contentious ground war in Afghanistan. Bergen points out how air wars lend themselves to censorship since journalists cannot accompany pilots during their missions or easily see what's happening from afar. "As a result," Bergen writes, "crews can only be interviewed before or after their missions, and journalists' reports can be supplemented by cockpit footage of bombings."[200]

In early 2016 the Justin Trudeau-led Liberal government withdrew fighter jets from the Middle East. At the same time they tripled the number of highly secretive Canadian special forces operating in Iraq.

***

As these short descriptions reveal, Canada's dynamic propaganda system is prepared to obfuscate, suppress and lie during war. This flagrant manipulation of public opinion is dangerous to democracy.

8. Conclusion

Just as this country's obsession with professional hockey does not just happen, Canadians' opinions about their country's role internationally is not a historical accident or 'natural' occurrence. Rather, it reflects the work of numerous institutions designed to influence public opinion, which together represent a powerful propaganda system.

On a number of occasions I've been told "Canadians don't care about the damage the government causes abroad." During speaking engagements questioners often say "what you're describing is terrible but it's been going on for a long time and the public isn't bothered."

Apparently, many politically conscious individuals believe Canadians are indifferent to Ottawa's international abuses. But, as this book shows, the foreign policy establishment doesn't believe this to be the case. If they did they wouldn't spend significant sums to obfuscate their international actions. Nor would they lie or censor information. In that sense DND and GAC's PR efforts represent a hopeful sign for internationalist political movements.

A central objective of this book has been to outline the obstacles Canadians face in understanding their country's place in the world. I hope readers find it empowering to learn why the public is so confused about Canada's international role. While indifference abounds, the primary explanation for the gap between what Canadians believe their government is doing abroad and their actions are the state and corporate forces that shape foreign policy discussion. (A second volume will detail how "the left" has contributed to confusion over Canadian foreign policy.)

The propaganda apparatus outlined also sheds light on the nature of Canadian foreign policy and political culture. A large PR machine is required when an institution seeks to obfuscate an

A Propaganda System

unsavoury reality. Barrick Gold's corporate social responsibility initiatives, for instance, are an effort to deflect criticism of its rights violations. Similarly, Ottawa's PR campaign in Afghanistan intensified alongside fighting and controversy over the war.

At a broader level, "do-gooder" foreign policy mythology is designed to lull the population into backing interventionist policies. If the public assumes the best of decision-makers they are unlikely to watch closely, particularly when an issue is far removed from their lives. In this way the benevolent mythology functions as a sort of 'free pass' for decision-makers when actual Canadian foreign policy history suggests the need for close attention.

And whose role is it to pay attention to what governments and corporations are doing?

This book should serve as a challenge and warning to journalists/academics regarding information control. On most domestic issues serious reporters don't simply puppet government press releases. But, journalists' "bullshit antennas" seem to weaken when covering Canada abroad. At the very least journalists have an ethical responsibility to investigate and mention opinions contradicting official foreign policy.

Beyond the moral question, journalists ought to be wary of DND/GAC propaganda for their own good. Former *Montréal Gazette* reporter Sue Montgomery's experience with the Canadian ambassador in Port-au-Prince highlights the matter. In "Parachute Journalism in Haiti: Media Sourcing in the 2003-2004 Political Crisis", Isabel Macdonald writes: "Montgomery recalled being given anti-Aristide disinformation when she called the Canadian embassy immediately after she had been held up by armed men while driving through Port-au-Prince days before the coup. Canada's ambassador to Haiti, Kenneth Cook, told her, 'We've got word that Aristide has given the order to the chimeres [purported pro-Aristide thugs] to do this kind of thing to international journalists because he's not getting any support.' According to Montgomery, Cook had urged her to tell the other international journalists who were staying at the same hotel: 'I think you should let all your colleagues at the Montana know that it's not safe for them.'"[1]

Given only two days to prepare for her assignment, Montgomery was ripe for official manipulation. Though she later realized the ambassador's claim was ridiculous, Montgomery told other journalists at Hotel Montana (where most international journalists stay in Port-au-Prince) that Aristide's supporters were targeting them. While Montgomery had both the courage and an avenue to admit her mistake, other reporters have probably had similar experiences without informing the public.

Since overthrowing a government, going to war or any number of other foreign policy decisions can lead to significant suffering, complicity in said affairs can weigh on one's conscience. And the growing accessibility of international news makes it increasingly difficult to avoid the ramifications of one's actions.

Information dissemination/opinion formation is especially important in relatively free societies. When the public has the right (in theory, if not always in practice) to vote, protest, speak freely etc. a hierarchical political system requires non-coercive means to "manufacture consent". In a military or totalitarian state Noam Chomsky notes, "you just hold a bludgeon over their heads and if they get out of line you just smash them over the head, but as societies become more free and democratic you lose that capacity and therefore you have to turn to the techniques of propaganda."[2]

Rather than controlling the population by force, the Canadian state/corporate nexus does so through control over information. The "father" of US public relations pointed this out nearly a century ago. In his 1928 book *Propaganda*, Edward Bernays writes, "the conscious and intelligent manipulation of the organized habits and opinions of the masses is an important element in democratic society. Those who manipulate this unseen mechanism of society constitute an invisible government which is the true ruling power of our country."[3]

***

An important, if rarely mentioned, rule of Canadian foreign policy enabled by the propaganda system outlined above, is the more impoverished a nation, the greater the gap is likely to be between what Canadian officials say and do. The primary explanation for the gap between what's said and done is that power generally defines what is considered reality. So, the bigger the power imbalance between Canada and another country the greater Ottawa's ability to distort their activities.

Haiti provides a stark example. In 2004 Ottawa helped overthrow Haiti's elected government and then supported an installed regime that killed thousands. Officially, however, Ottawa was "helping" the beleaguered country as part of the "Friends of Haiti" group. And the bill for undermining Haitian democracy, including the salaries of top coup government officials and the training of repressive cops, was largely paid out of Canada's "aid" to the country.[4]

A stark power imbalance between Ottawa and Port-au-Prince helps explain the gulf between Canadian government claims and reality in Haiti. Describing the country at the time of Aristide's ouster, former *Globe and Mail* foreign editor Paul Knox observed, "obviously, in the poorest country of the Americas, the government is going to have fewer resources at its disposal to mount a PR exercise or offensive if it feels itself besieged."[5]

With a $300 US million total budget for a country of eight million, the Haitian government had limited means to explain their perspective to the world either directly or through international journalists.[6] On the other hand, the Washington–Paris–Ottawa coup triumvirate had great capacity to propagate their perspective (CIDA and Foreign Affairs each spent 10 times the entire Haitian budget and DND 60 times). The large Canadian embassy in Port-au-

Prince worked to influence Canadian reporters in the country and their efforts were supplanted by the Haiti desks at CIDA and Foreign Affairs as well as the two ministries' communications departments.

While an imbalance in communications resources partly explains the coverage, there is also a powerful ideological component. The media's biased coverage of Haiti cannot be divorced from 'righteous Canada' assumptions widely held among the Canadian intelligentsia. CBC reporter Neil McDonald told researcher Isabel McDonald the Canadian government was "one of the most authoritative sources on conflict resolution in the world."[7] According to Isabel McDonald's summary, the prominent correspondent also said, "it was crazy to imagine Canada would be involved in a coup" and that "Canadian values were incompatible with extreme inequality or race-based hegemony", which Ottawa's policies clearly exacerbated in Haiti.[8]

The Canadian Council on Africa provides another example of the rhetoric that results from vast power imbalances and paternalist assumptions. Run by Canadian corporations operating on the continent, the council says it "focuses on the future of the African economy and the positive role that Canada can play meeting some of the challenges in Africa."[9]

Similar to the Canadian Council on Africa, the Canadian American Business Council, Canada China Business Council and Canada-UK Chamber of Commerce also seek to advance members' profit-making potential. But, the other lobby groups don't claim humanitarian objectives. The primary difference between the Canadian Council on Africa and the other regional lobby organizations is the power imbalance between Canada/the West and African countries, as well as the anti-African paternalism that dominates Canadian political culture. A group of Canadian corporations claiming their aim was to meet the social challenges of the US or UK would sound bizarre and if they said as much about China they would be considered seditious. (Ironically the

A Propaganda System

US-, Britain- and China-focused lobby groups can better claim the aid mantle since foreign investment generally has greater social spinoffs in more independent/better regulated countries.) But, paternalist assumptions are so strong — and Africans' capacity to assert themselves within Canadian political culture so limited — that a lobby group largely representing corporations that displace impoverished communities to extract natural resources is, according to the Canadian Council on Africa's mission statement, "committed to the economic development of a modern and competitive Africa."[10]

Chair of the Canadian Council on Africa Board, Benoit La Salle, provides a stark example of a 'humanitarian capitalist' abusing his power and 'good guy Canada' paternalism to wildly distort reality. In a 2012 *Gold Report* interview titled "First, Do Good When Mining for Gold: Benoit La Salle", the president of the Société d'Exploitation Minière d'Afrique de l'Ouest (SEMAFO) boasted about the company's social responsibility. La Salle said: "SEMAFO is not a company that mines gold, ships it out and, once that is done, breaks down camp and leaves. People see SEMAFO as being a very good corporate citizen. Today, many people believe that the CSR report is more important than our annual report."[11] This is a startling claim for an individual obligated to maximize investors' returns and a cursory look at the company's record suggests it has little basis in reality.

Those living near SEMAFO's Kiniero mine, reported *Guinée News* in 2014, felt "the Canadian company brought more misfortune than benefits."[12] The military killed three in a bid to drive away small-scale miners from its mine in southeast Guinea in 2008 and three years later protests flared again over the company's failure to hire local young people and the dissolution of a committee that spent community development monies.[13] In 2014 the Guinean government concluded that the Montréal firm evaded $9.6 million in tax, recommending that SEMAFO be fined and stripped of its mining rights in the country.[14]

To the east, SEMAFO opened the first industrial scale gold mine in Niger. In a 2007 interview La Salle described how the prime minister helped his company break a strike at its Samira Hill mine. "He gave us all the right direction to solve this legally," La Salle said. 'We went to court, we had the strike declared illegal and that allowed us to let go of some of the employees and rehire some of them based upon a new work contract. It allowed us to let go of some undesirable employees because they had been on strike a few times."[15]

The bitter strike led to a parliamentary inquiry regarding environmental damage caused by the mine, lack of benefits for local communities and treatment of miners. SEMAFO was also accused of failing to pay both taxes and dividends to the government. Despite owning a 20% share in the Samira Hill mine, the Guinean government received no direct payments from the Montréal-based majority owner between 2004 and 2010.[16]

Next-door, La Salle worked closely with President Blaise Compaoré for nearly two decades, traveling the globe singing the Burkina Faso government's praise. After leaving office the prime minister between 2007–2011, Tertius Zongo, was appointed to SEMAFO's Board of Directors and at a September 2014 Gold Forum in Australia SEMAFO officials lauded the Burkina Faso government as "democratic and stable".[17] The next month President Compaoré was ousted by popular protest after he attempted to amend the constitution to extend term limits. After ending Compaoré's 27-year rule community groups and mine workers launched a wave of protests against foreign, mostly Canadian, owned mining companies, including SEMAFO.

The Montréal company is an outgrowth of La Salle's work for Plan Canada, part of a $1 billion a year global NGO. La Salle said SEMAFO "was created in 1995 during my first visit to Burkina Faso as part of a mission with the NGO-Plan."[18] As Plan Canada's designated Francophone spokesperson La Salle got to know Compaoré who asked him to "help his country develop its mining sector."[19] La Salle procured mining expertise while Compaoré granted the Canadian a massive stretch of land to prospect. "The land package we have is way beyond what you'd see anywhere else in the world," La Salle boasted.[20] Compaoré was good to La Salle. The Canadian 'humanitarian' made millions of dollars from Burkina Faso's (and Niger and Guinea's) minerals. When he resigned after 17 years as president of SEMAFO in 2012, La Salle received a $3 million departure bonus, which was on top of his $1 million salary and the stock he owns in the firm.[21]

La Salle is just one in a long line of Westerners who've asked the world to believe what they say but ignore the results of what they do — a "spin-sploiter" — publicly professing humanitarian ideals all the while exploiting the world's most vulnerable. He knows the villagers and workers in Guinea or Burkina Faso, who may have a different view of SEMAFO's actions, aren't well placed to contradict his claims.

***

We need an organized system of truth telling about what Canada does abroad to counter the impact of the propaganda system outlined in this book. An element that could help in this regard, is an opposition party that seriously challenged Canadian foreign policy.

During Bernie Sanders' campaign to win the Democratic Party nomination for president in 2016 he criticized Washington's role in overthrowing Jacob Arbenz in Guatemala and Mohammed Mossadegh in Iran as well as the US war in Indochina and a number of other historic foreign policy decisions. It made me wonder if a leading Canadian politician had ever criticized a past foreign policy move. It's hard to imagine an NDP leader saying, "we shouldn't blindly follow Washington's war aims since that led Lester Pearson's government to deliver US bombing threats to North Vietnam in violation of international law." Nor can one imagine a politician saying, "as we evaluate our support for this UN mission let's not forget the blow Canadian peacekeepers delivered to central Africa when they helped undermine Congolese independence leader Patrice Lumumba."

Politicians don't even criticize destructive recent interventions such as Canada's participation in the 2011 war on Libya. It's as if there's a sign hanging in Parliament that says: "foreign policy mythologizers only."

While politicians largely refuse to criticize past foreign policy decisions, they happily mythologize their own decisions. On the tenth anniversary of the US-led invasion of Iraq former Prime Minister Jean Chrétien boasted that he never believed Iraq had amassed weapons of mass destruction and that staying out of the war was "a decision that the people of Muslim faith and Arab culture have appreciated very much from Canada, and it was the right decision."[22]

While the more liberal end of the dominant media regurgitated the former PM's claim, it's completely false to say Canada did not participate in the 2003 invasion of Iraq. As The Coalition to Oppose the Arms Trade's Richard Sanders has detailed, dozens of Canadian troops were integrated in US units fighting in Iraq; US warplanes en route to that country refuelled in Newfoundland; with Canadian naval vessels leading maritime interdiction efforts off the coast of Iraq, Ottawa had legal opinion suggesting it was technically at war with that country; Canadian fighter pilots participated in "training" missions in Iraq; three different Canadian generals oversaw tens of thousands of international troops there; Canadian aid flowed to the country in support of US policy.[23] As such, some have concluded that Canada was the fifth or sixth biggest contributor to the US-led war.

But the Chrétien government didn't do what the George W. Bush administration wanted above all else, which was to publicly endorse the invasion by joining the "coalition of the willing". Notwithstanding Chrétien's claims, this wasn't because he distrusted Bush's pre-war intelligence or because of any moral principle. Rather, the Liberal government refused to join the "coalition of the willing" because hundreds of thousands of Canadians took to the streets against the war, particularly in Québec. With the biggest demonstrations taking place in Montréal and Québecers strongly opposed to the war, the federal government feared that openly endorsing the invasion would boost the sovereignist Parti Québecois vote in the next provincial election.

So the Chrétien Liberals found a middle ground between the massive anti-war mobilization and Canada's long-standing ties to US imperialism. Most stories about Chrétien's decision on Iraq erased the role popular protest played in this important decision, focusing instead on an enlightened leader who simply chose to do the right thing.

Of course the Iraq war was not the first time that popular movements forced the hand of foreign policy decision-makers. Or the first time that the "official story" ignored the role of protesters. Or the first time that the myth makers twisted the truth to promote the notion of a benevolent Canadian foreign policy.

Take the example of Ottawa's move to adopt sanctions against apartheid South Africa in 1986. After Nelson Mandela died former Prime Minister Brian Mulroney and his Ambassador to the UN Stephen Lewis boasted that their government sanctioned South Africa. But, few in the media mentioned the two decades of international solidarity activism that exposed and opposed Canadian corporate and diplomatic support for the racist regime. (And, similar to the Liberals refusal to join the "coalition of the willing" in Iraq, Canadian sanctions against South Africa were half measures). Even though Ottawa prioritized corporate and geostrategic interests above the injustices taking place there for many decades, much is made about Canada's morally righteous position on apartheid South Africa.

The dynamics were similar with the 1973 coup in Chile. The Pierre Trudeau government was hostile to Salvador Allende's elected government and predisposed to supporting Augusto Pinochet's military dictatorship. In the midst of widespread torture and killings in the days after the coup against Allende, Canadian ambassador to Chile Andrew Ross cabled External Affairs: "Reprisals and searches have created panic atmosphere affecting particularly expatriates including the riffraff of the Latin American Left to whom Allende gave asylum ... the country has been on a prolonged political binge under the elected Allende government and the junta has assumed the probably thankless task of sobering Chile up."[24]

Canadian leftists were outraged at Ottawa's support for the coup and its unwillingness to accept refugees hunted by the military regime. Many denounced the federal government's policy and some (my mother among them) occupied various Chilean and Canadian government offices in protest. The Trudeau government was surprised at the depth of the opposition. A confidential 1974 cabinet document lamented that "the attention ... focused on the Chilean Government's use of repression against its opponents has led to an unfavourable reaction among the Canadian public — a reaction which will not permit any significant increase in Canadian aid to this country."[25]

Similar to Chrétien on Iraq, the Trudeau government tried to placate the protesters all the while pursuing a pro-US/pro-corporate policy. Canadian investment and business relations with Chile grew substantially after the coup. But, Ottawa allowed refugees from the Pinochet dictatorship asylum in Canada. As a result of the protests, thousands of refugees from the Pinochet (1973-90) dictatorship gained asylum in Canada, leaving many with the impression that Canada was somehow sympathetic to Chile's left. But, this view of Canada's relationship to Chile is as far from the truth as Baffin Island is from Tierra del Fuego.

Like Iraq, the partial activist victories regarding South Africa and Chile have been twisted to reinforce the idea that Canadian foreign policy is benevolent. And this myth, which obscures the corporate and geostrategic interests that overwhelmingly drive

Canadian foreign policy, is an obstacle to building effective opposition to Ottawa's destructive role in international affairs.

With politicians and establishment commentators refusing to credit activists, it is important militants write their own history. A better understanding of the power of solidarity and activist victories will strengthen challenges to Canadian foreign policy.

***

Social movement activism can force ideas onto the agenda and prompt people to pay attention. While the dominant media's subservience to the foreign policy establishment is more pronounced than most critics imagine, it's definitely not absolute. During three years of Haiti solidarity activism I witnessed a mix of hard to believe disinformation/omission, and ways dissidents can disseminate information via the dominant media.

Through timely, aggressive and creative interventions Haiti Action Montréal countered the dominant media's silence/deception. We did so by working with progressive elements within Montréal's large Haitian community, which opened up local media angles, and a pan Canadian network of solidarity activists who documented Ottawa's violent, antidemocratic, policies in Haiti.

Despite the hostile media climate in Québec, Haiti Action Montréal developed important relations with *La Presse* and *Montréal Gazette* journalists. By sending him press releases and invites to events Jooneed Khan helped us relay information to *La Presse* readers. While sympathetic to our work, the veteran international affairs writer was not in a position to communicate more than small bits of the rapidly unfolding story. But, in an indication of how a veteran journalist can circumvent institutional constraints, Khan used space made available to him by the February 2006 election upheaval in Haiti to briefly mention (twice) the meeting where Canadian officials discussed ousting President Aristide 13 months before the coup. This was the only time (to the best of my knowledge) that a corporate daily journalist mentioned the Ottawa Initiative on Haiti after the coup.

To bring Khan aboard we reached out and organized events, but relations with *Montréal Gazette* reporter Sue Montgomery demanded a different tack. Duped by Canadian officials and Ottawa-funded organizations in Haiti (see above), Montgomery was not generally a sycophant for the rich and powerful. In fact, a year earlier she condemned the Montréal police for sending 19 vehicles to arrest me for handing out leaflets at Concordia University. (For more about the arrest and my time as a Concordia Student Union vice president in the aftermath of the 2002 Benjamin Netanyahu protests see *Playing Left-Wing: From Rink Rat to Student Radical*) A few months after the coup I described Montgomery as "once progressive" in a piece criticizing her coverage of Haiti. The article sparked the hoped-for reaction, contributing to a re-evaluation of her position. Over the next year and a half she performed a 180° turn on the issue and during the 2006 federal election campaign Montgomery wrote an opinion piece titled "Voters should punish MPs for Haiti".[26] It argued that Foreign Minister Pierre Pettigrew and the prime minister's special advisor on Haiti, Denis Coderre, should lose their seats for undermining Haitian democracy. As the resident Haiti expert at the *Gazette*, Montgomery's change of position opened up a more sympathetic airing of Haiti Action Montréal's views by other reporters, notably Jeff Heinrich.

Montgomery and Khan helped Haiti Action Montréal relay critical information about Canada's devastating role in Haiti to the public. A small, all volunteer, group of committed activists pierced powerful bias through creative, timely and aggressive media work.

But, our media efforts took place alongside less 'sophisticated' activism. Haiti Action Montréal plastered thousands of event and demonstration posters and tens of thousands of "Canada out of Haiti" stickers across the city. Linked to a website, the stickers were a

A Propaganda System

way to reach people outside the dominant media (a quarter million stickers were distributed across the country). They even spurred *Montréal Mirror* editor Patrick Lejtenyi to publish a 2,500 word cover story critical of Canada's role in Haiti. The multipage spread in the free weekly included a picture and mention of the stickers covering the cityscape.

The *Montréal Mirror* story appeared during Haiti Action Montréal's campaign to defeat Foreign Minister Pierre Pettigrew in the 2006 election. We fashioned some posters featuring Pettigrew's image with the words "WANTED FOR CRIMES AGAINST HUMANITY IN HAITI". It wasn't subtle, but it had the virtue of being true. We saturated the riding, putting up 2,000 posters, handing out over 12,000 flyers and organizing a few actions. After Pettigrew lost his seat *La Presse* and *Le Devoir* credited our campaign with playing a spoiler role.

This suggests small groups, organized around telling the truth, can impact far-off policy. It also demonstrates that the public cares about what Canada does abroad, if they know about it.

As this book has outlined, the propaganda system enabling nefarious Canadian behaviour is well resourced and has influential friends, but this Goliath can be weakened by a small band of dedicated David activists armed with slingshots that spread the truth.

Bibliography

Abelson, Donald E. Do Think Tanks Matter? Assessing the Impact of Public Policy Institutes, McGill-Queen's University Press, 2002

Aitken, Ian. The Concise Routledge Encyclopedia of the Documentary Film, Routledge, 2013

Andersen, Robin. A century of media, a century of war, Peter Lang, 2006

Allen, Gene. Making National News: a History of Canadian Press, University of Toronto Press, 2013

Axelrod, Paul and John G. Reid, Youth, University and Canadian society: Essays in the Social History of Higher Education, McGill-Queen's University Press, 1989

Balawyder, Aloysius. In the Clutches of the Kremlin: Canadian–East European Relations, 1945–1962, Columbia University Press, 2000

Balzer, Timothy John. The Information Front, UBC Press, 2011

Bell, Ken and Desmond Morton. Royal Canadian Military Institute: 100 years, RCMI, 1990

Berman, Edward H. The influence of the Carnegie, Ford and Rockefeller Foundations on American Foreign policy, State University of New York Press, 1983

Berton, Pierre. Marching As to War: Canada's Turbulent Years, 1899-1953, Doubleday Canada, 2001

Beylerian, Onnig and Jacques Lévesque, Inauspicious Beginnings: Principal Powers and International Security, McGill-Queen's University Press, 2004

Bindon, Kathryn M. Queens men, Canada's men: the military history of Queen's University, Trustees of the Queen's University Contingent, 1978

Booh Booh, Jacques-Roger. Le patron de Dallaire parle: Révélations sur les dérives d'un général de l'ONU au Rwanda, Duboiris, 2005

Bourrie, Mark. The Fog of War: Censorship of Canada's Media in World War Two, Douglas & McIntyre, 2011

Bourrie, Mark. Fighting Words: Canada's Best War Reporting, Dundurn, 2012

Brandon, Laura. Art Or Memorial? The Forgotten History of Canada's War Art, University of Calgary Press, 2006

Brewster, Murray. The Savage War: The Untold Battles of Afghanistan, J. Wiley & Sons Canada, 2011

Brouwer, Ruth Compton. Canada's Global Villagers: CUSO in Development, UBC Press, 2013.

Brownlee, Jamie. Academia Inc.: How Corporatization Is Transforming Canadian Universities, Fernwood Publishing, 2015

Cahill, Jack. If You Don't Like the War, Switch the Damn Thing Off!, Musson Book Co., 1980

Cameron, Maxwell A. and Maureen Appel Molot. Canada Among Nations, 1995: Democracy and Foreign Policy, Carleton University Press, 1995

Carty, Robert, Virginia Smith and Latin American Working Group. Perpetuating poverty: the political economy of Canadian foreign aid, Between-the-lines, 1981

Chapnick, Adam. Canada's Voice: the public life of John Wendell Holmes, UBC Press, 2009

Comeau, Paul André, La démocratie en veilleuse: rapport sur la censure: récit de l'organisation, des activités et de la démobilisation de la censure pendant la guerre de 1939-45, Québec-Amérique, 1995

Comeau, Paul-André, Claude Beauregard and Edwidge Munn Come Conlin, Dan. War through the lens: the Canadian Army film and photo unit, Seraphim Editions, 2015

Cook, Tim. Clio's Warriors: Canadian Historians and the Writing of the World Wars, UBC Press, 2006

Dyer, Gwynne. Canada in the great game, Random House Canada, 2014

Edge, Marc. Asper Nation: Canada's Most Dangerous Media Company, New Star Books, 2007

Evans, Gary. John Grierson and the National Film Board: The politics of wartime propaganda, University of Toronto Press, 1984

Eglin, Peter. Intellectual Citizenship and the Problem of Incarnation, University Press of America, 2013

Engler, Yves and Anthony Fenton. Canada in Haiti: Waging War on the Poor Majority, Fernwood, 2005

Engler, Yves. Playing Left Wing: From Rink Rat to Student Radical, Fernwood, 2005

Fergusson, James G. Canada and ballistic missile defense, UBC Press, 2010

Forte, Maximilian C. The New Imperialism, Volume II: Interventionism, Information Warfare, and the Military-Academic Complex, Alert Press, 2011

Freedman, Jim. Transforming Development: foreign aid for a changing world, University of Toronto Press, 2000

Franck, Thomas M. and Edward Weisband, Secrecy and Foreign policy, Oxford University Press, 1974

Gendron, Robin S. Towards a Francophone Community: Canada's Relations with France and French Africa, 1945-1968, McGill-Queen's University Press, 2006

Grey, Jeffrey. The last word? Essays on Official History in the United States and British Commonwealth, Praeger, 2003

Hackett, Robert A. The Missing News: Filters and Blind Spots in Canada's Press, Garamond Press, 2000

Hampson, Fen Osler and Christopher J. Maule. Canada Among Nations, 1993-94: Global Jeopardy, Carleton University Press, 1994

Hale, James. Branching Out: the story of the Royal Canadian Legion, Royal Canadian Legion, 1995

Hall, James. Radio Canada International: voice of a middle power, Michigan State University Press, 1997

Haycock, Ronald G. Sam Hughes: the public career of a controversial Canadian, 1985 – 1916, Wilfrid Laurier Press, 1986

Heinbecker, Paul and Bessma Momani. Canada and the Middle East: in theory and practice, Wilfrid Laurier University Press, 2007

Herman, Edward and David Peterson. Enduring Lies: The Rwandan Genocide in the Propaganda System, 20 Years Later, The Real News Books, 2014

Ismael, Jacqueline and Tareq Ismael. Canada and the New American Empire, University of Calgary Press, 2004

James, Lawrence. The Savage Wars: British Campaigns in Africa, 1870-1920, St. Martin's Press, 1986

Keshen, Jeffrey A. Propaganda and Censorship during Canada's great war, University of Alberta Press, 1996

Klaehn, Jefferey. Filtering the News: essays on Herman and Chomsky's propaganda model, Black Rose Books, 2005

Klaehn, Jeffery. Bound by Power: Intended Consequences, Black Rose Books, 2006

Klassen, Jerome. Joining Empire: The Political Economy of the New Canadian Foreign Policy, University of Toronto Press, 2014

Klassen, Jerome and Greg Albo, Empire's Ally: Canada and the War in Afghanistan, University of Toronto Press, 2013

Klein, Ruth L. Nazi Germany: Canadian Responses Confronting Antisemitism in the Shadow of War, McGill-Queen's University Press, 2012

Langille, Peter. Changing the Guard: Canada's Defence in a World in Transition, University of Toronto Press, 1990

Larsen, Mike and Kevin Walby. Brokering Access: power, politics, and freedom of information process in Canada, UBC Press, 2012

Levine, Allan. Scrum war: The Prime Ministers and the Media, Dundurn Press, 1993

Macekura, Stephen J. Of Limits and Growth: The Rise of Global Sustainable Development in the Twentieth Century, Cambridge University Press, 2005

Maloney, Sean. Canada and UN peacekeeping: Cold War by other means, 1945-1970, Vanwell, 2002

Marcuse, Gary and Reginald Whitaker, Cold War Canada: The Making of a National Insecurity State, 1945-1957, University of Toronto Press, 1994

McFarlane, Peter. Northern shadows: Canadians and Central America, Between the Lines, 1989

McKay, Ian and Jamie Swift, Warrior Nation: Rebranding Canada in an Age of Anxiety, Between the Lines, 2012

McKay, Ian and Jamie Swift. The Vimy Trap: or, How We Learned To Stop Worrying and Love the Great War, Between the Lines, 2016

McQuaig, Linda. Holding the Bully's Coat: Canada and the U.S. Empire, Doubleday Canada, 2007

Miller, Robert. Aid as Peacemaker: Canadian Development Assistance and Third World Conflict, Oxford University Press, 1992

Miller, Duncan E. The Persian Excursion: the Canadian Navy in the Gulf War, Canadian Institute of Strategic Studies, 1995

Moreau, Nicolas and Audrey Laurin-Lamothe. The Montréal Canadiens: rethinking the legend, University of Toronto Press, 2015

Morrison, Alexander W. The Voice of Defence: the history of the Conference of Defence Associations: the first fifty years 1932-1982, Department of National Defence, 1982

Morrison, David. Aid and Ebb Tide: A History of CIDA and Canadian Development Assistance, Wilfrid Laurier University Press in association with the North-South Institute, 1998

Morton, Desmond. The Canadian General: Sir William Otter, Hakkert, 1974

Morton, Desmond. A Military History of Canada, Hurtig Publishers, 1985

Manera, Tony. A dream betrayed: The battle for the CBC, Stoddart, 1996

Nash, Knowlton. The Microphone Wars: A History of Triumph and Betrayal at the CBC, McClelland & Stewart, 1994

Newman, Peter C. The Canadian Establishment Volume 1, McClelland and Stewart, 1975

North, Liisa, Timothy David Clark and Viviana Patroni, Community Rights and Corporate Responsibility Canadian Mining and Oil Companies in Latin America, Between the lines, 2006

Off, Carol. The Ghosts of Medak Pocket, Random House Canada, 2004

Oja Jay, Dru and Nik Barry Shaw. Paved with Good Intentions: Canada's development NGOs from idealism to imperialism, Fernwood, 2012

Olechowska, Elzbieta. The age of international radio: radio Canada international (1945 – 2007), Mosaic Press, 2007

Onana, Charles. Les secrets de la justice internationale: enquêtes truquées sur le genocide rwandais, Duboiris, 2005

Pappé, Ilan. The Ethnic Cleansing of Palestine, Oneworld, 2006

Picard, Robert G. et al. Press concentration and monopoly: new perspectives on newspaper ownership and operation, Ablex Pub, 1988

Potter, Evan H. Branding Canada: Projecting Canada's Soft Power Through Public Diplomacy, McGill-Queen's University Press, 2009

Potter, Simon J. News and the British World: the emergence of an imperial press system, 1876-1922, Oxford University Press, 2003

Powley, E. Broadcast from the front: Canadian radio overseas in the second world war, Hakkert, 1975

Pratt, Cranford, Middle Power Internationalism: The North-South Dimension, McGill-Queen's University Press, 1990

Pratt, Cranford. Canadian International Development Assistance Policies: An Appraisal, McGill-Queen's University Press, 1994

Price, John. Orienting Canada: Race, Empire, and the Transpacific, UBC Press, 2011

Razack, Sherene. Dark Threats and White Knights: The Somalia Affair, Peacekeeping, and the New Imperialism, University of Toronto Press, 2004

Robinson, Paul, Nigel De Lee and Don Carrick. Ethics Education in the Military, Ashgate, 2008

Rutherford, Paul. When Television was Young: Primetime Canada 1952-1967, University of Toronto Press, 1990

Sandler, Stanley. The Korean War: An Encyclopedia, Garland, 1995

Sanger, Clyde. Half a loaf; Canada's semi-role among developing countries, Ryerson Press 1969

Scharfe, Sharon. Complicity: Human Rights and Canadian Foreign Policy: The Case of East Timor, Black Rose Books, 1996

Shoup, Lawrence H. and William Minter, Imperial Brain Trust, The Council on Foreign Relations and United States Foreign Policy, Authors Choice, 2004

Shoup, Laurence H. Wall Street's Think Tank: The Council on Foreign Relations and the Empire of Neoliberal Geopolitics, 1976-2014, Monthly Review Press, 2015

Skararup, Harold A. Out Of Darkness – Light, Vol 1, Iuniverse Inc, 2005

Smillie, Ian. The Land of Lost Content: A History of CUSO, Deneau, 1985

Stackhouse, John. Out of Poverty: And Into Something More Comfortable, Random House Canada, 2000

Stewart, Walter. Towers of gold, feet of clay: the Canadian banks, Collins, 1982

Stone, Diane and Andrew Denham. Think Tank Traditions: Policy Analysis Across Nations, Manchester University Press, 2004

Stone, I.F. The Hidden History of the Korean War, Monthly Review Press, 1969

Swift, Jamie and Brian Tomlinson. Conflicts of Interest: Canada and the Third World, Between the Lines, 1991

Taylor, Scott. Unembedded: Two Decades of Maverick War Reporting, Douglas & McIntyre, 2009

Taylor, Scott. Diary of an Uncivil War: The Violent Aftermath of the Kosovo Conflict, Esprit de Corps Books, 2002

Taylor, Scott. Tested mettle: Canada's peacekeepers at war, Esprit de Corps Books, 1998

Taylor, Scott. INAT: images of Serbia and the Kosovo Conflict, Esprit de Corps, 2000

Teigrob, Robert. Warming up to the Cold War: Canada and the United States Coalition of the Willing, from Hiroshima to Korea, University of Toronto Press, 2009

Tennyson, Brian Douglas. Canadian relations with South Africa: a diplomatic history, University Press of America, 1982

Tudiver, Neil. Universities for sale: resisting corporate control over Canadian higher education, J. Lorimer, 1999

Turk, James. The Corporate Campus: Commercialization and the Dangers to Canada's Colleges, J. Lorimer, 2000

Walker, John R. Third World news coverage: a survey of leading Canadian dailies, North-South Institute, 1989

Winter, James. Media Think, Black Rose Books, 2007

Winter, James, Common Cents: Media Portrayal of the Gulf War and Other Events, Black Rose Books, 1992

Wood, James. Militia Myths: ideas of the Canadian citizen soldier, 1896 – 1921, UBC Press, 2010

A Propaganda System

Endnotes

Chapter 1

1 Josh Campbell, Potash Ethics, Saskatoon Star Phoenix, Mar 7 2013 ; Bill Johnson, PotashCorp Ethical Saskatoon, Star Phoenix, Mar 9 2013
2 Marina Jimenez, Backyard Baghdad, Globe and Mail, Jan 22 2005
3 Yves Engler and Anthony Fenton, Canada in Haiti: Waging War on the Poor Majority, 89
4 Michael Ozanian, The Business of Hockey, Nov 24 2015 (http://www.forbes.com/teams/montreal-canadiens/)
5 Nicolas Moreau and Audrey Laurin-Lamothe, The Montréal Canadiens: rethinking the legend, 103
6 Ibid, 89-92
7 Ibid

Chapter 2

1 Ramsey M. Withers, A matter of education: It is the responsibility of the Department of National Defense to build and maintain a constituency for defence among Canada's citizens, Forum: Journal of Conference of Defence Associations Institute, Jan 1990
2 Ibid
3 Marie-Danielle Smith, DND gave minister more info on public opinion research than on ISIS operation, NATO, Embassy, Oct 28 2015
4 Carl Meyer, DND points to 'challenges' with former soldiers talking to media, Embassy, July 30 2014
5 Carl Meyer, DND: Military's 'values' shape 'Canada's identity', Embassy, Nov 23 2011
6 Ibid
7 David Pugliese, Fed up media officers desert DND, Ottawa Citizen, Sep 25 2011
8 Media Contacts (http://www.forces.gc.ca/en/contact-us/media-contacts.page)
9 Ibid
10 Defence Public Affairs Learning Centre (http://www.forces.gc.ca/en/training-establishments/defence-public-affairs-learning-centre.page)
11 Josée-Ann Paradis, The Military-Media Relationship: A Clash of Cultures? (http://www.cfc.forces.gc.ca/259/181/59_paradis.pdf); Paul Robinson, Nigel De Lee and Don Carrick, Ethics Education in the Military, 72
12 Robert Bergen, Censorship; the Canadian News Media and Afghanistan: A Historical Comparison with Case Studies, Calgary Papers in Military and Strategic Studies, 2009
13 Ibid
14 Carl Meyer, DND points to 'challenges' with former soldiers talking to media, Embassy, July 30 2014
15 Ibid
16 Marie-Danielle Smith, DND gave minister more info on public opinion research than on ISIS operation, NATO, Embassy, Oct 28 2015
17 Jerome Lessard, From news reporter to DND messenger, Belleville Intelligencer, Jan 22 2015 (http://www.intelligencer.ca/2015/01/22/from-news-reporter-to-dnd-messenger)
18 David Pugliese, Gen. Jon Vance responds to concerns over the "weaponization of public affairs" at DND, Sept 21 2015 (http://ottawacitizen.com/storyline/chief-of-the-defence-staff-gen-jon-vance-and-the-weaponization-of-public-affairs)
19 Ibid
20 Ibid
21 Scott Taylor, DND hits panic button over non-story, Halifax Chronicle Herald, June 9 2013 (http://thechronicleherald.ca/opinion/1134720-taylor-dnd-hits-panic-button-over-non-story?from=slidebox)
22 Ibid
23 Carl Meyer, DND points to 'challenges' with former soldiers talking to media, Embassy, July 30 2014
24 Meaghan Hobman, Soldiers Silenced? Freedom of Speech and the Canadian Armed Forces, CDA Institute Blog: The Forum, June 17 2014 (https://www.cdainstitute.ca/en/blog/entry/soldiers-silenced)
25 Meaghan Hobman, Loose lips: Free speech and the Canadian Forces, June 20 2014 (http://ipolitics.ca/2014/06/20/loose-lips-free-speech-and-the-canadian-forces/)
26 Ibid
27 Military staff ordered to clear online activity with superiors, CBC, Sep 28 2006 (http://www.cbc.ca/news/technology/military-staff-ordered-to-clear-online-activity-with-superiors-1.581999?ref=rss)
28 Carl Meyer, DND points to 'challenges' with former soldiers talking to media, Embassy, July 30 2014

A Propaganda System

29 Section 15 - International Affairs and Defence (http://www.oic-ci.gc.ca/eng/inv_inv-gui-ati_gui-inv-ati_section_15.aspx) ; Sharon Hobson, Operations Security and the Public's Need to Know, Canadian Defence and Foreign Affairs Institute, Mar 2011 ; David Pugliese, "Fade to Black", Ottawa Citizen, Sept 30 2006

30 Ibid

31 Sharon Hobson, Operations Security and the Public's Need to Know, Canadian Defence and Foreign Affairs Institute, Mar 2011 ; David Pugliese, "Fade to Black", Ottawa Citizen, Sept 30 2006

32 Appeal court slams DND's 3-year response to information request, Toronto Star, Mar 5 2015 (https://www.thestar.com/news/canada/2015/03/05/appeal-court-slams-governments-3-year-access-to-information-request.html)

33 David Pugliese, Military tried to cover up file on outspoken critic, Ottawa Citizen, July 13 2007

34 Ibid

35 Mike Larsen and Kevin Walby, Brokering Access: power, politics, and freedom of information process in Canada, 59

36 Peter Worthington, JTF2 - Canada's secret weapon or a place where trouble hides?, Sept 14 2010 (http://www.torontosun.com/comment/columnists/peter_worthington/2010/09/14/15351521.htm)

37 Alan Ng, The Media Analysis of the Canadian Navy Centennial How Military Publications and Civilian Publications Portray News Differently, CMNS 498 Simon Fraser University Honours Thesis, Spring 2011

38 Canadians in Korea (http://www.veterans.gc.ca/eng/remembrance/history/korean-war/valour-remembered)

39 Whitaker, Cold War Canada, 392

40 T Mirrlees, The Canadian armed forces "YouTube war": A cross-border military-social media complex, Global Media Journal - Canadian Edition, Vol 8 (http://www.gmj.uottawa.ca/1501/v8i1_mirrlees.pdf)

41 Christian Cotroneo, DND revs recruitment ads. Toronto Star, Nov 5 2006 ; The Disturbing Growth of Militarism in Canada, Collectif Échec à la guerre, May 2014 (http://echecalaguerre.org/wp-content/uploads/Disturbing-growth-of-militarism-in-Canada-May-2014-EAG.pdf)

42 David Pugliese, Xbox Live being used as a billboard for Canadian Forces recruiting ads, Ottawa Citizen, Sept 21 2014 (http://ottawacitizen.com/news/national/defence-watch/xbox-live-being-used-as-a-billboard-for-canadian-forces-recruiting-ads)

43 Michael Goodspeed, Identifying Ourselves in the Information Age (http://www.journal.forces.gc.ca/vo3/no4/doc/47-48-eng.pdf)

44 Janis L. Goldie, Fighting Change: Representing the Canadian Forces in the 2006–2008 Fight Recruitment Campaign, Canadian Journal of Communication, Vol 39 2014 (http://www.cjc-online.ca/index.php/journal/article/view/2768)

45 Luke F. Kowalski, The Public Face of the Royal Canadian Air Force: The Importance of Air Shows and Demonstration Teams to the R.C.A.F., For History 394 A02 Dr. Timothy Balzer, Apr 1 2013 (http://rusiviccda.org/wp-content/uploads/2013/05/The_Public_Face_of_the_Royal_Canadian_Air_Force.pdf)

46 The Disturbing Growth of Militarism in Canada, Collectif Échec à la guerre, May 2014 (http://echecalaguerre.org/wp-content/uploads/Disturbing-growth-of-militarism-in-Canada-May-2014-EAG.pdf)

47 Ibid

48 Noah Richler, War Games, Walrus, Apr 2012 (http://thewalrus.ca/war-games/)

49 Brett Clarkson, Celebrating the War of 1812 with a $28-million bang, QMI Agency, Oct 11 2011 (http://www.stcatharinesstandard.ca/2011/10/11/celebrating-the-war-of-1812-with-a-28-million-bang)

50 Carl Meyer, DND points to 'challenges' with former soldiers talking to media, Embassy, July 30 2014

51 Cost of 'Canada 150' commemorations comes out of military operations budget, Mar 14 2014 (http://www.cbc.ca/news/politics/cost-of-canada-150-commemorations-comes-out-of-military-operations-budget-1.2572425)

52 National Inventory of Canadian Military Memorials (http://www.veterans.gc.ca/eng/remembrance/memorials/national-inventory-canadian-memorials)

53 Archived - Community members pay tribute to Veterans in Barrie, Nov 4 2014 (http://news.gc.ca/web/article-en.do?nid=899979)

54 The Disturbing Growth of Militarism in Canada, Collectif Échec à la guerre, May 2014 (http://echecalaguerre.org/wp-content/uploads/

A Propaganda System

Disturbing-growth-of-militarism-in-Canada-May-2014-EAG.pdf)
55 Ibid
56 About the Museum (http://www.warmuseum.ca/about/about-the-museum/#tabs)
57 Quarterly Financial Report for the nine month period ended Dec 31 2015 (http://www.warmuseum.ca/wp-content/uploads/2016/02/quarterly-financial-statements-december-31-2015_e.pdf)
58 Jeff Noakes, The Canadian War Museum and Canadian Military History, July 30 2015 (http://www.history.army.mil/events/ahts2015/presentations/workshops/workshop9a_CanadianMilitaryProgram.pdf)
59 Canadian Military History (http://scholars.wlu.ca/cmh/) ; Studies in Canadian Military History Series (http://www.ubcpress.ca/books/series_military.html)
60 Laura Brandon, Art Or Memorial?: The Forgotten History of Canada's War Art, xix
61 Ibid
62 Museum Reference Guide NPP Standard Operating Procedures (https://www.cfmws.com/en/AboutUs/Library/PoliciesandRegulations/Finance/Documents/MuseumReference%20Guide_e.pdf) ; Serge Bernier, A Brief History of Canadian Forces Military Museums: 1919 to 2004 – Part 2 (http://www.journal.forces.gc.ca/vo6/no2/history-histoire-02-eng.asp)
63 Frequently Asked Questions (http://www.cmp-cpm.forces.gc.ca/dhh-dhp/faq/index-eng.asp?cat=museums&FaqID=56)
64 The Royal Canadian Regiment - In Touch - The Newsletter, Winter/Spring 2015 (http://thercr.ca/main/images/RCRAssn/assn_newsletters/Winter_Spring2015.pdf)
65 Organization of Military Museums of Canada (http://www.ommcinc.ca/#!home/mainPage)
66 Jeffrey Grey, The last word: essays on official history in the United States and British Commonwealth, 17
67 Tim Cook, Clio's Warriors: Canadian Historians and the Writing of the World Wars, 42
68 Ibid, 171
69 Ibid, 3
70 Official Histories (http://www.cmp-cpm.forces.gc.ca/dhh-dhp/his/oh-ho/index-eng.asp) Canada's Army in Korea: The United Nations Operations, 1950–53, and Their Aftermath: a Short Official Account ; Canadian Naval Operations in Korean Waters, 1950-1955 ; Strange Battleground: The Operations in Korea and Their Effects on Canada
71 Tim Cook, Clio's Warriors, 201
72 Ibid, 200
73 Jeffrey Grey, The last word?, 17
74 Roger Sarty, The Origins of Academic Military History in Canada, 1940-1967, Canadian Military History, Vol 23 Is. 2
75 Tim Cook, Clio's Warriors, 210/221
76 Ibid, 6
77 George Stanley (https://en.wikipedia.org/wiki/George_Stanley)
78 Ibid
79 Tim Cook, Clio's Warriors, 210
80 Ibid, picture after 182
81 J.L. Granatstein, Making history: The late historian Charles P. Stacey was a stickler for the truth, but his objectivity gave way to passion when it came to Mackenzie King, Globe and Mail, Sept 30 2000 (http://www.theglobeandmail.com/arts/making-history-the-late-historian-charles-p-stacey-was-a-stickler-for-the-truth-but-his-objectivity-gave-way-to-passion-when-it-came-to-mackenzie-king/article18426430/)
82 Wesley C. Gustavson, Missing the Boat? Colonel A. F. Duguid and the Canadian Official History of World War I, University of Calgary Master's Thesis, 1999, 89 ; Colonel Charles Perry Stacey (http://www.cmp-cpm.forces.gc.ca/dhh-dhp/adh-sdh/bio/index-eng.asp)
83 Tim Cook, Clio's Warriors, 137/154
84 Ibid, 183
85 Ibid, 173
86 Ibid, 197
87 Adam Chapnick, Where have all of Canada's diplomatic historians gone?, International Journal, Vol 65 No 3 Summer 2010 ; J.L. Granatstein, Making history, Globe and Mail, Sept 30 2000 (http://www.theglobeandmail.com/arts/making-history-the-late-historian-charles-p-stacey-was-a-stickler-for-the-truth-but-his-objectivity-gave-way-to-passion-when-it-came-to-mackenzie-king/article18426430/)
88 Adam Chapnick, Where have all of Canada's diplomatic historians gone?, International Journal, Vol 65 No 3 Summer 2010
89 Norman Hillmer (https://en.wikipedia.org/wiki/Norman_Hillmer)
90 Adam Chapnick, Where have all of Canada's diplomatic historians gone?, International Journal, Vol 65 No 3 Summer 2010

91 The Cadieux-Léger Fellowship (http://www.international.gc.ca/cip-pic/fellowship-bourse/cadieux-leger.aspx?lang=eng)

92 Adam Chapnick, Where have all of Canada's diplomatic historians gone?, International Journal, Vol 65 No 3 Summer 2010

93 Greg Donaghy, Documents on Canadian External Relations (http://www.diplomatie.gouv.fr/fr/IMG/pdf/ECcanada.pdf)

94 Greg Donaghy, Documenting the Diplomats: The Origins and Evolution of Documents on Canadian External Relations, The Public Historian, Vol 25 No 1 Winter 2003

95 About DHH: Who we are (http://www.cmp-cpm.forces.gc.ca/dhh-dhp/adh-sdh/index-eng.asp)

96 Military history brought to life, Western Sentinel, Apr 11 2013

97 Mallory Schwartz, War on the Air: CBC-TV and Canada's Military, 1952-1992, 269

98 Ibid, 126

99 Robert Bothwell, Randall Hansen and Margaret MacMillan, Controversy, commemoration, and capitulation: the Canadian War Museum and Bomber Command, Queen's Quarterly, Vol 115 Sept 2008

100 Audit of Financial Stewardship of Royal Military College of Canada, 7045-80, Nov 2012 (CRS) (http://www.crs-csex.forces.gc.ca/reports-rapports/2012/192p0909-eng.aspx)

101 Scott Taylor, Unembedded: Two Decades of Maverick War Reporting, 63

102 The Security and Defence Forum Backgrounder, Project number: BG-01.009, Apr 4 2001 (http://www.forces.gc.ca/en/news/article.page?doc=the-security-and-defence-forum/hnmx19or)

103 Ibid

104 Security and Defence Forum Year in Review, 2002–2003 (http://publications.gc.ca/collections/collection_2015/mdn-dnd/D3-18-2003-eng.pdf)

105 Ibid

106 Security and Defence Forum Year in Review, 2005–2006 (http://publications.gc.ca/collections/collection_2015/mdn-dnd/D3-18-2006-eng.pdf)

107 UNB's Toll of War project is 'propaganda,' historian says, Feb 2 2015 (http://www.cbc.ca/news/canada/new-brunswick/unb-s-toll-of-war-project-is-propaganda-historian-says-1.2940076)

108 Jane Kirby, Military Ties at Dalhousie's Centre for Foreign Policy Studies, Sept 7 2009 (http://halifax.mediacoop.ca/story/1874)

109 Ibid

110 Ibid

111 Security and Defence Forum Year in Review, 2002–2003 (http://publications.gc.ca/collections/collection_2015/mdn-dnd/D3-18-2003-eng.pdf)

112 Amir Attaran, When think tanks produce propaganda, Globe and Mail, Feb 21 2008

113 Ibid

114 Ibid

115 Jack Granatstein, Fort Fumble on the Rideau: Just say no to military academics, Globe and Mail, Aug 22 2011

116 Security and Defence Forum Year in Review, 2009–2010 (http://publications.gc.ca/collections/collection_2011/dn-nd/D3-18-2010-eng.pdf)

117 Evaluation of Security and Defence Forum (SDF) Class Grant Program, May 2010 (http://www.crs.forces.gc.ca/reports-rapports/pdf/2010/150P0921-eng.pdf)

118 Defense Minister Blais, House of Commons debates 1984, 3193

119 Onnig Beylerian and Jacques Lévesque, Inauspicious Beginnings: Principal Powers and International Security, viii ; Defence Management Studies (http://www.queensu.ca/dms/)

120 Danford W. Middlemiss, Dalhousie University's Centre for Foreign Policy Studies: a brief history, The Canadian political science Association Bulletin, Vol XXI May 1992

121 Ibid

122 Ibid

123 Ken Bell and Desmond Morton, Royal Canadian Military Institute: 100 years, 77

124 Paul Axelrod and John G. Reid, Youth, University and Canadian society: Essays in the Social History of Higher Education, 85 ; Kathryn M. Bindon, Queens men, Canada's men: the military history of Queen's University, 18

125 A call to revive university military training program, Universities News, Jan 25 2012 (http://www.universitiesnews.com/2012/01/25/a-call-to-revive-university-military-training-program/)

126 Ken Bell and Desmond Morton, Royal Canadian Military Institute: 100 years, 77

127 Civil Military Leadership Pilot Initiative Launched, July 8 2013, Project number: NR 13.220 (http://www.forces.gc.ca/en/news/article.page?doc=civil-military-leadership-pilot-initiative-launched/hjiq6l6c)

128 Ibid

129 Pilot program launched to help student soldiers

A Propaganda System

become leaders, July 8 2013 (https://uofa.ualberta.ca/news-and-events/newsarticles/2013/july/pilot-program-launched-to-help-student-soldiers-become-leaders#sthash.JLWrbV2z.dpuf)

130 Militarism and Canadian Universities June 15 2011 (http://anthrojustpeace.blogspot.ca/2011/06/militarism-and-canadian-universities.html)

131 Laura Beach, Canadian Academic Institutions, the Weapons Industry, and Militarist Ideology in Maximilian C. Forte, The New Imperialism, Volume II: Interventionism, Information Warfare, and the Military-Academic Complex

132 Ibid

133 Peter Langille, A few thoughts for the file on developing a Canadian Peace Institute (http://www.peace.ca/afewthoughts.htm)

134 Paul Weinberg, Peace Scholars See Shrinking Space for Dissent, IPS, Mar 2 2007 (http://www.ipsnews.net/2007/03/canada-peace-scholars-see-shrinking-space-for-dissent/)

135 Chief Executive Officer and Assistant Deputy Minister (Science and Technology), Dr. Marc Fortin (http://www.drdc-rddc.gc.ca/en/about/ceo-adm.page)

136 Defence Research and Development Canada (DRDC) collaborative activities with academic institutions to date encompass the following (http://www.drdc-rddc.gc.ca/en/partnerships-partenariats/academia.page)

137 Association of Canadian Community Colleges, Maintaining the Readiness of the Canadian Forces Through Training and Recruitment (https://www.collegesinstitutes.ca/wp-content/uploads/2014/05/20120301_DNDCommittee.pdf)

138 Ryan McNutt, Minister of Industry welcomes investment, May 16 2008 (http://www.dal.ca/news/2008/05/16/physics.html)

139 Ibid

140 Maximilian C. Forte, The New Imperialism, Volume II: Interventionism, Information Warfare, and the Military-Academic Complex Interventionism, Information Warfare, and the Military-Academic Complex, 35

Chapter 3

1 Royal Canadian Military Institute (https://en.wikipedia.org/wiki/Royal_Canadian_Military_Institute#cite_note-1)

2 About the RCMI (http://www.rcmi.org/About-Us-(1).aspx)

3 Eric Morse, The deadly chaos behind Putin's mysterious acts, Globe and Mail, Mar 24 2015 (http://www.theglobeandmail.com/opinion/the-deadly-chaos-behind-putins-mysterious-acts/article23595418/)

4 Desmond Morton, The Canadian General: Sir William Otter, 112

5 Ibid, 366 – 367

6 Ken Bell and Desmond Morton, Royal Canadian Military Institute, 28

7 Ibid, 34

8 Our History: More than a Century of Tradition (http://www.rcmi.org/About-Us-(1)/History.aspx)

9 Ken Bell and Desmond Morton, Royal Canadian Military Institute, 48

10 Ibid, 33

11 Desmond Morton, The Canadian General, 136

12 Ken Bell and Desmond Morton, Royal Canadian Military Institute, 79

13 James Wood, Militia Myths: ideas of the Canadian citizen soldier, 1896 – 1921, 197

14 The Canadian Woman's Annual and Social Service Directory 1915, 310

15 J. L. Granatstein, Canada's Army: Waging War and Keeping the Peace, 155

16 James Wood, Militia Myths, 198

17 Ibid, 204

18 Ibid, 197

19 Desmond Morton, A Military History of Canada, 122

20 CDA Institute Annual Conference on Security and Defence, Feb 18 2016 (http://www.veterans.gc.ca/eng/about-us/department-officials/minister/photos/gallery/786)

21 John Geddes, The CDA gets $100,000 a year from the Department of Defence, Macleans, Nov 15 2007 (http://www.ceasefire.ca/?p=187)

22 Alexander W. Morrison, The Voice of Defence, 191

23 Ibid, 129

24 2015 Ottawa Conference on Security and Defence, Mar 2015 (http://www.cdainstitute.ca/images/SD/March_2015_-_SD.pdf)

25 On Track, Vol 8 No 4 Dec 2003 (http://www.cdainstitute.ca/images/ontrack8n4.pdf)

26 Paul David Manson (https://en.wikipedia.org/wiki/Paul_David_Manson)

27 Jerome Klassen, Joining Empire: The Political Economy of the New Canadian Foreign Policy, 197

28 ON TRACK (http://www.cdainstitute.ca/en/research-and-publications/on-track)

A Propaganda System

29 Vimy Award (http://www.cdainstitute.ca/en/awards/vimy-award)

30 Alexander W. Morrison, The Voice of Defence: the history of the Conference of Defence Associations : the first fifty years 1932-1982, 22

31 Ronald G. Haycock, Sam Hughes: the public career of a controversial Canadian, 1985 – 1916, 138

32 Alexander W. Morrison, The Voice of Defence, 8

33 Ibid, 59

34 Harold A. Skararup, Out Of Darkness – Light, Vol 1, 225

35 Alexander W. Morrison, The Voice of Defence, 8

36 Ibid, 192 – 194

37 Ibid

38 Linda McQuaig, Holding the Bully's Coat: Canada and the U.S. Empire, 179

39 Ibid

40 Steven Staples, Breaking Rank: A citizens' review of Canada's military spending, The Polaris Institute, 2002

41 Steven Staples, CDA says media give new depth to the word 'shallow;' Steven Staples disagrees (http://www.rideauinstitute.ca/2008/08/04/cda-says-media-give-new-depth-to-the-word-shallow-steven-staples-disagrees/)

42 Ibid

43 Amir Attaran, When think tanks produce propaganda, Globe and Mail, Feb 21 2008 (http://www.theglobeandmail.com/opinion/when-think-tanks-produce-propaganda/article1051916/)

44 Ibid

45 Ibid

46 Peter Langille, Changing the Guard: Canada's Defence in a World in Transition, 109

47 Canadian Institute of Strategic Studies (http://www.policy.ca/policy-directory/Detailed/Canadian-Institute-of-Strategic-Studies-270.html)

48 CISS history - CDFAI (http://www.cdfai.org.previewmysite.com/PDF/CISS%20History.pdf)

49 Peter Langille, Changing the Guard, 116

50 Ibid

51 David Leyton-Brown, Canadian Annual Review of Politics and Public Affairs 1992, 121

52 CFB Baden–Soellingen (https://en.wikipedia.org/wiki/CFB_Baden%E2%80%93Soellingen)

53 Allan Woods, Support for Afghan mission can grow: Polls, Toronto Star, Aug 1 2007 (http://www.thestar.com/news/canada/2007/08/01/support_for_afghan_mission_can_grow_polls.html)

54 We Were Invincible, Résumé du livre (http://www.jcl.qc.ca/detail_livre/we-were-invincible/)

55 Major-General D.F. Holman, CD (Ret'd) (http://www.cfc.forces.gc.ca/136/385-eng.html)

56 David Pugliese, Former chief of defence staff Gen. Ramsey Withers dies, Ottawa Citizen, Dec 30 2014 (http://ottawacitizen.com/news/politics/former-chief-of-defence-staff-gen-ramsey-withers-dies)

57 Europe's Arctic Defence Agenda (http://www3.carleton.ca/csds/eventdetails/1011rudd.htm)

58 Canadian Institute of Strategic Studies (http://www.policy.ca/policy-directory/Detailed/Canadian-Institute-of-Strategic-Studies-270.html)

59 Alexander W. Morrison, The Voice of Defence, 231

60 Adam Chapnick, Canada's Voice: The Public Life of John Wendell Holmes, 206

61 Peter Langille, Changing the guard, 116

62 Ibid

63 Evaluation of the Pearson Peacekeeping Centre, Apr 2007 (http://publications.gc.ca/collections/collection_2016/mdn-dnd/D58-168-2007-eng.pdf)

64 Close peacekeeping centre, report urges, Victoria Times Colonist, Oct 6 2007 (http://www.pressreader.com/canada/times-colonist/20071006/281547991522258)

65 Evaluation of the Pearson Peacekeeping Centre, Apr 2007 (http://publications.gc.ca/collections/collection_2016/mdn-dnd/D58-168-2007-eng.pdf)

66 Alex Morrison (http://unac.org/2002/09/alex-morrison/)

67 Pearson Centre (https://en.wikipedia.org/wiki/Pearson_Centre#William_Morrison.2C_founder)

68 Sean Maloney, Canada and UN peacekeeping: Cold War by other means, 1945-197, xii

69 Bernd Horn, The Canadian Way of War: Serving the National Interest, 305

70 Howard D. Fremeth, Memory, Militarism and Citizenship: tracking the Dominion Institute in Canada's military-cultural memory network, Carleton University PHD Thesis, 2010, 228

71 Ibid, 207

72 Ian McKay and Jamie Swift, Warrior Nation: Rebranding Canada in an Age of Anxiety, 252

73 Howard D. Fremeth, Memory, Militarism and Citizenship: tracking the Dominion Institute in Canada's military-cultural memory network, Carleton University PHD Thesis, 2010, 69

74 Memory Project Newsletter, Winter 2016 (www.thememoryproject.com/newsletter/33:download)

75 Historica Canada (https://en.wikipedia.org/wiki/

A Propaganda System

Historica_Canada)
76 Howard D. Fremeth, Memory, Militarism and Citizenship: tracking the Dominion Institute in Canada's military-cultural memory network, Carleton University PHD Thesis, 2010, 196
77 Ian McKay and Jamie Swift, Warrior Nation, 280
78 Howard D. Fremeth, Memory, Militarism and Citizenship: tracking the Dominion Institute in Canada's military-cultural memory network, Carleton University PHD Thesis, 2010, 151/178
79 Ibid, 184
80 Ibid, 132
81 Donald Gutstein, Who funds the Fraser Institute? Teacher Newsmagazine, Vol 17 No 4 Jan 2005 (https://bctf.ca/publications/NewsmagArticle.aspx?id=7914)
82 Ibid
83 David Taras, The Winds of Right-wing Change in Canadian Journalism, Canadian Journal of Communication, Vol 21 No 4 (1996 (http://www.cjc-online.ca/index.php/journal/article/view/962/868)
84 Adam Chapnick, Canada's Voice, 193
85 Gerald Wright, About Contributors (https://www.opencanada.org/contributors/gerald-wright/)
86 Adam Chapnick, Canada's Voice, 206
87 Evaluation of Security and Defence Forum (SDF) Class Grant Program, May 2010 (http://www.crs.forces.gc.ca/reports-rapports/pdf/2010/150P0921-eng.pdf)
88 Canadian Defence and Foreign Affairs Institute (http://www.cgai.ca/exigencies_of_future_deployments)
89 2014 Annual Report: Overview (http://www.cgai.ca/annual_reports)
90 Barry Cooper, A Foreign Intelligence Service for Canada, Canadian Defence and Foreign Affairs Institute, Nov 2007 (www.cdfai.org.previewmysite.com/PDF/CFIS.pdf)
91 Without foreign sales, Canada's defence industry would not survive, Globe and Mail, Jan 11 2016 (http://www.theglobeandmail.com/report-on-business/rob-commentary/without-foreign-arms-sales-canadas-defence-industry-would-not-survive/article28100442/)
92 Lola Fakinlede, Inside the Canadian military journalism course, July 3 2013 (http://www.j-source.ca/article/inside-canadian-military-journalism-course)
93 Military Journalism Course (http://www.cgai.ca/military_journalism_course)
94 Lola Fakinlede, Inside the Canadian military journalism course, July 3 2013 (http://www.j-source.ca/article/inside-canadian-military-journalism-course)
95 David Williams, Canadian Journalism Students Visit the Regiment, June 9 2010 (http://www.strathconas.ca/canadian-journalism-students-visit-the-regiment)
96 Ross Munro Award 2010 (http://www.cgai.ca/ross_munro_award_2010)
97 Steven Staples, CDA says media give new depth to word 'shallow', Hill Times, Aug 5 2008 (http://www.ceasefire.ca/?p=232#sthash.WBdkpKDY.dpuf)
98 David Pugliese, Canadian Defence and Foreign Affairs Institute's Personal Attack on Ottawa Citizen's Lee Berthiaume Backfires…Big Time, May 20 2014 (http://ottawacitizen.com/news/national/defence-watch/canadian-defence-%E2%80%A8foreign-affairs-institutes-personal-attack-on-ottawa-citizens-lee-berthiaume-backfiresbig-time)
99 Security and Defence Forum – year in review, 2009-2010 (publications.gc.ca/collections/collection_2011/dn.../D3-18-2010-eng.pdf)
100 Ibid
101 Ian McKay and Jamie Swift, Warrior Nation, 230
102 Canadian defence and foreign affairs institute (http://www.gutenberg.us/articles/eng/Canadian_Defence_and_Foreign_Affairs_Institute)
103 Canadian Global Affairs Institute Speaker Series Archive (http://www.cgai.ca/speaker_series) ; Perrin Beatty (https://en.wikipedia.org/wiki/Perrin_Beatty)
104 About Us (http://www.legion.ca/who-we-are/)
105 Ian McKay and Jamie Swift, The Vimy Trap or, How We Learned To Stop Worrying and Love the Great War, 81
106 19 million poppies already sold in Canada ahead of Remembrance Day 2014 (http://www.vancitybuzz.com/2014/11/19-million-poppies-already-sold-canada-ahead-remembrance-day-2014/)
107 Royal Canadian Mint Commemorates 65th Anniversary of the End of Second World War with 25-Cent Circulation Coin Featuring Two Striking Red Poppies (http://www.mint.ca/store/news/royal-canadian-mint-commemorates-65th-anniversary-of-the-end-of-second-world-war-with-25cent-circulation-coin-featuring-two-

A Propaganda System

striking-red-poppies-10500002?cat=News+releases&nId=700002&parentnId=600004&nodeGroup=#.V73hdTXvbT8)

108 In Flanders Fields (https://en.wikipedia.org/wiki/In_Flanders_Fields)

109 Ibid

110 Alexander W. Morrison, The Voice of Defence, 231

111 Legion museums (https://en.wikipedia.org/wiki/Royal_Canadian_Legion#Legion_museums)

112 Lest We Forget Project (https://en.wikipedia.org/wiki/Lest_We_Forget_Project)

113 David Dean, Museums as conflict zones: the Canadian War Museum and Bomber Command, Museum and Society, Mar 2009 (https://www2.le.ac.uk/.../museumstudies/museumsociety/.../dean.pdf)

114 Ibid

115 Norman Hillmer, The Canadian War Museum and the Military Identity of an Unmilitary People, Canadian Military History Vol 19 Is. 3 2010

116 David Dean, Museums as conflict zones: the Canadian War Museum and Bomber Command, Museum and Society, Mar 2009 (https://www2.le.ac.uk/.../museumstudies/museumsociety/.../dean.pdf)

117 Mallory Schwartz, War on the Air: CBC-TV and Canada's Military, 1952-1992, 285

118 Historica Canada (https://en.wikipedia.org/wiki/Historica_Canada)

119 James Hale, Branching Out: the story of the Royal Canadian Legion, 26

120 Mallory Schwartz, War on the Air, 57

121 Ibid, 330

122 Ibid, 46

123 Ibid, 161

124 Ibid, 307/337 ; EJ Dick, The Valour and the Horror Continued: Do We Still Want Our History on Television?, Journal of the Association of Canadian Archivists, Spring 1993 (journals.sfu.ca/archivar/index.php/archivaria/article/viewFile/.../12854) ; James Hale, Branching out, 216

125 James Hale, Branching Out, 269/98

126 Ibid 218

127 Ibid, 114

128 Ibid, 33

129 The royal canadian legion application for membership

130 James Hale, Branching Out, 128

131 Ibid, 36/42/240

132 Ibid, 276/280 ; Spencer Perry, Veterans continue to rely on Royal Canadian Legion poppy fund (http://capitalnews.ca/politics-of-giving/veterans-continue-to-rely-on-royal-canadian-legion-poppy-fund/)

133 James Hale, Branching Out, 267-268

Chapter 4

1 Neil Tudiver, Universities for sale: resisting corporate control over Canadian higher education, 166

2 James Turk, The Corporate Campus: Commercialization and the Dangers to Canada's Colleges, 24

3 Neil Tudiver, Universities for sale, 166

4 James Turk, The corporate campus, 24

5 Ibid

6 Neil Tudiver, Universities for sale, 166

7 Editorial, Remembering the alma mater - Giving it back, Northern Miner, Vol 83 Nov 10 1997 (http://www2.northernminer.com/news/editorial--remembering-the-alma-mater--giving-it-back/1000162016/)

8 Munk School of Global Affairs Milestones, University of Toronto Magazine, Autumn 2015 (http://magazine.utoronto.ca/life-on-campus/munk-school-of-global-affairs-milestones/)

9 Ibid

10 Barrick and CIDA co-funding new World Vision project in Peru, Jan 15 2012 (http://barrickbeyondborders.com/people/2012/01/barrick-and-cida-co-funding-new-world-vision-project-in-peru/)

11 Minister Oda announces initiatives to increase the benefits of natural resource management for people in Africa and South America, Sept 29 2011 (http://www.acdi-cida.gc.ca/acdi-cida/acdi-cida.nsf/eng/CAR-929105317-KGD)

12 Barrick and CIDA co-funding new World Vision project in Peru, Jan 15 2012 (http://barrickbeyondborders.com/people/2012/01/barrick-and-cida-co-funding-new-world-vision-project-in-peru/)

13 Rick Arnold, Mining, CIDA partnership in Peru is pacification program, not development: Local indigenous rep writes to World Vision, Barrick Gold, CIDA asking them to stop, Embassy, Mar 5 2012 (http://protestbarrick.net/article.php?id=799)

14 Ibid

15 Allan Woods, Gold mine controversy awaits PM

A Propaganda System

in Santiago, Toronto Star, July 18 2007 (https://www.thestar.com/news/2007/07/18/gold_mine_controversy_awaits_pm_in_santiago.html)

16 Editorial, Bill C-300's defeat, Northern Miner, Nov 3 2010 (http://www.northernminer.com/regulatory-issues/editorial-bill-c-300-s-defeat/1000391175/)

17 Asad Ismi, Canadian Business in Chile, Peace Magazine May 1997 (http://peacemagazine.org/archive/v13n3p24.htm) ; Sheldon Kirshner, Munk gives Technion $7m gift for research centre, Canadian Jewish News, May 27 1999

18 Hal Weitzman, Bolivia's Morales vows to nationalise mining industry, Financial Times, May 8 2006 (http://www.ft.com/cms/s/2/feff7e00-ded6-11da-acee-0000779e2340.html#axzz3k2pQcSbH); Peter Munk, Stop Chavez' Demagoguery Before it is Too Late, Financial Times, Aug 22 2007

19 An interview with Peter Munk: You've got to hedge your bets, Economist, Apr 29 2014 (http://www.economist.com/blogs/schumpeter/2014/04/interview-peter-munk)

20 Open for Business: On What Terms, Canadian Association of University Teachers, Nov 2013, 64

21 Judith Deutsch, Munk School of Global Affairs and the Harper Government collaborate on "Direct Diplomacy" in Iran, May 22 2015 (http://scienceforpeace.ca/munk-school-of-global-affairs-and-the-harper-government-collaborate-on-direct-diplomacy-in-iran)

22 Seth Lubove and Oliver Staley, Schools Find Ayn Rand Can't Be Shrugged as Donors Build Courses, Bloomberg, May 5 2011 (http://www.bloomberg.com/news/articles/2011-05-05/schools-find-ayn-rand-can-t-be-shrugged-as-donors-build-courses)

23 Gerald Caplan, Money really can buy anything; even at the University of Toronto, Globe and Mail, Dec 17 2010 (http://www.theglobeandmail.com/news/politics/second-reading/money-really-can-buy-anything-even-at-the-university-of-toronto/article1320297/)

24 Dylan C. Robertson, Profs allege donor influence, The Varsity, Nov 29 2010 (http://thevarsity.ca/2010/11/29/profs-allege-donor-influence/)

25 Munk and U of T (https://munkoutofuoft.wordpress.com/munk-and-uoft/)

26 Dylan C. Robertson, Profs allege donor influence, The Varsity, Nov 29 2010 (http://thevarsity.ca/2010/11/29/profs-allege-donor-influence/)

27 Linda McQuaig, Universities' corporate temptation, Toronto Star, Dec 26 2012 (https://www.thestar.com/opinion/editorialopinion/2011/02/22/mcquaig_universities_corporate_temptation.html)

28 Ex-UofT President David Naylor gets named to Barrick Board, Dec 8 2013 (http://www.protestbarrick.net/article.php?id=940)

29 Judith Deutsch, Munk School of Global Affairs and the Harper Government collaborate on "Direct Diplomacy" in Iran, May 22 2015 (http://scienceforpeace.ca/munk-school-of-global-affairs-and-the-harper-government-collaborate-on-direct-diplomacy-in-iran)

30 Ex-UofT President David Naylor gets named to Barrick Board of Directors of Directors, Dec 8 2013 (http://toronto.mediacoop.ca/story/ex-uoft-president-david-naylor-gets-named-barrick/20347)

31 Ibid

32 Lionel Gelber Prize (http://munkschool.utoronto.ca/program/lionel-gelber-prize/)

33 Lipset Lecture Series (http://www.ned.org/seymour-martin-lipset-lecture-on-democracy-in-the-world/)

34 Toronto International Film Festival Presents Contemporary World Speakers, (http://munkschool.utoronto.ca/feature/toronto-international-film-festival-presents-contemporary-world-speakers-series/)

35 About: The Munk Debates are the world's preeminent public debating forum (https://www.munkdebates.com/about)

36 Election Debate: Date Announced for First Ever Federal Election Debate on Foreign Policy, Aug 14 2015 (http://munkdebates.com/election-debate)

37 Tom Rosenstiel, Turning subject experts into journalists: 9 good questions with Robert Steiner, Apr 24 2014 (https://www.americanpressinstitute.org/publications/good-questions/turning-subject-experts-journalists-9-good-questions-robert-steiner/)

38 Faculty (http://munkschool.utoronto.ca/journalism/faculty.php)

39 Former Globe and Mail editor-in-chief John Stackhouse joins Munk School, CNW, Apr 16 2014 (http://www.newswire.ca/news-releases/former-globe-and-mail-editor-in-chief-john-stackhouse-joins-munk-school-514098981.html)

40 Chris Selley, Margaret Wente is back in the good books, National Post, Nov 14 2012 (http://news.nationalpost.com/full-comment/chris-selley-

A Propaganda System

margaret-wente-is-back-in-the-good-books)
41 Stephen J. Toope,Canada needs to rethink foreign policy, Globe and Mail, Mar 28 2016
42 Canadian miners abroad learn wider responsibility, Globe and Mail, Jun 6 2011 (http://www.theglobeandmail.com/opinion/editorials/canadian-miners-abroad-learn-wider-responsibility/article582272/)
43 Ibid
44 Jen Moore, Canadian Development Aid No Longer Tied – Just Shackled to Corporate Mining Interests, Mar 27 2014 (http://miningwatch.ca/blog/2014/3/27/canadian-development-aid-no-longer-tied-just-shackled-corporate-mining-interests)
45 Ibid
46 Sakura Saunders, The Globe and Mail as Corporate Apologists: Behind the love affair with Barrick Gold (http://toronto.mediacoop.ca/story/globe-and-mail-corporate-apologists-behind-love-af/16338) ; Mining watchdog agency called 'bogus PR job', CBC News Oct 31 2011 (http://www.cbc.ca/news/canada/mining-watchdog-agency-called-bogus-pr-job-1.978674)
47 Campbell Clark, Ottawa backs using social media to boost Iran's dissidents, Globe and Mail May 10 2013 (http://www.theglobeandmail.com/news/politics/ottawa-backs-using-social-media-to-boost-irans-dissidents/article11847631/)
48 The Global Dialogue on the Future of Iran - Opening and Welcome, May 10 2013 (https://www.youtube.com/watch?v=1l7lvaphzFM)
49 Hebrew University Awards Honorary Doctorate to Dr. Janice Gross Stein, June 8 2012 (http://munkschool.utoronto.ca/blog/hebrew-university-awards-honorary-doctorate-to-dr-janice-gross-stein/) ; Niaz Salimi, Letter to Janice Stein, Munk school of global affair regarding two-day conference on Iran, titled "The global Dialogue on future of Iran" (http://www.ircan.com/letter-to-janice-stein-munk-school-of-global-affair-regarding-two-day-conference-on-iran/)
50 Yitzhak Benhorin, The man who fights Iran, Apr 26 2011 (http://www.ynetnews.com/articles/0,7340,L-4060499,00.html)
51 Mark Dubowitz (http://www.defenddemocracy.org/about-fdd/team-overview/dubowitz-mark/)
52 Munk School's Mark Dubowitz wins Intelligence Squared debate, May 28 2015 (http://munkschool.utoronto.ca/blog/munk-schools-mark-dubowitz-wins-intelligence-squared-debate/)
53 Irene Poetranto, After the Green Movement: Internet Controls in Iran, 2009-2012, Feb 15 2013 (https://opennet.net/blog/2013/02/after-green-movement-internet-controls-iran-2009-2012)
54 Projects (https://citizenlab.org/projects/)
55 John Lorinc, The New Cold War, Walrus, June 12 2012 (http://thewalrus.ca/the-new-cold-war/)
56 Ibid
57 Terry Lavender, Government of Canada backs digital public square from U of T's Munk School, Jan 6 2015 (https://www.utoronto.ca/news/government-canada-backs-digital-public-square-u-ts-munk-school)
58 Ibid
59 Ibid
60 Imperial Canada: Talon statement on "libel chill", May 14 2010 (http://talonbooks.com/news/imperial-canada-talon-statement-on-libel-chill-)
61 Philip Resnick, Those Bricks Barrick Gold Dropped, Apr 21 2010 (http://thetyee.ca/Mediacheck/2010/04/21/BarrickBricks/)
62 Tracey Tyler, Gold Firm Libelled on Web Sites, Court Rules, Toronto Star, June 5 2004
63 Ibid
64 William Spain, U.K. libel suit hits U.S. Web site, Aug 1 2001 (http://www.marketwatch.com/story/uk-libel-suit-hits-us-website)
65 Ibid
66 Ibid
67 Ex-U of T President David Naylor gets named to Barrick Board of Directors of Directors Dec 8 2013 (http://toronto.mediacoop.ca/story/ex-uoft-president-david-naylor-gets-named-barrick/20347)
68 Ibid
69 Canadian Institute of International Affairs Annual Report, 1990
70 J.L. Granatstein, Looking backwards: the Journal's first year, International Journal, Vol 33 No 1 Winter 1977-78
71 Canadian papers: 1933 prepared for the fifth biannual conference of the Institute of Pacific relations to be held in Banff, Canada August 14-28, 1933, preface
72 T.B. Millar, Commonwealth Institutes of International Affairs, International Journal, Vol 33 (winter 1977-8)
73 Lawrence T. Woods, John Nelson and the Origins of the Canadian Institute of International Affairs, International Journal, Vol 59 No 2 Spring 2004
74 Peter McFarlane, Northern shadows: Canadians

and Central America, 19

75 Ibid, 20

76 Walter Stewart, Towers of gold, feet of clay: the Canadian banks, 188

77 Donald E. Abelson, Do Think Tanks Matter?: Assessing the Impact of Public Policy Institutes, 42 ; E. D. Greathed, The Antecedents and Origins of the Canadian Institute of International Affairs,' University of Toronto thesis, 1966, 33

78 Carter Manny, The Canadian Institute of international affairs: 1928 to 1939: an attempt to 'enlighten' Canada's foreign policy, 24

79 Ibid, 83

80 Priscilla Roberts, Tweaking the Lion's Tail: Edgar J. Tarr, the Canadian Institute of International Affairs, and the British Empire, 1931–1950, Diplomacy and Statecraft, Vol 23 Dec 2012

81 Lawrence H. Shoup and William Minter, Imperial Brain Trust, The Council on Foreign Relations and United States Foreign Policy, 3

82 E. D. Greathed, The Antecedents and Origins of the Canadian Institute of International Affairs,' University of Toronto thesis, 1966, 2

83 Lawrence H. Shoup and William Minter, Imperial Brain Trust: The Council on Foreign Relations and United States Foreign Policy (http://www.thirdworldtraveler.com/New_World_Order/ImperialBrainTrust_CFR.html)

84 Lawrence H. Shoup and William Minter, Imperial brain trust, 12 ; E. D. Greathed, The Antecedents and Origins of the Canadian Institute of International Affairs,' University of Toronto thesis, 1966, 15

85 Priscilla Roberts, Tweaking the Lion's Tail: Edgar J. Tarr, the Canadian Institute of International Affairs, and the British Empire, 1931–1950, Diplomacy and Statecraft, Vol 23 Dec 2012

86 Carter Manny, The Canadian Institute of international affairs: 1928 to 1939, 22

87 E. D. Greathed, The Antecedents and Origins of the Canadian Institute of International Affairs,' University of Toronto thesis, 1966, 21 ; Diane Stone and Andrew Denham, Think Tank Traditions: Policy Analysis Across Nations, 29

88 History of the CIIA (http://cictoronto.ca/history/)

89 Donald Page, The Institute's 'Popular Arm': The League of Nations Society in Canada, International Journal, Vol 33 No 1 Winter 1977-78

90 Ibid

91 Ibid

92 D. J. Herperger, The League of Nations Society in Canada during the 1930s, University of Regina MA Thesis, 1978, 20/43

93 Donald Page, The Institute's 'Popular Arm': The League of Nations Society in Canada, International Journal, Vol 33 No 1 Winter 1977-78

94 History of the CIIA (http://cictoronto.ca/history/)

95 Carter Manny, The Canadian Institute of international affairs: 1928 to 1939, 73

96 History of the CIIA (http://cictoronto.ca/history/) ; Canada's Voice, 23-24

97 Diane Stone and Andrew Denham, Think Tank Traditions, 29

98 Adam Chapnick, Canada's Voice, 19

99 Diane Stone and Andrew Denham, Think Tank Traditions, 28

100 Ibid, 30

101 Carter Manny, The Canadian Institute of international affairs: 1928 to 1939, 97

102 Alex I. Inglis, The Institute and the Department, International Journal, Vol 33 No 1 Winter 1977/1978

103 Ibid ; Priscilla Roberts, Tweaking the Lion's Tail: Edgar J. Tarr, the Canadian Institute of International Affairs, and the British Empire, 1931–1950, Diplomacy and Statecraft, Vol 23 Dec 2012

104 Alex I. Inglis, The Institute and the Department, International Journal, Vol 33 No 1 Winter 1977-78

105 Ibid

106 Briefs concerning the aims, objectives and activities of the Canadian Institute of international affairs: presented for the information of the Royal commission on national development in the arts, letters and sciences, Apr 1950

107 Lawrence T. Woods, Rockefeller Philanthropy and the Institute of Pacific Relations: A Reappraisal of Long-Term Mutual Dependency, International Journal of Voluntary and Nonprofit Organizations, 1999

108 Ibid

109 Adam Chapnick, Canada's Voice, 25

110 History of the CIIA (http://cictoronto.ca/history/)

111 T.B. Millar, Commonwealth Institutes of International Affairs, International Journal, Vol 33 Winter 1977-8 ; Adam Chapnick, Canada's Voice, 142

112 Ibid, 143

113 Edward H Berman, The influence of the Carnegie, Ford and Rockefeller Foundations on American Foreign policy, 5

114 Adam Chapnick, Canada's Voice, 205

115 T.B. Millar, Commonwealth Institutes of International Affairs, International Journal, Vol 33 Winter 1977-8

116 Alex I. Inglis, The Institute and the Department, International Journal, Vol 33 No 1 Winter 1977-78

117 Canadian Institute of International Affairs Annual Report, 1988

118 Adam Chapnick, Canada's Voice, 181

119 Spotlight Canada: The Canadian Institute of International Affairs (https://anticommunistarchive.wordpress.com/edmund-burke-society/f-paul-fromm/spotlight-canada-the-canadian-institute-of-international-affairs/)

120 Donald E. Abelson, Do Think Tanks Matter?, 43

121 A Report on the Work of the Canadian Institute of International Affairs, 1982 – 1983 ; Canadian Institute of International Affairs Annual Report, 1993

122 Priscilla Roberts, Tweaking the Lion's Tail: Edgar J. Tarr, the Canadian Institute of International Affairs, and the British Empire, 1931–1950, Diplomacy and Statecraft, Vol 23 Dec 2012

123 A Report on the Work of the Canadian Institute of International Affairs, 1980 – 1981

124 Canadian Institute of International Affairs Annual Report, 1995 – 1996 ; Canadian Institute of International Affairs Annual Report, 1996 – 1997

125 A report on the work of the Canadian Institute of International Affairs, 1975 – 1976 ; A Report on the Work of the Canadian Institute of International Affairs, 1980 – 1981

126 Jim Balsillie leads in the creation of the new Canadian International Council, Sept 6 2007 (https://www.cigionline.org/articles/2007/09/jim-balsillie-leads-creation-new-canadian-international-council)

127 Jim Balsillie, Why international policy matters, Globe and Mail, Sept 6 2007 (http://www.theglobeandmail.com/report-on-business/why-international-policy-matters/article1081504/)

128 Jim Balsillie, Why we're creating the Canadian International Council, National Post, Oct 18 2007 (https://www.cigionline.org/articles/2007/10/why-we%E2%80%99re-creating-canadian-international-council)

129 Wall Street's Think Tank: The Council on Foreign Relations and the Empire of Neoliberal Geopolitics, 1976-2014 (http://monthlyreview.org/product/wall_streets_think_tank/)

130 CFR Convenes "Council of Councils" Linking Leading Foreign Policy Institutes From Around the World, Council on Foreign Relations, Mar 12 2012 (http://www.cfr.org/global-governance/cfr-convenes-council-councils-linking-leading-foreign-policy-institutes-around-world/p27612)

131 Munk and U of T (https://munkoutofuoft.wordpress.com/munk-and-uoft/)

132 Jeff Davis, New School Aims to Breath Life into Global Affairs, Embassy, Feb 20 2008 (https://www.cigionline.org/articles/2008/02/new-school-aims-breath-life-global-affairs)

133 Michael Valpy, Balsillie's disappointing foray into global affairs, Dec 16 2009 (http://www.theglobeandmail.com/news/national/balsillies-disappointing-foray-into-global-affairs/article1215757/)

134 Theresa Tedesco, The uneasy ties between Canada's universities and wealthy business magnates, National Post, Mar 9 2012 (http://business.financialpost.com/news/fp-street/influence-u-the-uneasy-ties-between-canadas-universities-and-wealthy-business-magnates)

135 About: Cigi Campus (https://www.cigicampus.org/about/)

136 Jeff Davis, New School Aims to Breath Life into Global Affairs, Embassy, Feb 20 2008 (https://www.cigionline.org/articles/2008/02/new-school-aims-breath-life-global-affairs)

137 Dominique Esser, Haiti Democracy Project: Supporting Coup Plotters since 2002 (https://www.indybay.orgnewsitems/2006/06/20/18281608.php)

138 Ahuva Balofsky, Media Mogul Haim Saban Would 'Bomb Living Daylights' out of Iran, Nov 12 2014 (http://www.breakingisraelnews.com/24182/media-mogul-haim-saban-bomb-living-daylights-iran/#YJhcxFRyO0FeIWgt.99) ; Philip Weiss, How fair is Martin Indyk, who says he was motivated by 'my… connection to Israel'?, July 22 2013 (http://mondoweiss.net/2013/07/how-fair-is-martin-indyk-who-says-he-was-motivated-by-my-connection-to-israel#sthash.Tcl2LT0J.dpuf)

139 Michael Valpy, Balsillie's disappointing foray into global affairs, Globe and Mail, Dec 16 2009 (http://www.theglobeandmail.com/news/national/balsillies-disappointing-foray-into-global-affairs/article1215757/)

A Propaganda System

140 CAUT Warns of Censure for Waterloo and Wilfrid Laurier (https://www.cautbulletin.ca/en_article.asp?ArticleID=3473)
141 Len Findlay, Investigation into the Termination of Dr. Ramesh Thakur as Director of the Balsillie School of International Affairs, affiliated with the University of Waterloo, Wilfrid Laurier University, and the Waterloo-based Centre for International Governance Innovation, Canadian Association of University Teachers, Sept 27 2010 (https://www.caut.ca/docs/default-source/af-ad-hoc-investigatory-committees/report-on-the-termination-of-dr-ramesh-thakur-as-director-of-the-balsillie-school-of-international-affairs-(2010).pdf?sfvrsn=4)
142 Ibid
143 Ibid
144 Ibid
145 Norman Paterson School of International Affairs (https://en.wikipedia.org/wiki/Norman_Paterson_School_of_International_Affairs)
146 J. L. Granatstein, A Man of Influence: Norman A. Robertson and Canadian Statecraft, 1929-68, 371
147 Ibid, 372/374
148 E. L. M. Burns (https://en.wikipedia.org/wiki/E._L._M._Burns)
149 Ibid
150 Michael Fry, Freedom and Change: Essays in Honour of Lester B. Pearson, Foreword
151 Norman Paterson School of International Affairs (https://en.wikipedia.org/wiki/Norman_Paterson_School_of_International_Affairs#cite_note-13)
152 Ibid
153 William and Jeanie Barton Chair in International Affairs (https://carleton.ca/npsia/about/william-and-jeanie-barton-chair-in-international-affairs/)
154 Faculty (http://carleton.ca/npsia/faculty/)
155 Ibid
156 Mary-Lou Schagena, CIGI celebrates 25th anniversary of Canada Among Nations book series, Apr 30 2010 (https://www.cigionline.org/articles/2010/04/cigi-celebrates-25th-anniversary-canada-among-nations-book-series)
157 Maxwell A. Cameron and Maureen Appel Molot, Canada Among Nations, 1995: Democracy and Foreign Policy, Preface ; Fen Osler Hampson and Christopher J. Maule, Canada Among Nations, 1993-94: Global Jeopardy, Preface

158 Encouraging the study of Islam: The State of Kuwait donates to the Institute of Islamic Studies, June 28 2007 (https://www.mcgill.ca/newsroom/channels/news/encouraging-study-islam-state-kuwait-donates-institute-islamic-studies-25900) ; Jennifer Campbell, Kuwait promotes Arabic studies, Ottawa Citizen, July 4 2007
159 King Abdullah Chair for Dialogue established at University of Toronto, June 29 2010 (https://www.saudiembassy.net/latest_news/news06291002.aspx) ; McGill's Institute of Islamic Studies receives $1.25 M gift from State of Qatar, Mar 26 2012 (https://www.mcgill.ca/newsroom/channels/news/mcgill%E2%80%99s-institute-islamic-studies-receives-125-m-gift-state-qatar-215711)
160 Executive Profile, James M. Stanford, O.C. Director, Omers Energy, (Inc.http://www.bloomberg.com/research/stocks/private/person.asp?personId=352855&privcapId=47056139) ; Barbara Black, $1.3 million Donation to MIGS for prevention project, Mar 20 2008 (http://cjournal.concordia.ca/archives/20080320/13_million_donation_to_migs_for_prevention_project.php)
161 Will to Intervene (W2I) (https://www.concordia.ca/research/migs/projects/will-to-intervene.html)
162 Anthony Fenton, Haiti and the Danger of the Responsibility to Protect (R2P), Dec 22 2008 (http://upsidedownworld.org/main/haiti-archives-51/1638-haiti-and-the-danger-of-the-responsibility-to-protect-r2p-)
163 Western To Establish New Chair In Central Banking Following $2-Million Gift From Jarislowsky Foundation (http://www.am980.ca/2016/05/09/jarislowsky-chair-western-donation/) (http://www.democracy.arts.ubc.ca/governance/merilees-chair/) ; Rhonda Spivak, U of M gets ME chair, Jewish Independent, Oct 12 2007 (http://www.jewishindependent.ca/oldsite/archives/oct07/archives07Oct12-03.html)
164 C.D. Howe Institute Annual Report, 2005 (https://www.cdhowe.org/pdf/annual_report_2005.pdf) ; Frederic Tomesco, SNC-Lavalin's top shareholder criticizes board for lax oversight before payments probe, Apr 30 2012 (http://business.financialpost.com/news/snc-lavalins-top-shareholder-criticizes-board-for-lax-oversight-before-payments-probe)
165 Peter C. Newman, The Canadian Establishment Volume 1, 146
166 Bronfman Chair Named, University of Toronto

A Propaganda System

Magazine, Autumn 2001 (http://magazine.utoronto.ca/life-on-campus/emanuel-adler-bronfman-chair-in-israeli-studies/)
167 Ibid
168 Paul Lungen, University of Toronto launches chair in Israeli studies, Canadian Jewish News Dec 11 1997
169 LIBI Fund - Supporting Our Soldiers, Haaretz, Feb 8 2009 (http://www.haaretz.com/news/libi-fund-supporting-our-soldiers-1.269673)
170 Champion: Sydney Kahanoff, Alberta Champions (http://www.albertachampions.org/champions-Sydney_Kahanoff.htm#.Vz4BX_krJaQ)
171 Laurie Monsebraaten, Shira Herzog, 61, was a progressive Canadian voice on Israel, Toronto Star, Aug 25 2014 (https://www.thestar.com/news/gta/2014/08/25/obituary_shira_herzog_61_was_a_progressive_canadian_voice_on_israel.html)
172 Naomi Azrieli, Azrieli Foundation donates $5 million to Concordia University, June 22 2011 (http://www.concordia.ca/cunews/main/releases/2011/06/22/azrieli-foundation-donates-5-million-to-concordia-university.html)
173 Ibid
174 Garry Marr, David Azrieli, Canadian billionaire and real estate tycoon, dies at age 92, July 9 2014 (http://business.financialpost.com/news/david-azrieli-canadian-billionaire-and-real-estate-tycoon-dies-at-age-92) ; Ilan Pappé, The Ethnic Cleansing of Palestine, 158
175 CUPE Boycott Petition (http://academicsforpeace.ca/petitions/archive/cupe-boycott/)
176 Sara DuBreuil, How can Israel become more sustainable? June 1-3: annual meeting of the Association for Israel Studies comes to Concordia, May 13 2015 (http://www.concordia.ca/cunews/main/stories/2015/05/13/israel-more-sustainable-association-israel-studies.html)
177 Gerald Steinberg, Learning lessons from Concordia, Canadian Jewish News, June 24 2015 (http://www.cjnews.com/news/israel/learning-lessons-concordia)
178 Nakina Stratos, Letters: BDS against Israel and the vote at Concordia, Montreal Gazette, Dec 18 2014 (http://montrealgazette.com/opinion/letters/letters-bds-against-israel-and-the-vote-at-concordia)
179 Faculty of Arts and Science launches campaign for Jewish Studies, Oct 16 2012 (http://boundless.utoronto.ca/news/faculty-of-arts-science-launches-campaign-for-jewish-studies/)
180 David Noble, The New Israel Lobby in Action, Nov 1 2005 (https://canadiandimension.com/articles/view/the-new-israel-lobby-in-action-david-noble)
181 McGill Jewish Studies department receives $1-million gift, June 6 2012 (http://academica.ca/top-ten/mcgill-jewish-studies-department-receives-1-million-gift)
182 Hillel Israel Guidelines (http://www.hillel.org/jewish/hillel-israel/hillel-israel-guidelines)
183 David Morrison, Aid and Ebb Tide: A History of CIDA and Canadian Development Assistance, 170
184 Ibid, 171
185 University Partnerships in Cooperation and Development Program Evaluation, Evaluation Division Performance and Knowledge Management Branch, Canadian International Development Agency, Feb 2007 (http://www.oecd.org/derec/canada/40690638.pdf)
186 CIDA funds the University of Calgary to help rebuild the education system in Kosovo, Canadian International Development Agency, Aug 20 2001 (http://reliefweb.int/report/serbia/cida-funds-university-calgary-help-rebuild-education-system-kosovo)
187 Leonora Angeles and Peter Boothroyd, Canadian Universities and International Development: Learning from Experience, Canadian Journal of Development Studies, Vol 24 No 1
188 Ian Smillie, The Land of Lost Content: A History of CUSO, 17
189 Ibid
190 Ibid, 35 ; David Morrison, Aid and Ebb Tide, 55
191 Ruth Compton Brouwer, Canada's Global Villagers: CUSO in Development, 198
192 Ibid
193 Ibid, 199
194 Dr. David Morrison (https://www.trentu.ca/morrison/bios.php)
195 Arja Vainio-Mattila, Kris Inwood and Aradhana Parmar, Perspectives on International Development Studies in Canadian Universities: The Canadian Consortium of University Programs in International Development Studies (CCUPIDS), Canadian journal of development studies, Vol 25 Mar 2004
196 IDRC: 40 years of ideas, innovation, and impact, 15

197 Ibid
198 Jim Freedman, Transforming Development: foreign aid for a changing world, 292
199 Madeleine Hardin, Faculty Members (http://www.ufv.ca/cmns/faculty-and-staff/faculty-members/madeleine-hardin/)
200 Membership Fee Increase, Sept 25 2015 (https://www.casid-acedi.ca/membership)
201 The Canadian Association for the Study of International Development: Organizational Strengthening 2012-2015 (https://www.idrc.ca/en/project/canadian-association-study-international-development-organizational-strengthening-2012-2015)
202 White paper on international development studies in Canada, The Canadian Association for the Study of International Development and The North-South Institute, Oct 2003 (http://citeseerx.ist.psu.edu/viewdoc/download;jsessionid=7450CCB3DA6202720968372DED465B16?doi=10.1.1.120.1199&rep=rep1&type=pdf)
203 InSight Canadian National Student's Conference in International Development Studies, 2005 (http://www.trentu.ca/stuorg/insight/2005programme.pdf) ; Andrew Hay, Session Proposals, Feb 28 2014 (http://undercurrentjournal.ca/session-proposals/)
204 Sponsors and Partners (http://www.icd-jci.ca/en/sponsors-and-partners)
205 Current and recent funding at ISID (https://www.mcgill.ca/isid/research/funding)
206 Global Learning (http://discover.utoronto.ca/learning/global-learning)
207 (http://www.queensjournal.ca/story/2011-06-01/news/students-conduct-research-south-africa/)
208 White paper on international development studies in Canada, The Canadian Association for the Study of International Development and The North-South Institute, Oct 2003 (http://citeseerx.ist.psu.edu/viewdoc/download;jsessionid=7450CCB3DA6202720968372DED465B16?doi=10.1.1.120.1199&rep=rep1&type=pdf)
209 David Morrison, Aid and Ebb Tide, 171
210 Ibid
211 Peter Eglin, Intellectual Citizenship and the Problem of Incarnation, 67
212 Jeffery Klaehn, Bound by Power: Intended Consequences, 244
213 Ibid
214 Peter Eglin, Intellectual Citizenship and the Problem of Incarnation, 63
215 Jeffery Klaehn, Bound by Power, 242
216 Liisa North, Timothy David Clark and Viviana Patroni, Community Rights and Corporate Responsibility Canadian Mining and Oil Companies in Latin America, 220
217 Mining Community Invests in New UBC Mining and Mineral Exploration Centre, Jan 16 2008 (https://science.ubc.ca/news/mining-community-invests-new-ubc-mining-and-mineral-exploration-centre)
218 Ivanhoe Mines, Laurentian University and the University of Limpopo Forge Educational Partnership to Provide Skills for South Africa's Miners of Tomorrow, Sept 9 2015 (http://www.marketwired.com/press-release/ivanhoe-mines-laurentian-university-university-limpopo-forge-educational-partnership-tsx-ivn-2053656.htm)
219 About Ian Telfer (http://www.telfer.uottawa.ca/en/about-us/about-ian-telfer) ; Theresa Tedesco, Canadian business mogul Joseph Rotman dies at age 80, Jan 27 2015 (http://business.financialpost.com/news/fp-street/canadian-business-mogul-joseph-rotman-dies-at-age-80)
220 Jamie Brownlee, Academia Inc.: How Corporatization Is Transforming Canadian Universities, 115
221 Bruce Cheadle, Donors, schools, profs seek peace after turmoil in education philanthropy, Dec 30 2012 (http://www.theglobeandmail.com/news/national/donors-schools-profs-seek-peace-after-turmoil-in-education-philanthropy/article6802598/)
222 Kim Mackrael, Huge opportunities' for Canadian mining industry to work in developing countries, The Globe and Mail June 19, 2013
223 Brief: The Canadian International Institute for Extractive Industries and Development (CIIEID) MiningWatch Canada, Mar 2014 (www.miningwatch.ca/files/ciieid_overview_march2014_.pdf)
224 Sam Heaton, Trudeau appoints NATO academic as foreign policy advisor, Feb 14 2016 (https://tonyseed.wordpress.com/2016/02/14/trudeau-appoints-nato-academic-as-foreign-policy-advisor/)
225 Margaret Biggs (http://www.queensu.ca/sps/margaret-biggs)
226 Adam Chapnick, Canada's voice, 206

Chapter 5

1 M. V. Naidu, From an idea to an institution: the Canadian Institute of International Peace and Security, Peace Research, Vol 16 No 3 Sept 1984
2 Ibid
3 Carleton Mourns Loss of William H. Barton, Nov 12 2013 (http://newsroom.carleton.ca/2013/11/12/carleton-mourns-loss-william-h-barton/)
4 George Gray Bell (https://en.wikipedia.org/wiki/George_Gray_Bell)
5 Geoffrey Pearson and Nancy Gordon, Shooting Oneself in the Head: the demise of CIIPS, in Canada Among Nations 1993 – 94 ; Roy McFarlane, Pearson Discusses Peace And Security Institute, Peace Magazine, May 1985 (http://peacemagazine.org/archive/v01n3p09.htm)
6 Geoffrey Pearson and Nancy Gordon, Shooting Oneself in the Head: the demise of CIIPS, in Canada Among Nations 1993 – 94
7 Ibid
8 Ibid
9 Geoffrey Pearson, New Opportunities for Peace Research, Peace Magazine, Oct 1989 (http://peacemagazine.org/archive/v05n5p20.htm)
10 Geoffrey Pearson and Nancy Gordon, Shooting Oneself in the Head: the demise of CIIPS, in Canada Among Nations 1993 – 94
11 About IDRC (https://www.idrc.ca/en/about-idrc)
12 IDRC: 40 years of ideas, innovation, and impact, 31
13 Ibid, 13
14 Liam Swiss, New IDRC Appointments: DFAIT Takeover? 19 Jun 2013 (http://blog.liamswiss.com/2013/06/19/new-idrc-appointments-dfait-takeover/)
15 Paul Heinbecker and Bessma Momani, Canada and the Middle East: in theory and practice, 147
16 Student wins $20,000 IDRC award (http://www.journalism.ubc.ca/ubc_journalismstudent_wins_21000_idrc_award/)
17 Jerome Klassen and Greg Albo, Empire's Ally: Canada and the War in Afghanistan, 317
18 Paul Heinbecker and Bessma Momani, Canada and the Middle East: in theory and practice, 149
19 Patrick Martin, Arab-Israeli group takes Canadian agency to court over terminated funding, Globe and Mail, July 1 2010 (http://www.theglobeandmail.com/news/world/arab-israeli-group-takes-canadian-agency-to-court-over-terminated-funding/article1215647/)
20 David Morrison, Aid and Ebb Tide, 111
21 Ibid
22 Edward H. Berman, The Influence of the Carnegie, Ford, and Rockefeller Foundations on American Foreign Policy, 141
23 Stephen J. Macekura, Of Limits and Growth: The Rise of Global Sustainable Development in the Twentieth Century, 149
24 David Morrison, Aid and Ebb Tide, 111
25 Ibid
26 45 Years of History (http://www.parlcent.org/en/who-we-are/our-story/) ; Thomas M. Franck and Edward Weisband, Secrecy and Foreign policy, 148
27 Cranford Pratt, Middle Power Internationalism: The North-South Dimension, 170
28 David Morrison, Aid and Ebb Tide, 111
29 Ibid, 87
30 Ibid
31 Clyde Sanger, Half a loaf; Canada's semi-role among developing countries, xi
32 David Morrison, Aid and Ebb Tide, 215
33 Ibid, 301
34 Kristiana Powell and Stephen Baranyi (http://www.nsi-ins.ca/publications/protect-africa/)
35 Athena Kolbe, Human rights abuse and other criminal violations in Port-au-Prince, Haiti: a random survey of households, Lancet, Sep 2 2006
36 Ramesh Thakur, UN breathes life into'responsibility to protect', Mar 21 2011 (https://www.thestar.com/opinion/editorialopinion/2011/03/21/un_breathes_life_intoresponsibility_to_protect.html) ; A victory for the Responsibility to Protect (http://www.uottawa.ca/articles/a-victory-for-the-responsibility-to-protect)
37 C. J. Chivers and Eric Schmitt, In Strikes on Libya by NATO, an Unspoken Civilian Toll, Dec 17 2011 (http://www.nytimes.com/2011/12/18/world/africa/scores-of-unintended-casualties-in-nato-war-in-libya.html?_r=0)
38 Paula Butler and Evans Rubara, Popularizing new neo-colonial governance processes for African minerals? An analysis of Canada's North-South Institute's 'Governing Natural Resources for Africa's Development' conference, Pambazuka, June 11 2013 (http://www.pambazuka.org/global-south/popularizing-new-neo-colonial-governance-processes-african-minerals)
39 Ibid
40 Ibid
41 Blair Crawford, Ottawa-based think tank

A Propaganda System

to close, Ottawa Citizen, Sept 10 2014 (http://ottawacitizen.com/news/local-news/north-south-institute-ottawa-based-think-tank-to-close)
42 Ibid
43 William Hipwell, Katy Mamen, Viviane Weitzner and Gail Whiteman, Aboriginal Peoples and Mining in Canada: Consultation, Participation and Prospects for Change, The North - South Institute, 2002 (caid.ca/MiningCons2002.pdf)
44 David Ignatius, Innocence Abroad: The New World of Spyless Coups, Washington Post, Sept 22 1991 (https://www.washingtonpost.com/archive/opinions/1991/09/22/innocence-abroad-the-new-world-of-spyless-coups/92bb989a-de6e-4bb8-99b9-462c76b59a16/)
45 Yves Engler, The Politics of Money Haiti and the Left (https://canadiandimension.com/articles/view/the-politics-of-money-haiti-and-the-left-yves-engler)
46 Ibid
47 Marina Jiménez, Author of Lancet article on Haiti investigated, Globe and Mail, Sept 7 2006 (http://www.theglobeandmail.com/news/national/author-of-lancet-article-on-haiti-investigated/article1103480/)
48 Harsha Walia, Aid or Corporate Raid? Oct 28 2006 (http://www.dominionpaper.ca/foreign_policy/2006/10/28/canadian_a.html)
49 Archived - Canada's New Government reinforces its commitment to enhance justice and the rule of law in Afghanistan July 12 2007 (http://news.gc.ca/web/article-en.do?crtr.sj1D=&mthd=advSrch&crtr.mnthndVl=&nid=340359&crtr.dpt1D=&crtr.tp1D=&crtr.lc1D=&crtr.yrStrtVl=2008&crtr.kw=&crtr.dyStrtVl=26&crtr.aud1D=&crtr.mnthStrtVl=2&crtr.yrndVl=&crtr.dyndVl=)
50 Lauryn Oates, The cultural relativists can't excuse evil, Ottawa Citizen Jan 28 2009
51 Lauryn Oates, Don't share a table with the Taliban, Globe and Mail, Nov 3 2006
52 James Hall, Radio Canada International: voice of a middle power, 83
53 Hansard May 14 1951, 3003
54 James Hall, Radio Canada International, 85
55 Ibid, 72
56 Hansard May 5 1953, 4829; Aloysius Balawyder, In the Clutches of the Kremlin: Canadian–East European Relations, 1945–1962, 12
57 Tony Manera, A dream betrayed: The battle for the CBC, 187 ; James Hall, Radio Canada

International, 184
58 Ibid, 89
59 Elzbieta Olechowska, The age of international radio: radio Canada international (1945 – 2007), 79
60 Ibid, 77
61 Ibid, 27
62 Evan H. Potter, Branding Canada: Projecting Canada's Soft Power Through Public Diplomacy, 160
63 Ibid, 129
64 Ibid, 130
65 Ibid, 129
66 Ibid, 130
67 Ibid, 105
68 Evaluation of the Canadian Foreign Service Institute (http://www.international.gc.ca/about-a_propos/oig-big/2007/evaluation/CFSI-ICSE.aspx?lang=eng)
69 Evan H. Potter, Branding Canada, 102
70 Audit of the Canadian Embassy Washington (Including the Consulate of Philadelphia), Nov 2007 (http://www.international.gc.ca/about-a_propos/oig-big/2007/washington.aspx?lang=eng)
71 R Norton, Canadian Advocacy in Washington, D.C., 2009 (www.revparl.ca/32/3/32n3_09e_Norton.pdf)
72 Simon J. Potter, News and the British World: the emergence of an imperial press system, 1876-1922, 78
73 Ibid, 79
74 Sheena Cameron, Extracting an ounce of truth: Mainstream media coverage of Canadian mining neoliberalism, Electronic Theses and Dissertations, Paper 4765, 102
75 Project profile: North-South Fellowships 2010-2012 (http://www.acdi-cida.gc.ca/cidaweb%5Ccpo.nsf/projEn/S065180001)
76 Archived - Toronto Filmmaker Wins 2006 Deborah Fletcher Award of Excellence in Filmmaking, Apr 21 2006 (http://news.gc.ca/web/article-en.do?crtr.sj1D=&mthd=advSrch&crtr.mnthndVl=&nid=208389&crtr.dpt1D=&crtr.tp1D=&crtr.lc1D=&crtr.yrStrtVl=&crtr.kw=deborah%2Bfletcher%2Baward&crtr.dyStrtVl=&crtr.aud1D=&crtr.mnthStrtVl=&crtr.yrndVl=&crtr.dyndVl=)
77 Eric Mark, Some journalists and news organizations took government funding to produce work: is that a problem?, July 17 2013 (http://www.j-source.ca/article/some-journalists-and-news-organizations-took-government-funding-

78 Ibid
79 Ibid
80 Ibid
81 Ibid
82 Ibid ; Madelaine Drohan, Teaching ethics to journalists: Are we reinventing the wheel?, Chumir Foundation for Ethics in Leadership, July 25 2007 (http://www.madelainedrohan.com/writing/teachingethicstojournalists.pdf)
83 Richard Sanders, Freedom Network (Réseau Liberté): Embedding CBC Reporters in Haiti's Elitist Media, Press for Conversion! 62 (http://coat.ncf.ca/our_magazine/links/62/CBC.htm)
84 Ibid
85 Isabel K. Macdonald, Covering the coup: Canadian news reporting, journalists, and sources in the 2004 Haiti crisis, York University: MA thesis, 2006, 140
86 Danny Glover, Stop the Political Persecution of Aristide and Fanmi Lavalas Once and for All, Sept 19 2014 (http://www.huffingtonpost.com/danny-glover/aristide-fanmi-lavalas-political-persecution_b_5852006.html)
87 Richard Sanders, Freedom Network (Réseau Liberté): Embedding CBC Reporters in Haiti's Elitist Media, Press for Conversion! 62 (http://coat.ncf.ca/our_magazine/links/62/CBC.htm)
88 Ibid
89 Ibid
90 François L'Écuyer, "Haiti: Militarisation de la paix: La MINUSTAH complice ?" Journal d'Alternatives, June 29 2005
91 Nikolas Barry-Shaw, Alternatives ... To What? Mr. Contra and Montreal-based NGO share same analysis on Haiti, ZNet, Aug 17 2005 (http://www.pavedwithgoodintentions.ca/debate/nikalternativestowhat)
92 Oxfam-Québec Etats financiers consolidés au 31 mars 2015 (http://oxfam.qc.ca/wp-content/uploads/2014/09/Oxfam-Qu%C3%A9bec_conso.pdf)
93 Steven Chase, Aid path undermining Karzai regime, expert warns, Globe and Mail, June 6 2008
94 J. L. Granatstein, The new peace movement, National Post, Aug 20 2008
95 Ibid
96 Peggy Mason, President (http://www.rideauinstitute.ca/directors-and-senior-advisors/)
97 Cranford Pratt, Canadian International Development Assistance Policies: An Appraisal, 101
98 David Morrison, Aid and Ebb Tide, 2
99 Dru Oja Jay and Nik Barry Shaw, Paved with Good Intentions: Canada's development NGOs from idealism to imperialism, 154
100 Robert Miller, Aid as Peacemaker: Canadian Development Assistance and Third World Conflict, 127
101 Dru Oja Jay and Nik Barry Shaw, Paved with Good Intentions,162
102 Kim Mackrael, Ottawa ignored CIDA green light when it halted aid group's funding, Globe and Mail, Oct 27 2010
103 Gerald Caplan, Is the Harper government playing the anti-Semitic card?, Globe and Mail, Dec 22 2009
104 Lee Berthiaume, Cutting out the development NGO 'heart', Embassy, June 9 2010

Chapter 6

1 Vastel, Haïti mise en tutelle par l'ONU?, L'actualité, Mar 15 2003 (http://www.lactualite.com/monde/haiti-mise-en-tutelle-par-lonu/) Ottawa Initiative on Haiti, Toronto Haiti Action Committee (http://thac.ca/ottawa-initiative-on-haiti/)
2 Michel Vastel, Haïti mise en tutelle par l'ONU?, L'actualité, Mar 15 2003 (http://www.lactualite.com/monde/haiti-mise-en-tutelle-par-lonu/)
3 Jacques-Roger Booh, Le patron de Dallaire parle: Révélations sur les dérives d'un général de l'ONU au Rwanda,161
4 Ibid, 71/95
5 Charles Onana, Les secrets de la justice internationale: enquêtes truquées sur le génocide rwandais, 127
6 Edward Herman and David Peterson, Enduring Lies: The Rwandan Genocide in the Propaganda System, 20 Years Later, 63
7 Lee Berthiaume, Israel urged Canadian government not to cut aid to Palestinians over UN vote: documents, National Post, July 9 2013 (http://news.nationalpost.com/news/canada/canadian-politics/israel-urged-canadian-government-not-to-cut-aid-to-palestinians-over-un-vote-documents)
8 Ibid
9 Ibid
10 Canada feared popular uprising in Haiti after quake, Canadian Press, Mar 31 2011 (http://www.ctvnews.ca/canada-feared-popular-uprising-in-haiti-after-quake-1.625850)

A Propaganda System

11 Ibid
12 Alycia Coulter and Lucy Ellis, The Canadian Armed Forces mark five years since earthquake in Haiti, Jan 12 2015 (http://www.forces.gc.ca/en/news/article.page?doc=the-canadian-armed-forces-mark-five-years-since-earthquake-in-haiti/i3yarmz7)
13 Don Peat, HUSAR Not up to Task, Feds Say: Search and Rescue Team Told to Stand Down, Toronto Sun, Jan 17 2010 (http://www.torontosun.com/news/haiti/2010/01/17/12504981.html)
14 Sheena Cameron, Extracting an ounce of truth: Mainstream media coverage of Canadian mining neoliberalism, Electronic Theses and Dissertations, Paper 4765, 127
15 Ibid
16 Dave Dean, 75% of the World's Mining Companies Are Based in Canada, July 9 2013 (http://www.vice.com/en_ca/read/75-of-the-worlds-mining-companies-are-based-in-canada)
17 Jeffery Klaehn, Corporate Hegemony. A Critical Assessment of the Globe and Mail's News Coverage of Near-Genocide in Occupied East Timor 1975–80, Gazette: The International Journal for Communication Studies Vol 64 No 4
18 Sharon Scharfe, Complicity: Human Rights and Canadian Foreign Policy: The Case of East Timor, 115
19 Ibid
20 Jefferey Klaehn, Filtering the News: essays on Herman and Chomsky's propaganda model, 145
21 Jeffery Klaehn, Corporate Hegemony. A Critical Assessment of the Globe and Mail's News Coverage of Near-Genocide in Occupied East Timor 1975–80, Gazette: The International Journal for Communication Studies Vol 64 No 4
22 Ibid
23 Ibid
24 Ibid
25 Joseph Jackson, Newspaper Ownership in Canada: An Overview of the Davey Committee and Kent Commission Studies, Dec 17 1999 (http://publications.gc.ca/Collection-R/LoPBdP/BP/prb9935-e.htm)
26 Media Convergence: How free is Canada's press?, CBC Digital Archives (http://www.cbc.ca/archives/entry/media-convergence-how-free-is-canadas-press)
27 Marc Edge, Asper Nation: Canada's Most Dangerous Media Company, 131
28 Marc Edge, Convergence and the "Black News Hole", Canadian Journal of Media Studies, Vol 2 No 1
29 Marc Edge, Asper Nation, 131
30 Clint Hendler, TNR's New Owners, The Nation, Mar 6 2007 (http://www.thenation.com/article/tnrs-new-owners/)
31 Ibid
32 Newspapers accused of misusing word 'terrorist', CBC, Sept 17 2004 (http://www.cbc.ca/news/canada/newspapers-accused-of-misusing-word-terrorist-1.489670)
33 Hansard Apr 6 1955, 2885
34 Jamie Swift and Brian Tomlinson, Conflicts of Interest: Canada and the Third World, 288
35 Robert G Picard et al, Press concentration and monopoly: new perspectives on newspaper ownership and operation, 113-114
36 Sheena Cameron, Extracting an ounce of truth: Mainstream media coverage of Canadian mining neoliberalism, Electronic Theses and Dissertations, Paper 4765, 52
37 Ibid, 52
38 (Bombardier board members were André Bérard and Jean Monty)
39 Board of Directors (http://thomsonreuters.com/en/about-us/board-of-directors.html)
40 Sheena Cameron, Extracting an ounce of truth: Mainstream media coverage of Canadian mining neoliberalism, Electronic Theses and Dissertations, Paper 4765, 42
41 Ibid, 42-43
42 Canada's leading advertisers in 2014 were: (http://www.adbrands.net/ca/top_advertisers_in_canada.htm)
43 Canada's Top 10 Military Producers, The Ploughshares Monitor, Winter 2003 Vol 24 Is. 4 (http://ploughshares.ca/pl_publications/canadas-top-10-military-producers/)
44 Knowlton Nash, The Microphone Wars: A History of Triumph and Betrayal at the CBC, 245
45 Elimination of advertising on CBC/Radio-Canada Services would be bad public policy (http://www.cbc.radio-canada.ca/en/reporting-to-canadians/reports/value/elimination/)
46 The Conservative Broadcasting Corporation, Friends of Canadian Broadcasting, Apr 26 2016 (https://www.friends.ca/blog-post/11728)
47 Knowlton Nash, The Microphone Wars, 19-22
48 A.E. Powley, Broadcast from the front: Canadian radio overseas in the second world war, 13 ; Leonard Walter Brockington, Behind the Diary: A

King's Who's Who Biographies (1888-1966) (https://www.collectionscanada.gc.ca/king/023011-1050.47-e.html)

49 Knowlton Nash, The Microphone Wars, 155-156

50 Alain Canuel, La censure en temps de guerre: Radio-Canada et le plébiscite de 1942, Revue d'histoire de l'Amérique française, Vol 52 No 2 1998

51 Arnold Davidson Dunton (http://www.thecanadianencyclopedia.ca/en/article/arnold-davidson-dunton) ; Mallory Schwartz, War on the Air: CBC-TV and Canada's Military, 1952-1992

52 History (http://www.rcinet.ca/english/about-us/historic/)

53 Mallory Schwartz, War on the Air: CBC-TV and Canada's Military, 1952-1992, 114

54 Ibid

55 Ibid,

56 Canadian Broadcasting Corporation : a brief history, 31

57 Mallory Schwartz, War on the Air, 98

58 Ibid, 71 ; Ian McKay and Jamie Swift, The Vimy Trap, 177

59 Mallory Schwartz, War on the Air, 112

60 Knowlton Nash, The Microphone Wars, 210

61 Mallory Schwartz, War on the Air, 81

62 Ibid, 81

63 Paul Rutherford, When Television was Young: Primetime Canada 1952-1967, 166

64 Ian Aitken, The Concise Routledge Encyclopedia of the Documentary Film, 134

65 Knowlton Nash, The Microphone Wars, 320

66 Tamara Baluja, 4.1 PR professionals for every journalist in Canada, Apr 7 2014 (http://www.j-source.ca/article/41-pr-professionals-every-journalist-canada)

67 Evan H. Potter, Branding Canada, 313 ; Canadian International Development Agency (https://www.tbs-sct.gc.ca/cla/idevi01-eng.asp)

68 David Pugliese, Veteran DND public affairs staff quitting over interference: report, Sept 25 2011 (http://news.nationalpost.com/news/canada/veteran-dnd-public-affairs-staff-quitting-over-interference-report)

69 Don Butler, New media training at Foreign Affairs aims to help officials avoid 'pitfalls', Ottawa Citizen, Jan 16 2014 (http://ottawacitizen.com/news/new-media-training-at-foreign-affairs-aims-to-help-officials-avoid-pitfalls)

70 Support to BCIU luncheon discussion with Major General Khaled Megawer, Mar 6 2016 (http://www.garda-world.com/news/entry/support-to-bciu-luncheon-discussion-with-major-general-khaled-megawer)

71 Barrick Gold 2015 Annual Report (http://www.barrick.com/files/annual-report/Barrick-Annual-Report-2015.pdf)

72 Dave Dean, 75% of the World's Mining Companies Are Based in Canada, July 9 2013 (http://www.vice.com/en_ca/read/75-of-the-worlds-mining-companies-are-based-in-canada)

73 Sheena Cameron, Extracting an ounce of truth: Mainstream media coverage of Canadian mining neoliberalism, Electronic Theses and Dissertations, Paper 4765

74 Anurag Dhir, Mines and mud-slinging, Montréal Mirror, Oct 11 2007

75 Ibid

76 Responsible Mining Activities Supported by Major Ecuadorian Indigenous Association, Marketwire, Dec 5 2007 (http://www.marketwired.com/press-release/corrientes-responsible-mining-activities-supported-major-ecuadorian-indigenous-association-tsx-ctq-799973.htm)

77 Jennifer Moore, How Good is Canada's Word? Vancouver's Corriente Resources in deep in Ecuador, Dominion Paper, Winter 2008 (http://s3.amazonaws.com/dominionfiles/pdf/dominion-issue55.pdf)

78 Ibid

79 John Ahni Schertow, Propaganda campaign against Mining Watch Canada, Oct 15 2007 (https://intercontinentalcry.org/propaganda-campaign-against-mining-watch-canada/)

80 Canada in the Hemisphere Perspective Paper, Apr 24 2015 (http://www.ccacanada.com/launch-of-the-the-ccas-first-canada-in-the-hemisphere-perspective-paper-may-7th-1150-130/#.V1ipB5VFDQw)

81 http://news.nationalpost.com/news/canada/canada-planning-to-sell-guns-and-military-equipment-to-developing-countries-to-maintain-domestic-arms-industry

82 Ian MacLeod, Social media powerful tool for terrorists, expert warns, Ottawa Citizen, Nov 26 2015 (http://ottawacitizen.com/news/politics/social-media-powerful-tool-for-terrorists-expert-warns)

83 The Aerospace Industries Association of Canada (AIAC) Submission to the Standing Committee on Finance's Pre-budget Consultations Immediate Measures to Maintain and Increase our Global

A Propaganda System

Aerospace Market Share, Aug 2011 (http://www.parl.gc.ca/Content/HOC/Committee/411/FINA/WebDoc/WD5138047/411_FINA_PBC2011_Briefs%5CAerospace%20Industries%20Association%20of%20Canada%20E.pdf) ; Stephanie Findlay, F-35 jet still popular with aerospace industry, Toronto Star, Apr 6 2012 (http://www.thestar.com/news/canada/2012/04/06/f35_jet_still_popular_with_aerospace_industry.html)

84 James G. Fergusson, Canada and ballistic missile defense, 1954 – 2009, 96

85 Kyle Duggan, Canada arms exports continue to rise, explosives sales double in 2013, Mar 10 2014 (http://www.davidmckie.com/canada-arms-exports-continue-to-rise-explosives-sales-double-in-2013/)

86 James G. Fergusson, Canada and ballistic missile defense, 96

87 John Spears, Munk takes on mine protesters, defends capitalism, Toronto Star, Dec 27 2012 (https://www.thestar.com/business/2010/04/28/munk_takes_on_mine_protesters_defends_capitalism.html)

88 Geoffrey York, Deadly clashes continue at African Barrick gold mine, Globe and Mail, Aug 26 2014 (http://www.theglobeandmail.com/report-on-business/international-business/deadly-clashes-continue-at-african-barrick-gold-mine/article20216197/)

89 Top 50 Socially Responsible Corporations, Macleans, June 14 2010 (http://www.macleans.ca/economy/business/social-responsible-corp-2010/)

90 Carolyn Leitch, Analysts upsize Gildan targets, Globe and Mail, Apr 11 2005 (http://www.theglobeandmail.com/report-on-business/analysts-upsize-gildan-targets/article1116830/)

91 John R. Walker, Third World news coverage: a survey of leading Canadian dailies, 13

92 Jacqueline Ismael and Tareq Ismael, Canada and the New American Empire, 33

93 Gene Allen, Making National News: a History of Canadian Press, 6

94 John Jirik, The world according to (Thomson) Reuters, Sur le journalisme - About journalism, Vol 2 No 1 2013

95 Mark Bourrie, Fighting Words: Canada's Best War Reporting, 316 ; Jack Cahill, If You Don't Like the War, Switch the Damn Thing Off!, 42

96 Alicia Upano, Will a history of government using journalists repeat itself under the Department of Homeland Security? The News Media and The Law, Winter 2003 (http://www.rcfp.org/browse-media-law-resources/news-media-law/news-media-and-law-winter-2003/will-history-government-usi#.dpuf) ; Jonathan Cook, CIA emails expose access journalist at work, Sept 5 2014 (http://www.jonathan-cook.net/blog/2014-09-05/cia-emails-expose-access-journalist-at-work/)

97 Jack Cahill, If You Don't Like the War, Switch the Damn Thing Off!, 142

98 Mallory Schwartz, War on the Air, 18

99 Five O'Clock Follies (https://en.wikipedia.org/wiki/Five_O%27Clock_Follies)

100 Mallory Schwartz, War on the Air: CBC-TV and Canada's Military, 1952-1992, 119

101 Ibid

102 Ibid

103 Daniel Terrance Hurley, Turning around a supertanker: media-military relations in Canada in the CNN age, Carleton University Masters, 2000,16

104 Peter Desbarats, Somalia Cover-up: a commissioners journal, 90

105 Eric Mark, Some journalists and news organizations took government funding to produce work: is that a problem?, July 17 2013 (http://www.j-source.ca/article/some-journalists-and-news-organizations-took-government-funding-produce-work-problem-)

106 Workshops conducted (http://www.madelainedrohan.com/train.html)

107 Madeleine Drohan (http://www.madelainedrohan.com/)

108 Alina Seagal, The Russian Enigma, Ryerson Review of Journalism, Mar 1 2008 (http://rrj.ca/the-russian-enigma/)

109 Jack Cahill, If You Don't Like the War, Switch the Damn Thing Off!, 192

110 Ibid, 42 ; John Stackhouse, Out of Poverty: And Into Something More Comfortable, 365

111 Ibid

112 Isabel K. Macdonald, Covering the coup: Canadian news reporting, journalists, and sources in the 2004 Haiti crisis, York University MA thesis, 2006, 140

113 Ibid

114 Ibid ; Richard Sanders, CIDA Bankrolled Coup`s Deputy Minister of Justice, Press for Conversion 61 (http://coat.ncf.ca/our_magazine/links/61/29-31.pdf)

115 Ibid

116 Robert Hackett, News and Dissent: The Press

and the Politics of Peace in Canada, 105/112
117 Ross Munro (https://en.wikipedia.org/wiki/Ross_Munro) Publishers to New Post, Ottawa Citizen, Dec 15 1975 (https://news.google.com/newspapers?nid=2194&dat=19751215&id=3r0yAAAAIBAJ&sjid=s-0FAAAAIBAJ&pg=2842,7499051&hl=fr)
118 Daniel Terrance Hurley, Turning around a supertanker: media-military relations in Canada in the CNN age, Carleton University Masters, 2000, 76
119 Ibid, 15
120 Ibid
121 Ibid, 16
122 Ibid, 17
123 Ibid, 17
124 Gene Allen, Making National News, 133
125 Legendary war correspondent always 'got the goods', Ottawa Citizen, Oct 19 2007 (http://www.canada.com/story_print.html?id=57494640-3d9f-4a14-8dfd-527935842ee6)
126 Gene Allen, News across the Border: Associated Press in Canada, 1894-1917, Journalism History, Vol 31 Winter 2006
127 Ibid
128 The Canadian Press history (http://www.thecanadianpress.com/about_cp.aspx?id=77)
129 Simon J. Potter, News and the British World, 202
130 Gene Allen, Making National News, 46 ; Gene Allen, News across the Border: Associated Press in Canada, 1894-1917, Journalism History, Vol 31 Winter 2006
131 Paul Knox, News for the World?, Literary Review of Canada, Dec 2010 (http://reviewcanada.ca/magazine/2010/12/news-for-the-world/
132 Ivanhoe Mines Responds to Misinformed and Damaging Comments Contained in Bloomberg Story, Oct 8 2014 (http://www.marketwired.com/press-release/ivanhoe-mines-responds-misinformed-damaging-comments-contained-bloomberg-story-tsx-ivn-1955916.htm)
133 Ibd
134 Geoffrey York, Robert Friedland's mining showdown in South Africa, Globe and Mail, Jan 9 2015 (http://www.theglobeandmail.com/report-on-business/international-business/robert-friedlands-mining-showdown-in-south-africa/article22390288/)
135 Noir Canada (https://fr.wikipedia.org/wiki/Noir_Canada)
136 Philip Resnick, Those Bricks Barrick Gold Dropped, Apr 21 2010 (http://thetyee.ca/Mediacheck/2010/04/21/BarrickBricks/)
137 Mike Fegelman, Backgrounds, biases need to be declared, QMI Agency Mar 27 2010 (http://www.lfpress.com/comment/2010/03/26/13372171.html)
138 Ibid
139 Pierre Chauvin, A Decade After: A Look Back at the 2002 Netanyahu Riot, Sept 11 2012 (http://thelinknewspaper.ca/article/a-decade-after/)
140 Yves Engler, Playing Left Wing: From Rink Rat to Student Radical, 125
141 James Adams, Shoppers Drug Mart removes Adbusters magazine, Globe and Mail, Nov 2 2010 (http://www.theglobeandmail.com/arts/shoppers-drug-mart-removes-adbusters-magazine/article1241416/)
142 Ibid
143 David Pugliese, Gen. Jon Vance responds to concerns over the "weaponization of public affairs" at DND, Sept 21 2015 (http://ottawacitizen.com/storyline/chief-of-the-defence-staff-gen-jon-vance-and-the-weaponization-of-public-affairs)
144 Ibid
145 Gwynne Dyer, Canada in the great game, 2
146 Ibid
147 Ibid
148 Mallory Schwartz, War on the Air: CBC-TV and Canada's Military, 1952-1992, 307/337
149 E.J. Dick, The Valour and the Horror Continued: Do We Still Want Our History on Television?, Journal of the Association of Canadian Archivists, Spring 1993 (journals.sfu.ca/archivar/index.php/archivaria/article/viewFile/.../12854)
150 We weren't always "the one that's read.", History (http://espritdecorps.ca/about/)
151 Scott Taylor, Unembedded, 39
152 Ibid, 62
153 Ibid, 63
154 Scott Taylor, Unembedded, 145
155 Ibid
156 Edward Herman and Noam Chomsky, A Propaganda Model Excerpted from Manufacturing Consent, 1988 (https://chomsky.info/consent01/)

Chapter 7

1 Patrick Cain, In the line of fire, Ryerson Review of Journalism, Aug 1 1996 (http://rrj.ca/in-the-line-of-fire/)

A Propaganda System

2 Robert Page, The Boer War and Canadian Imperialism, Canadian Historical Association Booklets Vol 44, 15

3 Lawrence James, The Savage Wars: British Campaigns in Africa, 1870-1920, 69

4 Kelley S. Kent, Propaganda, Public Opinion, and the Second South African Boer War 2013, Vol 5 No 10 (http://www.inquiriesjournal.com/articles/781/2/propaganda-public-opinion-and-the-second-south-african-boer-war)

5 Pierre Berton, Marching As to War: Canada's Turbulent Years, 1899-1953, 30

6 Allan Levine, Scrum war: The Prime Ministers and the Media, 54

7 Ibid, 56

8 Brian Douglas Tennyson, Canadian relations with South Africa: a diplomatic history, 29

9 Kate Barker, Breaking the News by Following the Rules: Canadian War Correspondents in World War Two Continued a Tradition of Bending to Authority, Submitted to Prof. Horn, Aug 1 2013 (www.katebarker.com/pdfs/MRPfinal.pdf)

10 Simon J. Potter, News and the British World, 51

11 Kate Barker, Breaking the News by Following the Rules: Canadian War Correspondents in World War Two Continued a Tradition of Bending to Authority, Submitted to Prof. Horn, Aug 1 2013 (www.katebarker.com/pdfs/MRPfinal.pdf)

12 Ibid ; Mark Bourrie, Fighting Words, 133 ;

13 Carman Miller, Research Resources on Canada and the South African War, Archivaria Archives and Military History, Summer 1988 (http://archivaria.ca/index.php/archivaria/article/view/11496)

14 Ibid

15 Ibid

16 Simon J. Potter, News and the British World, 51

17 Ibid

18 Autumn 1899 (Age 24) "World-Famous Overnight" (http://www.winstonchurchill.org/the-life-of-churchill/young-soldier/1896-1900/2841-autumn-1899-age-24)

19 Ibid, 179

20 Mark Bourrie, Canada's evolving military censorship, Apr 30 2010 (http://ottawawatch.blogspot.ca/2010/04/canadas-evolving-military-censorship.html)

21 Jeffrey A. Keshen, The War on Truth, Canada's History, Vol 95 Is. 4 Aug 2015

22 Kate Barker, Breaking the News by Following the Rules: Canadian War Correspondents in World War Two Continued a Tradition of Bending to Authority, Submitted to Prof. Horn, Aug 1 2013 (www.katebarker.com/pdfs/MRPfinal.pdf)

23 Mark Bourrie, The Fog of War: Censorship of Canada's Media in World War Two, 22

24 Robert Bergen, Censorship; the Canadian News Media and Afghanistan: A Historical Comparison with Case Studies Calgary Papers: In Military and Stratigic Studies

25 Word warriors and camera combatants unite, The Maple Leaf, Vol 16 No. 5 May 2013 (http://publications.gc.ca/site/archivee-archived.html?url=http://publications.gc.ca/collections/collection_2013/dn-nd/D12-7-16-5-eng.pdf)

26 Lord Beaverbrook (http://www.warmuseum.ca/firstworldwar/history/after-the-war/history/lord-beaverbrook/)

27 Donald Page, 'Canadians and the League of Nations before the Manchurian Crisis,' a discussion of Canadian public opinion and pressure groups during the 1920s, University of Toronto PhD thesis 1972, 66

28 Mark Bourrie, The Fog of War, 23

29 War Measures Act (http://www.canadahistoryproject.ca/1914/1914-04-war-measures-act.html)

30 Pearce J. Carefoote, Censorship in Canada (http://hpcanpub.mcmaster.ca/case-study/censorship-canada)

31 Jeffrey A. Keshen, Propaganda and Censorship during Canada's great war, 66

32 http://www.biographi.ca/en/bio/chambers_ernest_john_15E.html

33 Jeffrey A. Keshen, Propaganda and Censorship during Canada's great war, 66

34 Ernest John Chambers, The Great War Album (http://greatwaralbum.ca/Great-War-Album/About-the-Great-War/Unrest-on-the-homefront/Ernest-John-Chambers)

35 Kate Barker, Breaking the News by Following the Rules: Canadian War Correspondents in World War Two Continued a Tradition of Bending to Authority, Submitted to Prof. Horn, Aug 1 2013 (www.katebarker.com/pdfs/MRPfinal.pdf)

36 Jeffrey A. Keshen, The War on Truth, Canada's History, Vol 95 Aug 2015 ; Mark Bourrie, The Fog of War, 23

37 Ibid

38 Jeffrey A. Keshen, Propaganda and Censorship during Canada's great war, 73

39 Kate Barker, Breaking the News by Following

A Propaganda System

the Rules: Canadian War Correspondents in World War Two Continued a Tradition of Bending to Authority, Submitted to Prof. Horn, Aug 1 2013 (www.katebarker.com/pdfs/MRPfinal.pdf)
40 Pearce J. Carefoote, Censorship in Canada (http://hpcanpub.mcmaster.ca/case-study/censorship-canada)
41 Jeffrey A. Keshen, Propaganda and Censorship during Canada's great war, 79
42 Jeffrey A. Keshen, The War on Truth, Canada's History, Vol 95 Is. 4 Aug 2015
43 Mark Bourrie, Fighting Words, 144
44 L. Ruth Klein, Nazi Germany, Canadian Responses Confronting Antisemitism in the Shadow of War, 59
45 Timothy John Balzer, The Information Front: The Canadian Army, Public Relations, and War News during the Second World War, 2
46 Ibid
47 Holly Bridges, Canadian military photographers: The silent witnesses of war, Lookout, Dec 3 2012 (http://www.lookoutnewspaper.com/canadian-military-photographers-the-silent-witnesses-of-war/)
48 Dan Conlin, War through the lens: the Canadian Army film and photo unit, 159
49 About Canada's Military Photographers (https://www.collectionscanada.gc.ca/faces-of-war/025014-1000-e.html)
50 Eric Thompson, Canadian Warcos in World. War II: Professionalism, Patriotism and Propaganda, Mosaic 23 Summer 1990
51 Wartime Information Board (https://en.wikipedia.org/wiki/Wartime_Information_Board)
52 Gary Evans, John Grierson and the National Film Board: The politics of wartime propaganda, 3
53 Timothy John Balzer, The Information Front, 198
54 Mallory Schwartz, War on the Air: CBC-TV and Canada's Military, 1952-1992, 126
55 Eric Thompson, Canadian Warcos in World War II: professionalism, patriotism and propaganda
56 Knowlton Nash, The Microphone Wars, 178
57 Ibid, 187
58 Ibid, 186
59 Ibid
60 Kate Barker, Breaking the News by Following the Rules: Canadian War Correspondents in World War Two Continued a Tradition of Bending to Authority, Submitted to Prof. Horn, Aug 1 2013

(www.katebarker.com/pdfs/MRPfinal.pdf)
61 Timothy John Balzer, The Information Front, 31
62 Béatrice Richard, Dieppe The Making of a Myth, Canadian Military History, Vol 21 Iss. 4
63 Ibid
64 Kate Barker, Breaking the News by Following the Rules: Canadian War Correspondents in World War Two Continued a Tradition of Bending to Authority, Submitted to Prof. Horn, Aug 1 2013 (www.katebarker.com/pdfs/MRPfinal.pdf)
65 Ross Munro Award 2010, Mr. Murray Brewster (http://www.cgai.ca/ross_munro_award_2010)
66 Timothy John Balzer, The Information Front, 6
67 Robert Bergen, Censorship; the Canadian News Media and Afghanistan: A Historical Comparison with Case Studies, Calgary Papers in Military and Strategic Studies, 2009 ; Mark Bourrie, The Fog of War, 45
68 Comeau, Paul-André, Claude Beauregard and Edwige Munn, La démocratie en veilleuse: rapport sur la censure: récit de l'organisation, des activités et de la démobilisation de la censure pendant la guerre de 1939-45, 21
69 Mark Bourrie, Between Friends: Censorship of Canada's Media in World War II University of Ottawa PHD thesis, 153-53/434
70 Ibid ; James Naylor, Pacifism or anti-imperialism? The CCF response to the outbreak of World War II, Journal of the Canadian historical Association, Vol 8 No.1, 1997
71 Robin S. Gendron, Towards a Francophone Community: Canada's Relations with France and French Africa, 1945-1968, 24
72 Robert Teigrob, Warming up to the Cold War: Canada and the United States Coalition of the Willing, from Hiroshima to Korea, 185
73 Robert Bergen, Censorship; the Canadian News Media and Afghanistan: A Historical Comparison with Case Studies, Calgary Papers in Military and Strategic Studies, 2009
74 Robert Teigrob, Warming up to the Cold War, 188
75 Robin Andersen, A century of media, a century of war, 37
76 Daniel Fazio: Censorship in the Korean War. Press-Military Relations, June 1950-January 1951, Australasian Journal of American Studies, Vol 26 No. 2 Dec 2007
77 Canadian Forum, Military Censorship, Feb 1951
78 Stanley Sandler, The Korean War: An Encyclopedia, 271

A Propaganda System

79 Canadian Forum, Military Censorship, Feb 1951

80 John Price, Orienting Canada: Race, Empire, and the Transpacific, 264

81 Ibid

82 Friends, colleagues remember legendary war correspondent Bill Boss, Oct 18 2007 (http://www.cbc.ca/news/canada/toronto/friends-colleagues-remember-legendary-war-correspondent-bill-boss-1.642236) ; Mike's Korean War Pictures, Jan 25 2010 (http://webcache.googleusercontent.com/search?q=cache:b6kvBiS9HGQJ:www.hillmanweb.com/rivers/av/Korea2.pps+&cd=4&hl=en&ct=clnk&gl=ca)

83 John Price, Orienting Canada, 264

84 I.F. Stone, The Hidden History of the Korean War, 258

85 John Price, Orienting Canada, 271

86 Arnold Davidson Dunton (http://www.thecanadianencyclopedia.ca/en/article/arnold-davidson-dunton) ; Mallory Schwartz, War on the Air, 34

87 John Price, Orienting Canada, 275

88 Ibid, 279

89 James Gareth Endicott (https://en.wikipedia.org/wiki/James_Gareth_Endicott)

90 Gary Marcuse and Reginald Whitaker, Cold War Canada, 375

91 Ibid, 369

92 Ibid, 375-377

93 Canadian journalists say they are frustrated by censorship, Vancouver Sun, Jan 24 1991

94 Gulf War: Truth or propaganda? (http://www.cbc.ca/archives/entry/gulf-war-truth-or-propaganda) ; Nayirah (testimony) (https://en.wikipedia.org/wiki/Nayirah_(testimony))

95 Joshua Holland, The First Iraq War Was Also Sold to the Public Based on a Pack of Lies, June 27 2014 (http://billmoyers.com/2014/06/27/the-first-iraq-war-was-also-sold-to-the-public-based-on-a-pack-of-lies/)

96 Torie Rose DeGhett, The War Photo No One Would Publish, The Atlantic, Aug 8 2014 (http://www.theatlantic.com/international/archive/2014/08/the-war-photo-no-one-would-publish/375762/)

97 James Winter, Common Cents: Media Portrayal of the Gulf War and Other Events, 3

98 Tim Harper, CF-18 mission reports under strict censorship, Vancouver Sun, Jan 23 1991

99 Scott Taylor, Unembedded, 53

100 Ibid, 60

101 Duncan E. Miller, The Persian Excursion: the Canadian Navy in the Gulf War, 210

102 Robert Bergen, Censorship; the Canadian News Media and Afghanistan: A Historical Comparison with Case Studies, Calgary Papers in Military and Strategic Studies, 2009

103 Ibid ; Duncan E. Miller, The Persian Excursion, 204

104 Daniel Terrance Hurley, Turning around a supertanker: media-military relations in Canada in the CNN age, 24

105 Ibid, 25

106 Duncan E. Miller, The Persian Excursion, 205

107 David Taras and Christopher Waddell, How Canadians Communicate IV: Media and Politics (http://www.aupress.ca/books/120205/ebook/99Z_Taras_Waddell_2012-How_Canadians_Communicate_IV.pdf/), 217

108 Robert W. Bergen, Balkan Rats and Balkan Bats: The art of managing Canada's news media during the Kosovo air war, University of Calgary PhD dissertation, 2005, 93/369

109 The Missing News: Filters and Blind Spots in Canada's Press, 125

110 Mark Fineman, The Oil Factor in Somalia Los Angeles Times, Jan 18 1993 (http://articles.latimes.com/1993-01-18/news/mn-1337_1_oil reserves)

111 Sherene Razack, Dark Threats and White Knights: The Somalia Affair, Peacekeeping, and the New Imperialism, 4

112 Daniel Terrance Hurley, Turning around a supertanker: media-military relations in Canada in the CNN age, Carleton University Masters, 2000, 11

113 Somalia Inquiry Executive Summary (http://www.queensu.ca/dms/DMS_Course_Materials_and_Outline/Readings-MPA834/NDHQ%20Somalia%20Inquiry%20Executive%20Summary.pdf)

114 Ibid

115 David Salters, Medak Pocket: Canada's forgotten battle, Toronto Star, Sept 16 2013 (http://www.thestar.com/news/insight/2013/09/14/medak_pocket_canadas_forgotten_battle.htm)

116 Carol Off, The Ghosts of Medak Pocket, 10

117 Ibid, 273; Scott Taylor, INAT: images of Serbia and the Kosovo Conflict, 15

118 David Salters, Medak Pocket: Canada's forgotten battle, Toronto Star, Sept 16 2013 (http://www.thestar.com/news/insight/2013/09/14/medak_pocket_canadas_forgotten_battle.htm)

A Propaganda System

119 Scott Taylor, INAT, 17

120 Scott Taylor, Tested mettle: Canada's peacekeepers at war, 207

121 Ibid

122 Scott Taylor, INAT, 38

123 Chris Wattie, Forces refused U.S. Request out of Iraq fears, National Post, Sept 10 2004

124 Kosovo War (https://en.wikipedia.org/wiki/Kosovo_War#Civilian_losses)

125 Daniel Terrance Hurley, Turning around a supertanker: media-military relations in Canada in the CNN age, Carleton University Masters, 2000, 179

126 James Winter, Media Think, 77

127 Scott Taylor, Diary of an Uncivil War: The Violent Aftermath of the Kosovo Conflict, 12

128 Scott Taylor, INAT, 144

129 James Winter, Media Think, 72

130 Scott Taylor, INAT, 146

131 Scott Taylor, Unembedded, 212

132 David Taras and Christopher Waddell, How Canadians Communicate IV: Media and Politics (http://www.aupress.ca/books/120205/ebook/99Z_Taras_Waddell_2012-How_Canadians_Communicate_IV.pdf/), 217

133

134 Robert W. Bergen, Balkan Rats and Balkan Bats: The art of managing Canada's news media during the Kosovo air war, University of Calgary PhD dissertation, 2005, 275

135 Ibid

136 Ibid

137 Ibid, 276

138 Ibid

139 Ibid, 369

140 The Canadian Armed Forces in Afghanistan, Introduction (http://www.veterans.gc.ca/eng/remembrance/history/canadian-armed-forces/afghanistan)

141 Kim Mackrael, Canada's role in Iraq could mirror Afghanistan, foreign minister says, Globe and Mail, Mar 5 2015 (http://www.theglobeandmail.com/news/politics/foreign-affairs-minister-nicholson-to-speak-about-secret-trip-to-iraq/article23305564/)

142 Captain Ray Wiss, Line in the Sand: Canadians at War in Kandahar ; DND financing books praising Afghan war, Dec 24 2008 (http://www.ceasefire.ca/?p=643#sthash.U9df3dtK.dpuf)

143 Lt.-Col Michael Vernon, Desert Lions

144 Sharon Hobson, Operations Security and the Public's Need to Know, Prepared for the Canadian Defence and Foreign Affairs Institute, Mar 2011 (https://d3n8a8pro7vhmx.cloudfront.net/cdfai/pages/41/attachments/original/1413662074/Operations_Security_and_the_Publics_Need_to_know.pdf?1413662074) ; Robert Bergen, Censorship; the Canadian News Media and Afghanistan: A Historical Comparison with Case Studies, Calgary Papers in Military and Strategic Studies, 2009

145 James Laxer, It's time to recalibrate Canada's mission, Globe and Mail, July 22 2008 (http://www.theglobeandmail.com/opinion/its-time-to-recalibrate-canadas-mission/article1057765/)

146 Chris Wattie, Embedded in Ontario as military hones media skills, National Post, July 12 2003

147 Semi Chellas, Good to Go, Walrus, Feb 2007 (http://thewalrus.ca/2007-02-media/)

148 Bob Bergen, Disarming the Media, Alberta Views, Apr 2007 (https://albertaviews.ab.ca/wp-content/uploads/2014/08/Disarming-the-Media-Bob-Bergen.pdf)

149 Ibid

150 Allan Thompson, Outside the wire, Canadian Association of Journalists, Vol 12 Winter 2007 (http://caj.ca/wp-content/uploads/2010/mediamag/winter2007/mediawinter2007.pdf)

151 Jay Janzen, Op ATHENA ROTO 0 Embedded Media, Canadian Army Journal Fall/Winter 2004 (http://publications.gc.ca/collections/Collection/D12-11-7-3-4E.pdf)

152 Robert Bergen, Censorship; the Canadian News Media and Afghanistan: A Historical Comparison with Case Studies, Calgary Papers in Military and Strategic Studies, 2009 ; (http://www.theglobeandmail.com/news/national/pms-office-sought-a-positive-spin-from-reporters/article959572/)

153 Sharon Hobson, The Information Gap: Why the Canadian Public Doesn't Know More About its Military, Prepared for the Canadian Defence and Foreign Affairs Institute, June 2007 (http://dspace.africaportal.org/jspui/bitstream/123456789/10386/1/The%20Information%20Gap%20%20Why%20the%20Canadian%20Public%20Doesnt%20Know%20More%20About%20its%20Military%202007.pdf?1)

154 Sherry Wasilow, Hidden Ties that Bind: The Psychological Bonds of Embedding Have Changed the Very Nature of War Reporting, Stream, Vol 4 No 1 2011

A Propaganda System

155 Ibid

156 Vern Huffman, As Generals Send the Nation to War, Canadian Dimension, Nov 2006 (https://canadiandimension.com/articles/view/as-generals-send-the-nation-to-war-vern-huffman)

157 Jay Janzen, Op ATHENA ROTO 0 Embedded Media, Canadian Army Journal Fall/Winter 2004 (http://publications.gc.ca/collections/Collection/D12-11-7-3-4E.pdf)

158 Sharon Hobson, The Information Gap: Why the Canadian Public Doesn't Know More About its Military, Prepared for the Canadian Defence and Foreign Affairs Institute, June 2007 (http://dspace.africaportal.org/jspui/bitstream/123456789/10386/1/The%20Information%20Gap%20%20Why%20the%20Canadian%20Public%20Doesnt%20Know%20More%20About%20its%20Military%202007.pdf?1)

159 Murray Brewster, The Savage War: The Untold Battles of Afghanistan, 263

160 Louise Bourbonnais, Pas d'indépendants en Afghanistan, Trente, Dec 2007 (http://www.fpjq.org/opinion-pas-dindependants-en-afghanistan/)

161 Scott Taylor, Military passes on touching photo op, Halifax Chronicle-Herald, Jan 29 2007

162 Lyndsie Bourgon, Reporting from the front lines, King's Journalism Review, Feb 19 2008 (http://thekjr.kingsjournalism.com/reporting-from-the-front-lines/)

163 Ulrich Mans, Christa Meindersma and Lars Burema, Eyes Wide Shut? The Impact of Embedded Journalism on Dutch Newspaper Coverage of Afghanistan, The Hague Centre for Strategic Studies, Apr 2008

164 Rebecca Lamarche, The challenges of embedded war reporting, King's Journalism Review, Jan 24 2013 (http://thekjr.kingsjournalism.com/tag/canadian-forces/feed/)

165 J Sheppard, Globe columnist, reporters on 'embedded' journalists, Globe and Mail, June 8 2006 (http://www.theglobeandmail.com/opinion/globe-columnist-reporters-on-embedded-journalists/article1100382/?page=all)

166 Rebecca Lamarche, The challenges of embedded war reporting, King's Journalism Review, Jan 24 2013 (http://thekjr.kingsjournalism.com/tag/canadian-forces/feed/)

167 Ashley Walters, All Disquiet on the Western Front, This Magazine, Jan 2009

168 CDA and Matthew Fisher rush to military's defence, May 5 2009 (http://www.ceasefire.ca/?p=1302#sthash.NScPlpWh.dpuf)

169 Authorities watching embedded reporters closely, Canadian Press, Sept 13 2009 (http://www.ctvnews.ca/authorities-watching-embedded-reporters-closely-1.433999)

170 Ashley Walters, All Disquiet on the Western Front, This Magazine, Jan 2009

171 Ulrich Mans, Christa Meindersma, Lars Burema Eyes Wide Shut? The Impact of Embedded Journalism on Dutch Newspaper Coverage of Afghanistan April, 2008

172 Benjamin W. Hadaway, Lampreys under a shark: embedded news reporters and the military in the 21st century, Carleton University Thesis 2006, 109

173 Ibid

174 Rebecca Lamarche, The challenges of embedded war reporting, King's Journalism Review, Jan 24 2013 (http://thekjr.kingsjournalism.com/tag/canadian-forces/feed/)

175 Christopher Waddell, Inside the Wire, Literary Review of Canada, Apr 2009 (http://reviewcanada.ca/magazine/2009/04/inside-the-wire/)

176 Robert Bergen, Censorship; the Canadian News Media and Afghanistan: A Historical Comparison with Case Studies, Calgary Papers in Military and Strategic Studies, 2009

177 David Pugliese, Shadow Wars : Special Forces in the New Battle Against Terrorism, 109

178 Sharon Hobson, Operations Security and the Public's Need to Know, Canadian Defence and Foreign Affairs Institute, Mar 2011

179 Harper on defensive over media ban on return of dead soldiers CBC News, Apr 25, 2006 (http://www.cbc.ca/news/canada/harper-on-defensive-over-media-ban-on-return-of-dead-soldiers-1.598979)

180 Robert Bergen, Censorship; the Canadian News Media and Afghanistan: A Historical Comparison with Case Studies, Calgary Papers in Military and Strategic Studies, 2009

181 Omar El Akkad, Detainee file was overseen by 'Tiger Team', Globe and Mail, Jan 3 2008 (http://www.theglobeandmail.com/news/national/detainee-file-was-overseen-by-tiger-team/article665892/)

182 Ibid

183 Sharon Hobson, Operations Security and the Public's Need to Know, Prepared for the Canadian Defence and Foreign Affairs Institute, Mar 2011

184 PM shuts down Parliament until March, CBC,

A Propaganda System

Dec 30 2009 (http://www.cbc.ca/news/politics/pm-shuts-down-parliament-until-march-1.829800)

185 Canada won't try again for Security Council seat, Canadian Press, Dec 28 2011 (http://www.cbc.ca/m/touch/politics/story/1.1123224)

186 Patrick Cockburn, Amnesty questions claim that Gaddafi ordered rape as weapon of war, Independent, June 23 2011 (http://www.independent.co.uk/news/world/africa/amnesty-questions-claim-that-gaddafi-ordered-rape-as-weapon-of-war-2302037.html)

187 Ibid

188 Archived - Statement by the Prime Minister of Canada paying tribute to troops who served on Libyan mission, Nov 24 2011 (http://news.gc.ca/web/article-en.do?nid=639909)

189 Peter Oborne, Voices from Benghazi: 'We have lived through the worst five years', Jan 2 2016 (http://www.spectator.co.uk/2016/01/voices-from-benghazi-we-have-lived-through-the-worst-five-years/)

190 David Taras and Christopher Waddell, How Canadians Communicate IV (http://www.aupress.ca/books/120205/ebook/99Z_Taras_Waddell_2012-How_Canadians_Communicate_IV.pdf/), 223

191 Ibid, 225

192 Canadian CF-18 jet bombs Libyan weapons depot, Mar 25 2011 (http://www.telegraph.co.uk/news/worldnews/africaandindianocean/libya/8405986/Canadian-CF-18-jet-bombs-Libyan-weapons-depot.html)

193 David Pugliese, The Libya Mission One Year Later: A victory, but at what price?, Ottawa Citizen, Feb 18 2012 (http://www.ottawacitizen.com/news/Libya+Mission+Year+Later+victory+what+price/6178518/story.html)

194 Jerome Lessard, Belleville Intelligencer, Tight restrictions for media during deployment at CFB Trenton, Oct 2014 (http://www.intelligencer.ca/2014/10/16/tight-restrictions-for-media-during-deployment-at-cfb-trenton)

195 David Pugliese, Sssssh.....don't let anyone know the Canadian military will be operating out of Kuwait, Ottawa Citizen, Oct 17 2014 (http://ottawacitizen.com/news/national/defence-watch/sssssh-dont-let-anyone-know-the-canadian-military-will-be-operating-out-of-kuwait)

196 Stephen M. Saideman, Adapting in the Dust: lessons learned from Canada's war in Afghanistan, 145

197 Kelsey Berg, DND Decides that Silence is the Best Policy, Aug 28 2015 (http://natoassociation.ca/dnd-decides-that-silence-is-the-best-policy/)

198 Lee Berthiaume, Military intelligence warns of terrorists harassing Canadian Forces personnel, families online, Ottawa Citizen, Mar 24 2015

199 David Taras and Christopher Waddell, How Canadians Communicate IV (http://www.aupress.ca/books/120205/ebook/99Z_Taras_Waddell_2012-How_Canadians_Communicate_IV.pdf/), 217

200 Ibid, 216

Chapter 8

1 Isabel Macdonald, Parachute Journalism" in Haiti: Media Sourcing in the 2003-2004 Political Crisis, Canadian Journal of Communication, Vol 33 2008

2 On Propaganda: Noam Chomsky interviewed by unidentified interviewer WBAI, Jan 1992 (https://chomsky.info/199201__/)

3 (http://www.thirdworldtraveler.com/Propaganda/Propaganda_Bernays.html)

4 Richard Sanders, CIDA Bankrolled Coup's Deputy Minister of "Justice", Press for Conversion! 61 (http://coat.ncf.ca/our_magazine/links/61/29-31.htm)

5 Isabel K. Macdonald, Parachute Journalism" in Haiti: Media Sourcing in the 2003-2004 Political Crisis, Canadian Journal of Communication, Vol 33 2008

6. Isabel K Macdonald, Covering the coup: Canadian news reporting, journalists, and sources in the 2004 Haiti crisis, York University MA thesis, 2006, 147

7 Isabel Macdonald, Parachute Journalism" in Haiti: Media Sourcing in the 2003-2004 Political Crisis, Canadian Journal of Communication, Vol 33 2008

8 Ibid

9 About Us (http://ccafrica.ca/about-us/)

10 Ibid

11 Brian Sylvester, First, Do Good When Mining for Gold: Benoit La Salle, The Gold Report, May 23 2012 (http://www.theaureport.com/pub/na/first-do-good-when-mining-for-gold-benoit-la-salle)

12 Alpha Condé suspend le secrétaire général du ministère des mines pour la vente « illicite » des mines d'or de Kiniero, June 5 2014 (http://guineenews.org/alpha-conde-suspend-le-secretaire-general-du-ministere-des-mines-pour-la-vente-illicite-des-mines-dor-de-kiniero/)

A Propaganda System

13 Three said killed in army crackdown on small scale miners in central east Guinea, BBC Monitoring Africa – BBC Worldwide Monitoring, June 6 2008

14 Semafo caught out by Mazars law, Africa Mining Intelligence, Mar 24 2015

15 Don MacDonald, Local Miner a Major Force in Niger, Montreal Gazette, Apr 16 2007

16 Lawrence Williams, Semafo Facing an African Gold Take-Away?, Sept 1 2010 (http://www.mining.com/semafo-facing-an-african-gold-take-away/)

17 Burkina Faso coup highlights African investment risks, The West Australian, Nov 2014

18 Daouda Emile Ouedraogo, Benoît La Salle, PDG de la SEMAFO: "Le secteur minier sera un des moteurs du développement du Burkina Faso", May 28 2007 (http://www.lefaso.net/spip.php?article21052)

19 Yan Barcelo, Midas Touch: A CA discovers an El Dorado in West Africa, CA magazine, Aug 2010 (file:///C:/Users/n_hausf/Downloads/CAmagazine-August-2010.pdf)

20 Peter Koven, The benefactor turns a profit; SEMAFO grew out of a charitable visit to Africa, National Post, July 29 2010

21 Sylvain Larocque, Le fondateur de Semafo quittera le conseil, La Presse, Apr 8 2013 (http://affaires.lapresse.ca/economie/energie-et-ressources/201304/08/01-4638807-le-fondateur-de-semafo-quittera-le-conseil.php)

22 Kim Mackrael, Canada has lost international stature, Chrétien says, Globe and Mail, Mar 12 2013 (http://www.theglobeandmail.com/news/politics/canada-has-lost-international-stature-chretien-says/article9707000/)

23 Richard Sanders, Canada's Covert War in Iraq (http://coat.ncf.ca/articles/Canada_Iraq.htm)

24 Peter McFarlane, Northern Shadows: Canadians and Central America, 136

25 Robert Carty, Virginia Smith, Latin American Working Group, Perpetuating poverty: the political economy of Canadian foreign aid, 66

26 Sue Montgomery, Voters should punish MPs for Haiti, Montreal Gazette, Jan 15 2006

About the Author

Dubbed "Canada's version of Noam Chomsky" (Georgia Straight), "one of the most important voices on the Canadian Left today" (Briarpatch), "in the mould of I. F. Stone" (Globe and Mail), "part of that rare but growing group of social critics unafraid to confront Canada's self-satisfied myths" (Quill & Quire), "ever-insightful' (rabble.ca), "Chomsky-styled iconoclast" (Counterpunch) and a "Leftist gadfly" (Ottawa Citizen), Yves Engler's eight previous books are:

>Canada in Africa: 300 Years of Aid and Exploitation
>The Ugly Canadian: Stephen Harper's Foreign Policy
>Lester Pearson's Peacekeeping: the Truth May Hurt
>Stop Signs: Cars and Capitalism on the Road to Economic, Social and Ecological Decay (with Bianca Mugyenyi)
>Canada and Israel: Building Apartheid
>The Black Book of Canadian Foreign Policy
>Canada in Haiti: Waging War on the Poor Majority (with Anthony Fenton)
>Playing Left-Wing: from Rink Rat to Student Radical

For more information about Yves go to his Web page at www.yvesengler.com